THE CORE CURRICULUM IN PROFESSIONAL PSYCHOLOGY

CALIFORNIA SCHOOL OF PROFESSIONAL PSYCHOLOGY

LOS ANGELES

1991

Published and distributed by the American Psychological Association

Washington, DC

THE CORE CURRICULUM IN PROFESSIONAL PSYCHOLOGY

Edited by: Roger L. Peterson
James D. McHolland
Russell J. Bent
Elizabeth Davis-Russell
Glenace E. Edwall
Kenneth Polite
David L. Singer
George Stricker

Published by
American Psychological Association
Washington, DC

Copies may be ordered from
APA Order Department
P.O. Box 2710
Hyattsville, MD 20784

Typeset by AAH Graphics, Fort Valley, VA
Printed by Patterson Printing, Benton Harbor, MI
Technical Editing: Mary Day McCoy
Production Coordination: Deborah Segal

Library of Congress Cataloging-in-Publication Data

Core curriculum in professional psychology/National Council of Schools of Pro-
    fessional Psychology; edited by, Roger L. Peterson . . . [et al.].
        p.   cm.
    Based on a conference held in San Antonio, Tex. in Jan. 1990.
    Includes bibliographical references.
    ISBN 1-55798-143-4: (on acid-free paper) $30.00 ($24.00 to members)
    1. Psychology—Study and teaching—Congresses. 2. Clinical psychology—
Study and teaching—Congresses. 3. Psychology, Applied—Study and teaching—Congresses. I. Peterson, Roger L., 1944- . II. National Council of Schools
of Professional Psychology (U.S.)
    [DNLM: 1. Clinical Competence—congresses. 2. Curriculum—congresses.
3. Psychology, Clinical—education—congresses. WM 18 C797 1990]
BE77.C65 1991
150'.71`1—dc20
DNLM/DLC
for Library of Congress   91-31516
                                                                                CIP

Printed in the United States of America.
First Edition

TABLE OF CONTENTS

Part III—Broadening the Core Curriculum

Part IV—Conference Resolutions

PREFACE

Roger L. Peterson

Antioch New England Graduate School
Keene, New Hampshire

It is now a little over 3 years since the 1988 summer meeting of the National Council of Schools of Professional Psychology (NCSPP), which preceded the American Psychological Association's annual meeting. In hotel meeting rooms and air-conditioned restaurants in Atlanta, I first discussed the work that led to the San Antonio conference on the Core Curriculum in Professional Psychology and ultimately to this book. Though by no means clear then, I am impressed now that this vision of the core curriculum is fundamentally and profoundly "social." This seems evident in at least 5 ways:

First, social, social constructionist (cf. Gergen, 1982, 1985), and historical analyses of the core curriculum in professional psychology (Peterson, chaps. 1 & 3; Weiss, chap. 2) provide the intellectual ground and context.

Second, the centerpiece of the book is the most definitive articulation of the professional psychology competency areas to date. They are derived from and organized around an analysis of the social circumstances, the needs, and the demands of psychological practice, not the traditional areas of university psychological science (chaps. 10–16). It is obsolete to view professional psychologists narrowly as simply applying the findings of their experimental colleagues from mainline universities. Indeed Trierweiler and Stricker's notion (chap. 14) of the "local clinical scientist" suggests that practitioners have a social role to play as scientists (not only caregivers) within their local communities.

Third, this book advocates for a broadened, socially responsible, and responsive conceptualization of the core that includes explicit attention to women (Edwall, chap. 17; Edwall & Newton, chap. 19) and to ethnic diversity (Davis-Russell, Forbes, Bascuas, & Duran, chap. 20). Furthermore, the proposals about inclusion in the core of material relevant to the self of the professional psychologist and to experience is tantamount to arguing for the importance of person-focused social and interpersonal sorts of educational experiences (Singer, Peterson, & Magidson, chap. 28).

Fourth, using perspectives derived from social psychology, there is explicit attention to the educational contexts in which the core curriculum is embedded. Schools of professional psychology (Morrison, O'Connor, & Williams, chap. 6) and individual faculty (Borden & Mitchell, chap. 7) are polled for their opinions. Teaching is examined with an emphasis on the importance of modeling (Lubin & Stricker, chap. 5). The process and problems surrounding curricular change are examined from a social–organizational perspective (Cannon & McHolland, chap. 9).

Fifth, the social, interpersonal, and organizational processes that produced this

conference and this book were of sufficient importance to deserve the narrative attention I gave to them in chapter 1, rather than being segregated solely into a grateful preface. In my view, this is equally true for other similar conferences, even though the current
convention is to artificially separate the knowledge products from the knowers. On a
more personal basis, knowing the interests, attitudes, and styles of the editors of this
book, the social emphasis cannot be surprising. Moreover, the NCSPP presidency of
James McHolland, during which this work took place, had a strong and effective theme
of inclusion and respect for diversity. No doubt the temporal context of this NCSPP conference—between one focused on diversity in 1989 and one on women in professional
psychology in 1991—influenced its content. More generally, though, all three conferences were responding to larger necessary and fundamental social changes in professional psychology.

During a comment period following a presentation based on this material at the
1991 American Psychological Association annual meeting in San Francisco, a colleague
of mine remarked that these ideas are "radical" (L. Mangione, personal communication,
August 19, 1991). There seemed to be agreement all around. At the same time, in the
age that has produced behaviorism, it is hard to see as particularly remarkable the suggestions that reinforcement conditions in university and health care settings have
shaped psychology or that the demands of practice ought to influence training. Readers
may find that the ideas in this book seem both radical and commonplace at the same
time.

In my view, the NCSPP has come of age. It follows then that the social process of
dissemination is increasingly a focus. Our hope would be to stimulate broad-based conversations about the ideas in this book—both radical and commonplace, both obvious
and subtle, both practical and conceptual—within and beyond the boundaries of
schools who identify with the professional psychology movement, among mainstream
Boulder model clinical faculty, at institutions with master's degree programs, at undergraduate colleges, at internship and practicum training agencies, and among all who
care about the shape of education in professional psychology in years to come.

PART I
CORE CURRICULUM:
GENERAL CONSIDERATIONS

1

THE SOCIAL, RELATIONAL, AND INTELLECTUAL CONTEXT OF THE CORE CURRICULUM AND THE SAN ANTONIO CONFERENCE

Roger L. Peterson
Antioch New England Graduate School
Keene, New Hampshire

The pronouncements of training conferences are not born, fully grown, from the forehead of Zeus, but rather come from a particular group of people, with particular relationships and allegiances, meeting in a particular social and historical context (cf. Weiss, chap. 2). In my view, the minimization or sometimes even blindness to the importance of context has led psychology into many discouraging corners. Therefore, I begin with sketches of the social, relational, and intellectual context of the National Council of Schools of Professional Psychology (NCSPP), its conference on the core curriculum in professional psychology, the core curriculum in general, and, in this process, this volume itself. This book emerged during a period of 3 years from the work of a group of people associated with NCSPP who, during a time of intense activity halfway through the process, came together for 3 days. They met in a fine hotel, recycled from its days as a college, stuccoed, with balconies along the river walk in San Antonio, Texas, in January 1990.

The National Council of Schools of Professional Psychology

Founded in 1974, NCSPP is an organization of professional programs in psychology whose mission is enhancement and enrichment of professional psychology training as well as mutual support. It currently consists of 27 member and 10 associate-member schools, 25 of which are accredited by the American Psychological Association (APA). For the last several years, after identifying a number of critical issues in professional psychology, NCSPP has designated committees to study and organize relevant information, bring together a series of working papers, and design a midwinter conference for the larger membership.

This volume is the fourth in a series that has emerged from this process and the resulting annual training conference. The first of these volumes was *Quality in Professional Psychology Training: A National Conference and Self-Study* (Callan, Peterson, & Stricker, 1986). Arising from what has come to be known as the Mission Bay conference, the second volume was *Standards and Evaluation in the Education and Training of Professional Psychologists: Knowledge, Attitudes, and Skills* (Bourg et al., 1987). A third volume, *Toward Ethnic Diversification in Psychology Education and Training* (Stricker et al., 1990), based on the 1989 Puerto Rico conference, was published in 1990. NCSPP has scheduled a 1991 conference on women in professional psychology and a 1992 conference on evaluation in professional psychology training.

San Antonio Conference Participants and Structure

The participants at the San Antonio conference were representatives of the member institutions of NCSPP and their invited guests, as listed at the end of this volume. NCSPP began as an organization with one representative from each institution, usually a dean or another with a similar role. Before the 1989 Puerto Rico conference on ethnic diversification, typically one or two top administrators, the great majority being men, represented each program. After that conference and following some political developments (the details of which are unclear), a third institutional delegate could come who brought ethnic or gender diversity to the group. Authors of papers were invited to San Antonio, as were special guests from seven other organizations that are concerned with psychological training. It is interesting to note that, in contrast to some other training conferences, many of the conferees knew one another quite well and had working relationships going back a number of years. At the same time, there were people new as institutional representatives and therefore new to the organization and the group. Of the 78 participants, 72% (56) were men, 28% (22) were women, and 18% (14) brought ethnic diversity to the conference.

In a process that began 17 months earlier in Atlanta, contributors of papers were selected by an informal process that depended on the NCSPP representatives and their networks. A preconference volume was sent to each registrant in early December 1989. It contained draft versions of most of the material in this book. Given rigidly restricted and sometimes controversial page limitations, the authors were later asked to revise their work assuming a postconference perspective, which included knowledge of the conference resolutions.

The conference itself was composed of six sessions and a banquet. The first three of these sessions began with a plenary session and a framing address. Then, prearranged, intentionally diverse work groups, composed of 10 participants and led by steering committee members, met to discuss the issues and to develop resolutions. The steering committee met between sessions to compile, collate, and edit the notes of each group into a single product. Resolutions were reworked and approved during another series of plenary sessions. All the plenary sessions were held in a spacious ballroom with draped tables organized in a large rectangle; the podium and the steering committee were at one end, and the coffee was behind the seats at the other. This light and airy room was conducive both to comfort and to lofty ideas.

For the most part, participants arrived the day before the opening conference plenary session, attended NCSPP committee meetings and a reconnecting cocktail party, and then sampled San Antonio's cuisine. Reshaped to provide a sense of immediacy, to convey the intellectual context of the meeting, and at the same time to introduce this book, the next sections intentionally preserve some of the text and tone of my initial address and identify the central themes.

Opening Plenary Session: Social and Relational Context

So here we are this morning, reasonably awake, remembering each other's names and faces, wondering what this will actually be like. You know, I have found that carrying a book of preconference papers in my briefcase for 8 working days is equivalent to reading the papers: The knowledge goes up my arm and directly into long-term memory. Too late now, though, you will actually have to read.

Recently, I came across the following wonderful dictionary definition of *core:* "the central, innermost, or most essential part of anything" (Urdang & Flexner, 1969, p. 298). In a world where sometimes it seems as if no one is talking about anything important, we get to spend 3 days discussing the central, innermost, and most essential parts of the professional psychology curriculum. In addition, we are going to have a good time together. We have the opportunity to converse with respected colleagues—in the context of developing friendships—about matters that we have all considered deeply, complained about, and struggled with. We have a structure that allows small groups to get to know one another and to work to construct resolutions that will be considered by all of us in plenary sessions. If we use vision and creativity, our work will impact positively on training in professional psychology for years to come. We will eat well, relax, leave behind some aggravations from home, even pick up a few new ones here (maybe even in this chapter).

Some of my closest colleagues and friends from Antioch are here, with whom I share day-to-day enthusiasms and discouragements, who know my virtues and vices both, perhaps in more details than they or I would wish. There are others back home I carry in my head: more than 100 students who have entrusted to us their professional training, years of their lives, and many thousands of dollars; and 20 or so talented faculty who, oddly enough, do not always agree with me about everything. Here I have made some friends in this group with whom I have learned and laughed since 1983 when I first started coming. By the end of this meeting, there will be new developments in old relationships and some new relationships as yet unknown. Through this organization and particularly through the steering committee work for this conference, I have had the opportunity to work with talented psychologists. The most senior of these, Russell Bent and George Stricker, were finishing their doctorates while I was in high school. They are people whose work I respected long before I knew anyone who even knew them, let alone whether they were purported to have a sense of humor. Although none are here today, among NCSPP members are a professor who sat on my dissertation committee, a dean who was once my undergraduate student, and a person who in 1971 interviewed a thinner me for a job I did not get. (Do you think he remembers?)

My point is not to welcome you with a narcissistic tour through my personal scrapbook. Instead, I believe that my own array of relationships are not at all unusual, but rather are typical of the experience of each of you around the room. Here is the key: As with all other training conferences, the conversations we have, the positions we develop, the scientific and professional work we do here this week will grow out of and be a product of our relationships, the social and interpersonal context of our lives, and this meeting.

I am, of course, aware that the relational and contextual positions that I am articulating have much in common with some feminist views of psychology. The further exploration of these enormously important personal, professional, and organizational issues will be our work for the 1991 NCSPP conference on women in professional psychology.

Let me digress for a moment to say that I have become fond of the term *conversation* to characterize what goes on between people in relationships: between friends (or enemies), colleagues, and psychologists and clients. The philosopher Richard Rorty (1979) suggested that the exploration of conversation is the "ultimate context within which knowledge is to be understood" (p. 389). Conversation seems more balanced, more graceful, more respectful, less jargony, and a bit more universal than exchange, debate, or dialogue. I learned it from Bill Lax (personal communication, January 13, 1990), a constructivist and systemic psychologist who cited both Rorty (1979) and Goolishian (Anderson & Goolishian, 1988).

Certainly, it is true that the results of meetings of historians or lawyers discussing curriculum are just as influenced by relationships and social context. However, the circumstances of professional psychology are enormously different in three ways. First, relationships are central to almost every aspect of the work of professional psychologists. Second, as I argue in my chapter on the social construction of the core curriculum (chap. 3), the systematic neglect of social and interpersonal context in scientific psychology underlies many of the problems in both the science and the profession today. Third, in a profound sense, this conference is about relationships. Let me discuss each in turn and identify some of the major themes.

Core Curriculum: General Considerations

An understanding of the core curriculum is necessarily based on a series of general social, historical, scientific, and epistemological considerations. These global concerns are addressed in this introduction, in Weiss' thought-provoking historical analysis (chap. 2), in my own social constructionist perspective (chap. 3), and in a discussion of academic – scientific issues by Webbe, Farber, Edwall, and Edwards (chap. 4).

Centrality of Relationships in Professional Psychology

Perhaps the most unanimous belief of the people in this room is the foundational primacy of, in Kenneth Polite's and Edward Bourg's words, "the basic ability to establish, understand, and maintain an authentic and appropriate relationship" (chap. 11, p. 83) to all the functions of the professional psychologist. On the basis of the resounding level of agreement, let me say no more and turn to more controversial areas.

Social and Contextual Elements of Psychological Science

Relationships of all kinds are not in opposition to scientific psychology; rather, they are its very foundation. Elsewhere, I have asserted that "any particular piece of psychological research or practice is embedded in a particular context: its historical time and its culture" (chap. 3, p. 24). Our science is fundamentally nonobjective, a product of the attitudes of psychologists and the relationships they have had with those whom they study. Along with Sarason (1981) and others, I see all too much of psychology—both experimental and professional—as fundamentally asocial and a product of those gifted, typically male, White, upper-middle-class professors who populate elite research institutions using disengaged and distant methods, where, for example, factors that could give a piece of research ecological validity come to be defined as error. I argue for a strengthened scientific psychology where "the development of psychological knowledge is changed from the universal to the contextual, from the distant and objective to the close and engaged, from ivory tower isolation to community embeddedness" (chap. 3, p. 25).

Reflexivity is a name for that process by which one can step out of the ongoing flux of living and, by a reflective glance, examine actions and behaviors in the past tense (Gergen, 1982, p. 18). Although it has long been a central element of our science and our practice (chap. 2 and chap. 18), I would like to see psychology formally differentiate itself from, say, astrophysics and geology and commit itself to identifying systematically the ramifications of this reflexivity inherent in the discipline.

I certainly do not want to give the impression that I want to eliminate university science or that I somehow think it is all bad or useless. I would like academic psychology to acknowledge forthrightly two essential points. First, as science fiction writer David Zindell (1988) said, "We don't see things as they are; we see things as we are" (p. 371). Second, every element of theory or data about human beings is understandable only in a social context, whether we are talking about the rise of behaviorism in the other-directed 1950s or Freud's insights about sexuality as a product of the intellectual ferment of turn-of-the-century Vienna that produced the visual artists Klimt and Schiele (Varnedoe, 1986).

Perhaps I can convey it metaphorically. Back in New Hampshire, I live on Spofford Lake, which I can see from my desk, located in a study high over the water surrounded by wood the color of piano keys. (Yes, I am afraid this *is* sort of a rustic, ivory tower metaphor.) In the winter the lake is frozen flat. When the sun is out, it gleams and glistens like silver, clean and orderly. Not many people are there in the winter. Oh yes, from time to time skaters, snowmobilers, or cross-country skiers come across it. I can see them now; the people are tiny dots of various sizes. The lake has a crisp, forbidding coldness about it. (This is why we northerners came to San Antonio, right?)

A universal conclusion about this scene such as "most people believe it is best to stay inside where it is most comfortable" is changed substantially by the contextual clause "in the New Hampshire winter." Nor would one wish to generalize from these observations that "arch-conservative New Hampshire citizens believe always in covering the entire body except for a small area on the face."

I count myself among those who continue to respect and admire even the most austere and wintery elements of psychological science: multiple regression, for example. I am attracted to the clarity and comfort provided by those large windows near my desk at this time of year. Still, sometimes it seems as if traditional academic psychology wants me to adopt a "scientific" perspective that seems to say I can know all of what I need to know sitting inside by myself, protected, warm, looking out on a January afternoon.

The summer, of course, is a different story. The lake is filled with life, families of all shapes and sizes, swimming, boating, having fun. People are actually in the water, without their overcoats on. During the weekends, there is a buzz of excitement, an interesting complexity, although admittedly a certain human messiness.

I am not against winter, as long as it does not stay year-round and is not put forward as the critical nature of all reality. I want to include in professional psychology the view with friends and family, of men, women, and kids from different parts of the world down by that summer beach. Furthermore, I would like us all to actually be able to go in the water and even go out on boats. We may get wet, and there are bugs in the summer, but it is worth it.

Of course, professional psychology is not and cannot be antiscience. Our students must know that psychology is not something we or others just make up as we go along to fit the moment. We must, respectfully, test our thoughts, our observations, and our visions in the context of relationships with the human participants in research, according to systematic changeable rules derived during academic conversations. The conversation needs to focus on the nature of that science, its breadth, the sorts of science that are practiced by professional psychologists, and the sort of training that best prepares them. There must be a way to both do and appreciate this science on a summer day by the shore.

In this context, then, a theme of this conference is the development of a broad and inclusive vision of scientific psychology. Beyond the simple rote learning of quasiexperimental design and analysis of variance, a sense of tolerance should emerge from carefully cultivated, discipline-based training in critical thinking that eradicates attitudes characterized by "who knows?" or "anything goes." The scientific disciplinary core courses should be taught in such a way that the science and the profession are brought together. Generations of students have had the totally unnecessary experience in which material purporting to be foundational to clinical practice was taught in an alienating abstruse manner. If these courses are taught by academic faculty with only a minimal appreciation of the clinical enterprise or by clinical faculty with only a modest knowledge of the science, then these faculty will continue to model and create the very split that continues to plague our discipline.

As reflected in its label, the research and evaluation competency, of course, belongs in both the academic – scientific knowledge base (cf. Webbe, Farber, Edwall, & Edwards, chap. 4) and the professional core competencies. The integrative vision developed by Trierweiler and Stricker (chap. 14) brilliantly put psychological research in the context of real people in the relationships constituting professional psychology. Their commentary and vision of local science deserve careful scrutiny for both what they propose and the further thinking they stimulate. Science provides particularly important and illuminating kinds of conversations. In my view, these scientific conversations must include more diverse people who speak according to more flexible rules and must occur at the local level according to local needs. Furthermore, professional psychologists must converse about other things as well.

Pedagogy

All of us who have been taught, who teach, and who hire faculty know that pedagogy is critical to what students actually experience. I am talking about the sorts of teaching relationships that should be shared by faculty and students. It is embarrassing that a profession that says learning is a central focus has had so little involvement with quality education. I would like us to assert that quality teaching is the sine qua non of professional education, long before research credentials and scholarly productivity. If close relationships with faculty are central, if being mentored is a core experience, if students are to be treated with respect, if modeling is pivotal as Lubin and Stricker (chap. 5) suggest, let us say so. If, as Rudestam suggests (chap. 8), national networks of personal computers are critical to the education of tomorrow, let us begin to put them in place today.

Empirical Work

Empirical studies of curricular issues are rare. Morrison and O'Connor (chap. 6) surveyed NCSPP programs with regard to program elements that make up the six competency areas. Seeing their centrality to professional education, Borden and Mitchell (chap. 7) surveyed the views of NCSPP faculty (rather than administrators) regarding the competency areas. Both studies found that the consultation and education and the management and supervision competencies are not well promulgated, and, in my view, they deserve expanded attention. These studies contribute to the literature about what is currently being done and about what faculty think, but, as Weiss (chap. 2) repeatedly and convincingly argues, no studies have shown whether particular curriculum elements explicitly lead to identifiable competencies in newly trained professional psychologists.

Curricular Change

Curricular change is not an easy process, as Cannon and McHolland (chap. 9) show us. This topic directs attention to the relationships between program leaders and faculty and students at home institutions. How many times have David Singer and I come back home from national training meetings all jazzed up with some clearly brilliant new possibility only to be treated as if we had had a strange acid trip or been kidnapped by religious fanatics? In faculty meetings, I have heard a conservative faculty member confidently propose a purported "innovation" that would take us into a time warp back to the 1950s. In spite of inherently conservative faculties, we must find ways to weave considerations of diversity, gender, and sexual orientation into the fabric of the curriculum. Working both ends, we can inspire our faculties to train the psychologists of the future while generating systematic contingencies for development and innovation.

Training Conferences and Relationships

Training conferences, including the San Antonio conference, are about relationships, not simply about our academic discipline. In the academic world, the term *discipline* is used "to refer to the knowledge and information base of a broad field of study and instruction" (Fowler, 1990, p. 2). In a broad sense, then, deeply embedded in the discipline, the core curriculum must prepare students for the professional relationships in which they will spend their lives. Even in a very narrow sense, curriculum can be seen as the content of the very special conversation that occurs in the relationships that compose doctoral training in professional psychology.

At the conference, our initial work focused on the attitudes and values underlying the core curriculum and gave rise to the general preamble in the resolutions (chap. 21).

All too often, comments on the core curriculum have focused narrowly on the content of courses. Afterward, indeed almost as an afterthought, have come statements about values and ethics. "Learn this stuff, be a scientist, take a practicum, oh yes, and be ethical and for diversity too," someone might have said. Admittedly, our own Mission Bay conference had a bit of this character as well. If certain attitudes and values are indeed the bedrock of the profession, they must be given an overarching priority in curricular conversations.

Our conversation about core attitudes and values is about the sorts of relationships we should have with our clients, our communities, and one another. It should speak to how we are to treat the others with whom we are in professional relationships: colleagues, students, and clients alike. We need, I believe, most of all an increased level of respectfulness. One of the most discouraging things about the academic rugged individualism Sarason (1981) described is that it makes some of our professional organizations and affairs—like some elements of the accreditation process, some purported actions of Council of Graduate Departments of Psychology (COGDOP) (in the not too distant past), and an unquotable critique of the American Psychological Association by a member of the American Psychological Society—seem as if they were written by the author of "How the West Was Won." Now I admit to enjoying a spirited debate as well as the next person. (Here I probably *should* say "next man.") However, I imagine these "competitions" might be more like friendly games of tennis than gladiatorial combat to the death. I further admit to having enjoyed, from time to time, a full and embarrassingly satisfying dinner at the table of professional disdain. (I was not there alone; there was a crowd.)

Singer, Magidson, and I (chap. 18) discuss related issues in the context of specifying the importance of the self-in-role and in relation to others as core. The development of a sense of self-in-relationship that guarantees a sense of collaborative colleagueship is absolutely critical to professional psychology and is no easy business. I want to advocate for a professional psychology of engaged clinicians who bring their real selves to conversations with clients in authentic relationships. People who want to use their verbal skills to win can go to law school; there is room in medicine for those who wish to treat people's parts rather than their whole.

Professional Core Competency Areas

After the Mission Bay conference, I think we have a consensus on the areas of the professional core. There are six "competency areas that specify the generic core [that] require basic proficiency": relationship, assessment, intervention, research and evaluation, consultation and teaching, and management and supervision (including ethics) (Bourg, Bent, McHolland, & Stricker, 1989, p. 70). Training is to include relevant knowledge, skills, and attitudes. We should keep in mind that particular skills and attitudes within these competency areas define the sorts of relationships in which professional psychologists participate.

Along with the relevant resolutions, each of six chapters in Part II provides a particular conceptualization and basic background material for each competency area. Polite and Bourg on the relationship competency (chap. 11), Gold and De Piano on assessment (chap. 12), and Bent and Cox on intervention (chap. 13) are anchoring points for professional psychology, for the core curriculum, and for this book. Trierweiler and Stricker on research and evaluation (chap. 14) delineate their striking new vision of the "local clinical scientist" for professional psychology. The consultation and education competency, according to Illback, Maher, and Kopplin (chap. 15), and the management and supervision competency, in the eyes of Bent, Schindler, and Dobbins (chap. 16) are underdeveloped in training programs. Curriculum in these areas must be expanded to better prepare tomorrow's psychologists, ironically, for what today's psychologists are actually doing in their own local contexts.

Broadening the Core Curriculum

On one level, a theme of the conference and of the book is broadening the core curriculum beyond traditional content "to include material relevant to the self of the professional psychologist, to experience, to women, and to ethnic diversity. . . . [We need] a broadened conceptualization of the core curriculum, beyond definitions by content, beyond traditional university science, and beyond the frame provided by the competencies" (Edwall, chap. 17, p. 129).

After Edwall's moving introduction, Singer, Magidson, and I (chap. 18) put forward that there should be "systematic attention to the nature of the relationship between the self of the student and the work of professional psychology" (p. 133). As mentioned earlier, we suggest that reflexivity, the ability to reflect on actions and behaviors in the past (Gergen, 1982, p. 18; Smedslund, 1985), must be in the center of training in professional psychology. Perhaps this is the area that is most obviously and directly about relationships. In a notion that is at the same time common and radical, it seems to me that the core curriculum should include the authentic self of each student in a way that necessitates particular, intense sorts of relationships to his or her colleagues and faculty. It is time for us to bring this sort of personal reflexivity into the core curriculum.

Edwall and Newton (chap. 19) make the case for a broadened psychological epistemology based on the contributions of feminist scholarship and examine the core structure of professional training curricula, experiences, and processes from the perspective of women. Then, Davis-Russell, Forbes, Bascuas, and Duran (chap. 20) discuss the necessity of understanding current psychological paradigms and of adopting a new one to effectively evaluate and generate knowledge pertaining to ethnic diversity. In asking where women and ethnic diversity fit into the core curriculum, we are asking how we are to relate across genders and to those we see as different from ourselves, those who are "the other." This process demands systematic curricular attention in ways only partly understood, particular knowledge, and a respectful willingness to explore the basis for conversations with others whose experiences may be quite different from our own. We need to commit ourselves to developing a nonalienating science to help us construct ways in which this can be done. We should be proud that NCSPP's midwinter conferences on diversity in 1989 and on women in 1991—as well as this one—should help to bring psychology along.

Conference Resolutions

The conference produced a remarkable and striking array of detailed resolutions beginning with the explicit identification of four curricular values: a broadened view of the educational domain of professional psychology, which includes humanities and personal and professional experience; the affirmation of multiple ways of knowing, both objective and subjective; the demonstrated mastery of professional knowledge, skills, and attitudes; and the preparation for lifelong learning. The conferees also affirmed the value of "diversity and inclusiveness as fundamental elements of human experience" (chap. 21, p. 159); the necessity of education of the personal and professional self of the student; the importance of preparation for multiple professional roles; a broadly defined vision of curriculum; the centrality of relationships to the clinical enterprise; and "the [absolute] importance of the responsible use of power and authority" (chap. 21, p. 155).

Conclusion

As is clear by now, this book was the product of many other sorts of effort beyond the putting of words on a page and moving them around. I want to recognize by name the particular people who served on the steering committee, thereby creating the conference and this volume, although I will resist the temptation to characterize each of their particular contributions in a sentence or a phrase. They are (in alphabetical order) Russell Bent, Elizabeth Davis-Russell, Glenace Edwall, James McHolland, Ethel Magidson, Kenneth Polite, David Singer, and George Stricker. I am proud of these talented people, proud of the quality of conferees present, proud of having taken the high road, proud of our friendships, our respectfulness, and our caring, and proud of the work we have done together.

I want to close by returning to the question of relationships, particularly who we at NCSPP want to be to one another. I suppose, because we occupy similar roles, we have been mirrors for each other, often sharing with impassioned empathy. As the professional psychology movement has been and continues to be embattled, we have been a foxhole family. Struggling along this sometimes rugged road, I have believed that the Thomas Jeffersons and the Samuel Adams of the professional psychology movement are up there in front. Ground has been gained, but there still are redcoats just on the other side of the hill. I have worried at moments that Valley Forge was ahead of us, not behind us.

Sometimes the metaphor of revolution in professional psychology training seems apt. Regardless of rhetoric, that revolution is one that has more in common with religion than with science. Religious wars that have dominated the greater part of this first century of psychology are fomented by programs teaching their students the one and only true faith. I am for conversations with strong opinions, persuasively expressed, but such opinions should not be put forward as canon, to use Glenace Edwall's phrase (personal communication, August 8, 1989).

In our curricular conversations, we need to continue to keep two simple things in mind. First, as every student of learning knows, behavior responds to contingencies, and one learns best what one practices most. Contingencies designed to produce the best of practitioners are more likely to produce them than contingencies designed to produce university science researchers. Second, we have seen that there are people in need of us, less than they could be, imprisoned by their pasts, abused, frightened; people trapped by the intolerant and derogatory ideas of others; people run down by poverty and the economic system; and people ensnared by their own habits and thoughts. The ultimate task of our educational programs is to prepare professional psychologists who are willing to share their pain and to reach out a hand.

2

TOWARD A COMPETENCY-BASED CORE CURRICULUM IN PROFESSIONAL PSYCHOLOGY: A CRITICAL HISTORY

Bruce J. Weiss

Massachusetts School of Professional Psychology
Dedham, Massachusetts

The history of the search for a core curriculum in clinical psychology has been influenced more by the profession's search for identity than by empirical findings. Although psychologists are fond of thinking of the debate on this issue as being influenced by philosophical, epistemological, and empirical factors, a fresh look at the reasons for promulgating a core curriculum may be needed if the profession is to break an impasse that has existed for the last 40 years.

Curriculum and training standards can be framed in at least three ways. *Content-based* standards identify particular content areas that must be in the curriculum, such as the familiar list that includes cognitive – affective, individual, social, and biological bases of behavior, history and systems, and so on. Programs demonstrate compliance essentially by means of syllabi. *Competency-based* standards indicate competencies that graduates are to have. At least in the ideal situation, program compliance would be demonstrated by providing evidence of student competence. Presumably, in a manner that encourages diversity and creativity, programs might develop a variety of ways of teaching particular competencies, always subject to empirical scrutiny. *Structural* standards identify particular organizational or educational structures that programs must have. Controversial examples include the proportion of full-time faculty, free-standing versus university-based programs, a concrete definition of residency requirements, and whether internships are full or part time and concurrent with or after course work. Content-based standards and structural standards typically are not based on data.

In this chapter, I argue that the profession has held stubbornly to the concept of a content-based core curriculum in spite of the fact that there is no evidence that it is related to the efficacy of practitioner training. To understand this persistence, I examine the different developmental stages of the profession as reflected in key conferences. Certain pivotal events occurred, each of which placed demands on the profession that it was not fully prepared to meet. At each point, activists within organized psychology seized these opportunities to move the profession forward at the cost of having to justify policies of standardization that had been established.

The major national conferences sponsored by the American Psychological Association (APA) have been critical in providing this justification. According to Bickman (1987), the profession has used these conferences as problem-solving mechanisms. Conferences that have been held during periods of consensus and that reflect such consensus in their conclusions have been viewed as successful. These conferences, along with accreditation practices, have been powerful instruments in psychology's efforts to shape and to promote the profession.

APA Conferences (1949–1987)

Boulder Conference (1949)

It is commonly agreed that World War II signaled the beginning of clinical psychology as a profession. After the war, the Veterans Administration (VA) asked organized psychology to identify appropriate graduate programs from which it could select interns to help staff its hospitals. Because preparatory work had to be completed quickly, APA formed a Committee on Training in Clinical Psychology, chaired by David Shakow, to formulate a recommended graduate course of study. The report (APA Committee on Training in Clinical Psychology, 1947) established a core curriculum and indicated that there must be study in general psychology, psychodynamics, diagnostic methods, research methods, psychotherapy, and related disciplines.

The Boulder conference was convened at least partially to justify decisions that already had been made. During the 2 years before the Boulder conference, the VA already had received its requested list of qualified programs, and 35 clinical psychology training programs had been accredited. In view of recent concern about the proliferation of clinical psychology training programs, it is ironic that 22% of the 155 clinical psychology programs that were accredited through 1988 (APA, 1988) had been granted accreditation in the 2 years before the 1949 Boulder conference. The Boulder conferees asserted that there should be a common core of training for clinical psychologists, but denied that there was "one best way" (Raimy, 1950, p. 55) to arrange subject matter, as the Shakow report attempted to do. They spoke strongly for this decision to be left to the universities.

The Boulder report warned that "overspecification can present a facade of logical integration that may well be contrary to the facts" (Raimy, 1950, p. 55) and called for the encouragement of diversity. It cautioned that this diversity might be blocked by accrediting agencies that "insist upon uniformity as a short-sighted means of achieving immediate goals" (p. 31).

The turf of clinical psychology, however, already had been established. By then, 35 programs, primarily from distinguished research and large state universities, had been accredited. Psychology, which had been identified primarily as a scientific discipline, had made a rapid transition into a profession as well.

As an aspect of establishing itself as a profession, clinical psychologists demarcated a distinct vocabulary, necessary for what Larson (1977) called the "negotiation of cognitive exclusiveness" (p. 24). As Willensky (1964) explained, this has been a traditional step in turning an occupation into a profession. Unless its vocabulary can be made sufficiently unfamiliar to lay people, a group will have difficulty staking out its jurisdiction or claiming a monopoly on certain skills. This is particularly important for an occupation grounded in human-relations skills.

By the time the Boulder conference ended, the conferees had patched together the scientist–practitioner model and had taken another traditional step in the development of a profession. For a profession to develop, a group must be cohesive enough to be able to persuade others that the propagation of one paradigm of education is in everyone's best interests (Friedson, 1970). At the Boulder conference, this task obviously was made easier by the homogeneous composition of the participant group. Among the 53 university-affiliated psychologists, 51 represented programs that had been accredited before the conference convened (Raimy, 1950).

Clinical psychologists had agreed to define the profession in response to an external force (viz., the VA request for a list of appropriate training programs). Not surprisingly, this expeditious definition included accommodation by the profession to psychology's long-standing battle for prestige as a research discipline within academe. With this definition in place, only 28 additional programs were accredited during the next 18 years (1950–1967).

Miami Conference (1958)

At the Miami conference, the participants approached the core curriculum very differently. They emphasized that (a) the profession would grow best by adding and deleting areas from the curriculum, (b) flexibility must be stressed, and (c) such experimentation was essential to the improvement of clinical training. They warned that accreditation must not be allowed to become a destructive force that pushed programs into conformance (Roe, Gustad, Moore, Ross, & Skodak, 1959).

There was an ironic pledge of allegiance to the profession's commitment to the notion of a core curriculum: Loyalty prevailed when the Miami conferees confirmed that there is a common core, but irony prevailed when they refused to specify what that core should be. The participants chose to leave that to each program to determine. The conferees, however, did endorse the need for some central oversight for clinical training and named APA accreditation as the mechanism for that oversight. Endorsement of the profession's enforcement arm was every bit as potent, if not more so, than intellectual validation of the core-curriculum concept would have been.

Chicago Conference (1965)

A second major event in the history of the profession was the Community Mental Health Centers Act of 1963 because it created the demand for a considerably greater number of psychologists to staff the proposed community mental health centers. With the impact of this legislation as the background, the major theme of the Chicago conference became dissatisfaction with the state of clinical training. The participants warned of the futility of seeking only one solution regarding curricular requirements and encouraged the development of multiple models. It was clear that most programs were not meeting the need for adequate training.

The Chicago conferees adamantly refused to focus on the content of doctoral programs and *what* should be taught; instead, they examined *how* psychology should be taught. They adopted the resolution that the "notion of a core curriculum is no longer viable" (Hoch, Ross, & Winder, 1966, p. 88). The participants did not take a position on APA accreditation, but they commented that "organizational and institutional forces seemed to ward off diversity, because uniformity was easier to control and programs found it easier to pattern themselves after those already in existence" (Hoch et al., 1966, p. 75).

The Chicago conferees encouraged more diversity in training than the participants at previous conferences had done. Furthermore, they helped to open the door for psychology to play a greater part in the new mental health movement in the country. The pace of program accreditation increased after the Chicago conference. Beginning in 1968, and during the next 5 years, 30 programs became accredited: In 1972, 13 programs were accredited, the most in any one year since the group was formed.

Vail Conference (1973)

At the 1973 Vail conference, disenchantment with graduate psychology education was at its peak. By this time, there were many more employment opportunities for psychologists, and there were many more qualified applicants for graduate schools than there were slots in the research-oriented university programs. However, there were still only two accredited professional school programs and no accredited Doctor of Psychology (PsyD) programs.

Clearly, it was time for the status quo to be given a jolt, and the Vail conferees did just that. A more diverse group of participants than at previous conferences, the Vail conferees urged explicit recognition of an alternative doctoral degree, the PsyD, and the establishment of the practitioner model. The participants proposed more flexible curriculum building and advocated that students have a voice in planning their own individualized curriculum. They recommended creating an educational environment in which societal needs would be able to lead quickly to modification of curriculum (Korman, 1974).

Accreditation was described as "not equal to the task of adequately evaluating the efficacy of training, the quality of graduates, and the value of the services to the ultimate recipient" (Korman, 1974, p. 445). The Vail conferees recommended that the profession examine the functional relationship between content and the roles for which programs were preparing future professionals. They called for a demonstration project to revise the accreditation process by focusing on the competencies of graduates rather than the content they had learned. After the Vail conference, however, there was no demonstration project. Indeed, no such demonstration project ever occurred, although, as early as 1949, Shakow had urged APA to support validation studies of accreditation (APA Committee on Training in Clinical Psychology, 1949).

During the 14 years (1974 – 1987) after the Vail conference, 22 of the 53 clinical psychology programs that were accredited were explicitly professional programs with practitioner models. In 1979, APA, in response to the development of these programs, revised its accreditation standards to allow for (a) more flexible faculty staffing patterns, (b) multiple models of internship, (c) recognition of the PsyD, and (d) acceptance of free-standing institutions outside the traditional university system (APA, 1979). Seventeen of the 22 practitioner programs that became accredited from 1974 to 1987 were PsyD programs, and 7 were in free-standing institutions.

These revised standards, however, did not free up curricular requirements. During the 1970s, two developments helped to determine that there would be greater rather than lesser specification of the curriculum in the new accreditation standards. First, during this decade there was optimism that psychology might be included as a primary health-care provider in national health insurance. Organizations such as the National Register insisted on more standardization of educational criteria to ensure this outcome. Second, in 1975, in a judicial decision that allowed a clearly nonqualified applicant to sit for the licensure examination in Washington, DC, Judge MacKinnon said psychology is an "amorphous, inexact, and even mysterious discipline [and] possession of a graduate degree in psychology does not signify the absorption of a corpus of knowledge as does a medical, engineering or law degree" (cited by Wellner, 1978, p. 6). Quoting this excerpt proved to be one of the most powerful arguments used by the prostandardization forces.

The threat that psychologists could be excluded from national health insurance by court challenges to the identity of the profession drew a strong response. Reacting to Judge MacKinnon's assessment of psychology, the profession, as it had done almost 30 years earlier, allowed an external force to dominate its decision as to how to define itself. Wellner (1978) called for a national consensus on the core curriculum for clinical psychology programs, and such a consensus, at least among the major regulatory bodies in psychology, seems to have been reached. APA, the American Association of State Psychology Boards, the National Register, and most state licensing boards specified similar core-curriculum requirements: scientific and professional ethics and standards; research design and methodology; statistics; psychological measurement; history and systems; individual, biological, cognitive – affective, and social bases of behavior; practica; and internships.

Salt Lake City Conference (1987)

The most recent major conference cited the recurrent issue of a core curriculum as the central issue needed for the unity of the profession (Bickman, 1987). Although the Salt Lake City conferees made the usual call for program independence for specification of the core content, at the same time they endorsed the basic areas specified by APA for programs seeking accreditation in professional psychology (National Conference on Graduate Education, 1987). Because APA accreditation is almost essential for a clinical psychology program to survive, this endorsement is tantamount to preserving the status quo.

Therefore, during the last 10 years, psychology training has been shaped by a liberal definition of organizational structure and type of degree offered but by a standardized definition of the core curriculum. The result is that many programs offer the PsyD and operate out of an explicit practitioner model, but their curricula are increasingly similar to more traditional programs (Kopplin, 1986).

National Council of Schools of Professional Psychology Conferences (1978–1987)

In addition to the conferences supported by APA, there have been several conferences sponsored by the National Council of Schools of Professional Psychology (NCSPP), an organization founded in 1977 to develop standards for education and training of professional psychologists. NCSPP has taken a different approach to issues such as core curriculum, perhaps because it has the singular mission of promoting the best training for professional psychologists, not the responsibility of defending the dual aspects of the scientist–practitioner model.

Virginia Beach Conference (1978)

In the first NCSPP conference at Virginia Beach in 1978, one key resolution was that the curricula of the practitioner and scientist–practitioner models need to be evaluated through outcome research, because there is no evidence regarding the effectiveness of curriculum models in producing competent practitioners (Watson, Caddy, Johnson, & Rimm, 1981).

La Jolla Conference (1981)

In 1981 at the La Jolla conference, NCSPP participants continued to call for a research-based approach to establishing quality assurance. In addition, they agreed to publish descriptive information about what actually goes on in professional psychology programs (Callan et al., 1986). In a preconference paper, Gianetti, Peterson, and Wilkins (1986) exposed the historical concept of the core curriculum, as reflected in accreditation criteria, as nothing more than the collective agreement of organized psychology. They noted that collective agreement could merely generate hypotheses about what curricula would result in desirable outcomes, but it did not confirm such hypotheses.

Gianetti et al. (1986) warned that strictly adhering to consensually defined practices would merely reduce the variation in the practice. The conferees resolved to continue research on these issues in an effort to move beyond description toward the ability to perform evaluative, criterion-based research. Unfortunately, if one views program curricula as an independent variable (Gustad, 1958), reduction of innovative curricula reduces the variance and makes such research much more difficult.

In two separate conference papers (Bent, 1986; Kopplin, 1986), the notion was introduced that core-curriculum development and evaluation must focus on a set of competencies rather than content areas. If a competency-based core curriculum were adopted, curricula could be evaluated in terms of their success at developing these competencies in students.

Mission Bay Conference (1987)

At NCSPP's Mission Bay conference in 1987 (Bourg et al., 1989), the participants resolved that there should be a core curriculum in professional psychology based on six identifiable competency areas: relationship, assessment, intervention, research and evaluation, consultation and education, and management and supervision. The conferees concluded that understanding the relation between knowledge bases and professional applications is more important than knowledge from a content-based curriculum alone.

The need to evaluate curricula in terms of competence, asserted by NCSPP members at the Virginia Beach conference, the La Jolla conference, and the Mission Bay conference, is not new and can be traced back to the 1973 APA Vail conference. The Vail participants believed that a lack of concern for program evaluation was inconsistent with clinical psychology's stated pride in evaluation research and in being a data-based discipline (Korman, 1973). Similarly, Koocher (1979) was curious about the lack of attention that had been paid to establishing the validity of licensing requirements. He asserted that the cost of promulgating nonvalid measures was often ignored by organized psychology. Stern (1984) stated that the lack of empirically based methods for assessing competence in professional psychology prevented adequate evaluation of any training models and left little basis for stating that particular educational practices ensured professional competence.

Resistance to a Competency-Based Core Curriculum

There are a number of reasons for organized psychology's resistance to the task of tying the core curriculum to professional competencies. The most prevalent arguments are as follows:

1. This type of research is complex and expensive (Menne, 1981).
2. Competency-based education might lead to a lock-step curriculum and diminished academic freedom (Bent, 1986).
3. Focusing on phenotypic skills may be the wrong approach; genotypic abilities, such as that of inquiry, should be the focus of training in psychology. Stern (1984) believed that the goal should be genotypic competence that allows one to do many jobs well. Teaching should focus on intellectual processes and methods, such as active learning, criticizing and integrating a body of research literature, and being able to compare psychological theories, rather than emphasizing particular content. Stern (1984) indicated that this is what Flexner (1910) really wanted medical education to include. Starr (1982) agreed and reported that, contrary to common perceptions, Flexner (1925) would have preferred that medical education have the flexibility of arts and sciences graduate education and that Flexner (1925) became increasingly disenchanted with the rigid educational standards that became identified with his name. McHolland, Peterson, and Brown (1987) stated what seems to be a summary of NCSPP's position on this issue: Metacognitive skills, such as a student's ability to evaluate oneself in professional applications, are very important. "We maintain only that both phenotypic and genotypic skills need to be assessed and that appraisal of the former is likely to be easier than appraisal of the latter" (p. 117).
4. Psychology would become a collection of specific skills or occupations rather than a profession, and education or experience requirements would be irrelevant (Menne, 1981). This last criticism seems to provide the best explanation for organized psychology's resistance to competency-based education or, for that mat-

ter, to education geared to the training of the professional self and metacognitive skills. The profession has labored to establish a corpus of knowledge that defines clinical psychology, and it has relied on core-curriculum requirements to maintain its cognitive exclusiveness.

According to Stern (1984), psychology must begin to differentiate its economic – political agenda from its educational agenda. The former defines psychology and educational practices in a way that protects and advances the economic interests of psychology, whereas the latter is concerned only with the best training for practitioners. Both agendas are important, but can result in contradictory definitions. Stern argued that a content-based core curriculum may best serve the economic – political agenda, but only a competency-based core curriculum can advance the scientific investigation of what constitutes the best educational practices.

Rather than being drawn into a bona fide debate on the relative merits of these two models, organized psychology is actively considering the addition of new structural, non-data-based educational requirements to reassert its exclusiveness and control. In a preconference paper at Salt Lake City, Altman (1987) admonished that a reactionary orientation might be about to form, and this has historically taken the form of "excluding free-standing schools, reinstituting lengthy core curriculum requirements, [and] insisting on traditional patterns of education" (p. 1068).

This warning should be heeded because such reactionary attitudes, indeed, are on the rise. In 1987, the APA Salt Lake City conferees called for the abolition of free-standing schools by 1995 (National Conference on Graduate Education, 1987). At a recent conference on internship training (Belar et al., 1989), the participants recommended that (a) the internship requirement be lengthened to 2 years, (b) all interns be selected from APA-accredited educational programs, and (c) all internship training take place in APA-accredited internships. Furthermore, in 1989, the members of the APA Task Force on the Scope and Criteria for Accreditation (American Psychological Association, 1989) made the following regressive recommendations: (a) a return to primary reliance on full-time faculty members; and (b) restriction of student internships to the period after completion of the educational program rather than in concurrence with some academic work.

It appears that the most savvy leaders of reactionary forces in organized psychology have come to understand what critical observers of the history of medical education already know: Psychology does not need its own Flexner (1910) report to reduce the number of educational programs and students in professional psychology. As Starr (1982) noted, in the 5-year period *before* the Flexner report was published (1906 – 1910), 31 medical schools closed their doors. In the 5 years after the publication of the report (1911 – 1915), only 36 more closed. It was not the Flexner report, as commonly believed, that closed the medical schools. Rather, it was the steadily rising requirements (e.g., lengthening the curriculum, adding internship requirements) imposed by licensing boards and other regulatory authorities that altered the economics of medical education and decreased the number of students and graduates.

Conclusion

A certain amount of nonsense is to be expected in the interpretations of what best serves the profession. However, some of these resolutions threaten to alter permanently models of education and possibly to close successful programs without any evidence that these models or programs are any less successful than traditional programs in producing effective psychologists.

Gianetti et al. (1986) noted that "debates [about the core curriculum] are mainly rhetorical and emotional since they are based on beliefs and political considerations rather than on empirical evidence" (p. 165). An example of this sort of rhetoric is Eriksen's (1958) comment that psychology valued experimentation and academic freedom more than it did uniformity and standardization. He stated, "It will be a sad day when we agree on the content of the core curriculum" (p. 58). In another example, Fox and Barclay (1989) provided a genuine disincentive for psychologists to examine critically the issue of the core curriculum by asserting that "resistance to the definition of such a core for the education and training of clinical psychologists is based on shadow rather than substance" (p. 56). A final example of rhetoric is contained in my own transposition of Fox and Barclay's (1989) quote—the belief that a content-based definition of a core curriculum is based on shadow rather than substance: The shadow is cast by organized psychology's economic–political agenda.

I hope it is time for the profession of clinical psychology to go beyond such rhetoric. The participants at the NCSPP San Antonio conference, the midwinter 1989–1990 meeting, reaffirmed the notions that (a) the core competency areas should be the organizing principle for curriculum construction, and (b) a content-based core curriculum should not be an end in itself. The conferees also supported variety in curricular designs and called for attempts to validate the effect of different curricular designs on the development of professional competencies in students.

However, it will require more than the San Antonio resolutions to change clinical psychology's 40-year preoccupation with a content-based core curriculum or to prevent the establishment of new nonfunctional educational requirements. Since the 1949 Boulder conference, the participants at every major training conference have warned that accreditation practices can stifle needed experimentation with curriculum development, and this is exactly what has happened. Since 1949, participants at curriculum and training conferences have called for validation studies of educational practices. Whether professional psychology has reached a stage in its development when it will follow through on these studies is still to be determined.

3

SOCIAL CONSTRUCTION OF THE CORE CURRICULUM IN PROFESSIONAL PSYCHOLOGY

Roger L. Peterson
Antioch New England Graduate School
Keene, New Hampshire

Most traditional professional psychologists have grown up with the belief that there is an underlying core discipline in psychology with particular knowledge and methods, however unclear the elements of that discipline might be at a certain historical moment. In this view, there are human universals waiting to be discovered by closer attention to patterns of reinforcement or the decoding of unconscious meanings, although few imagine that the equivalent of a better telescope or a space probe would unveil that basic nature of the psychological solar system. Traditional psychologists believe in a deterministic world where there must be stable and predictable underlying patterns, even if these patterns are seldom apparent in our own lives or in our own times. Conveyed through a constantly developing core curriculum, advancements in the discipline that would solve psychological problems and provide a firm base for practice would emerge over time by adhering to objective, disinterested, value-free scientific methods that produce empirical data. Although each of us questioned some part or another of this viewpoint, these common beliefs were perhaps a naive version of logical positivist metatheory of the sort communicated by generations of introductory psychology textbooks.

Of course, we all understood that there were social pressures on this science: the politics of universities and academic departments, the growth of clinical psychology after World War II, the community mental health movement, research support, and so on. Even so, the core discipline was thought to be sound, protected by the timeless and improving methods and procedures of science, such as physics and astronomy. At worst, the social pressures would lead to waste or faddish research or perhaps would contribute experimental error. The current version of this position is expressed by Matarazzo's (1987) vision of the "one psychology" with "many applications" (p. 893), with its articulated faith in a content-based core curriculum. In this perspective, the disciplinary science is in the foreground against a vague and not especially important social context.

In strong contrast, the application of social constructionist metatheory, a social epistemology (Gergen, 1982, 1985), reverses the figure and the ground. The accumulated knowledge of the human, social aspects of psychology are a product and creation of particular social contexts. In this chapter I examine the core curriculum in professional psychology—its historical background, as it exists today, and as it might develop—through the lens of social constructionism.

In the context of the core curriculum, I argue for vastly increasing the importance of an intellectually coherent, general social frame in the training of professional psychologists (cf. Leary & Maddux, 1987). After summarizing some relevant elements of social constructionist thought, I examine the social culture and history of professional psychology and the increasing importance of cross-cultural and ethnic psychology. Then I apply a similar analysis to the current training context and to the professional school movement. Next I discuss social reflexivity, along with its ramifications (Gergen, 1982; Smedslund, 1985), as particular characteristics of the discipline of psychology on the personal, personal – professional, professional, and cultural levels. Social interactional and social individual elements are mentioned only briefly because they are mostly beyond the scope of this chapter. I conclude the chapter with a discussion of social responsibility. Throughout the chapter, I refer to various cores (e.g., a core for the future, a social responsibility core). My point in using this language is to emphasize that the core can be thought of in ways other than as a course in this area and a course in another area.

Social Constructionist Epistemology

Gergen (1982), in his book *Toward Transformation in Social Knowledge* as well as in his more accessible 1985 article, applied the social constructionist position to the field of psychology. He showed convincingly how the social knowledge on which the science and ultimately the profession depend is embedded in a particular culture and history, influenced by the scientific "rules" that have been developed primarily in university contexts, formed by power relationships and economics, and based on value-laden foundations (Gergen, 1982). In contrast to the traditional view, this frame "removes knowledge from data-driven and/or cognitively necessitated domains and place[s] it in the hands of people in relationship" (Gergen, 1985, p. 272). It is a mistake to try to understand the core curriculum as a disembodied product of empirical science.

Gergen (1982) doubted whether there are any universal human truths or transhistorically valid principles to be discovered. Any particular piece of psychological research or practice is embedded in a particular context: its historical time and its culture. Specific influences on knowledge products include local, regional, national, ethnic, economic, and gender-based characteristics. Furthermore, the very language of psychological description is rooted in a specific culture (p. 30).

Much social and behavioral research is based on the questionable assumption of the underlying stability of human behavior. Although research moves forward based on a "limited set of systematically constrained experiences," there is a "multitude of disordered and discontinuous events taking place outside the scientific sanctum" that more accurately reflect real human phenomena (Gergen, 1982, p. 2). If human behavior is much more responsive to situations and is less internally driven, the straightforward, traditional idea that a professional psychologist learns the basic scientific facts and then applies them to clients becomes questionable. The information necessary to understand and to influence another is primarily available in the local social circumstances rather than in traditional psychological studies. Therefore, the acquisition of core professional skills and processes that will allow access to the necessary, locally relevant information may be more central to the profession than acquisition of supposedly general psychological knowledge.

Furthermore, according to Gergen (1982), this fundamentally nonobjective behavioral science theory affirms the ultimate value of empirical research but changes its context and interpretation. Some argued that ideological interests in the behavioral sciences are masked by laying claim to objectivity, which in fact rationalizes an enhanced position of authority or power and suggests that knowledge is best gained from distant relationships rather than from trusting, intimate, or collegial ones (Gergen, 1982, pp. 32–33).

> *Criteria for rigorous research demand personal distance between the observer and the observed. A deep and intimate acquaintance between the two would threaten the ostensible validity of the research findings. Yet the implicit message contained within methods designed by this criterion is that superior knowledge in the social sphere is gained through alienated relations. Intimate relations are implicitly blind and unrealistic. (Gergen, 1982, p. 33)*

Although the concept of "alienated relations" (Gergen, 1982, p. 33) between scientist and subject may have little to do with the study of the atmosphere on Mars, it is critical to the study of the atmosphere of intimate relationships and race relations in cities. Far from being universal, the objective standpoint may have within it a strong, potentially self-serving and negative, almost antisocial bias. Research developing from this tradition cannot be the primary basis for an interpersonally connected professional psychology.

The *scientific* and *empirical* context of the development of psychological knowledge is changed from the universal to the contextual, from the distant and objective to the close and engaged, from ivory tower isolation to community embeddedness. It illuminates the present, puts the past in context, is much more pragmatic, and obliges a systematic consideration of the moral standards inherent in our science and profession. We must situate "ourselves within a much more diffuse and flowing realm of activity; simply, we must begin from within our actual everyday life situation . . . whatever *that* is" (Shotter, 1985, p. 168). Most striking, this perspective heals the long-standing schism between clinician and researcher with a cooperative vision of "local science" (see Trierweiler & Stricker, chap. 14). Gergen (1982, 1985) called this new, more human, and humane vision of the behavioral sciences "sociorationalism." Systematic, rational scholarship and research explicitly embedded in particular social contexts help to provide significance and meaning for human communities.

Social constructionism and psychology itself have a context. Marginalized or victimized groups quite reasonably come to question the nature of the social knowledge put forward as science by the dominant political groups. Hawkesworth's (1989) superb article on epistemologies in feminist scholarship presented the alternative worldviews in a way that is relevant to the issues inherent in the social science of all disenfranchised groups. She identified four epistemologies, which I present in a general, rather than in her feminist, frame. The first of these parallels Gergen's (1982, 1985) descriptions of traditional positivistic, empirical psychology. The second is standpoint theory, which argues that there is a privileged perspective that emerges from people who are oppressed that "can pierce ideological obfuscations and attain correct and comprehensive understanding of the world" (Hawkesworth, 1989, p. 536). The third is postmodernism, a deconstructionist position that "rejects the very possibility of a truth about reality" and argues for the "situatedness" of each observer (Hawkesworth, 1989, p. 536). This perspective involves "profound skepticism regarding universal (or universalizing) claims about the existence, nature, and powers of reason" (Hawkesworth, 1989, p. 536). The fourth perspective, for which Hawkesworth ultimately argued, is based on "cognition as a human practice" (Hawkesworth, 1989, p. 536). To a substantial degree it parallels social constructionism as presented here, although the language is different and rationalism is not central.

In the context of standpoint theory and postmodern views, the social constructionist perspective, with its confidence in rationality and contextual empiricism, seems downright conservative. All of psychology faces a challenge: The concerns of women, minorities, and third-world people (cf. Moghaddam, 1987) ultimately must be addressed within the context of our science if it is to remain viable over the long term. These issues, too, must be addressed in the core curriculum.

Social Culture and History

Scientific as well as professional knowledge are historically dependent on the prevailing meaning systems and conceptual structures of the times (cf. Gergen, 1982, p. 17). If psychology and its core curriculum have been created by people "in relationship" (cf. Gergen, 1985, p. 272) at a particular historical moment and in a particular subculture, all of these elements merit scrutiny.

Certainly, social contexts draw together compatible people who in turn further develop the contexts. A discussion of the sorts of people who have created American psychology can emphasize their social context or their personalities. The first position is that psychology has within it two cultures (Kimble, 1984) or two sorts of people (Dana, 1987) variously defined. One of these cultures is said to be inhabited generally by the sorts of faculty described later, which Sampson (1985) spoke of as dominated by "egocentric control," Shotter (1989) identified as governed by the text of "possessive individualism," and Dana (1987) labeled "alpha persons," the bad (mostly) guys or the real scientists depending on one's perspective. The other culture—Sampson's (1985) "sociocentric" and Dana's (1987) "beta persons"—is said to consist of the good guys, women, minorities, and creative-intuitive, humanistic types or soft-headed antiscientists.

There are moments where this sort of argument seems persuasive. However, I believe that a rigorous professional psychology demands a particular sort of contextual, engaged, related, and committed science, not the elimination of science and substitution of a similarly valuable but substantially different humanism embodied in different sorts of people. According to the social constructionist position, neglect of social context in psychological science has led to error and misunderstanding within the context of the traditional, "egocentric" culture by its own internal standards, not simply to immorality and alienation as viewed by the outsider "sociocentrics."

The second position is that people create knowledge products consistent with who they are, the culture in which they find themselves, and the people and questions they study. A historical examination of the profession within the context of the characteristics of university faculties and university life should illuminate the past and pave the way for future changes in training and ultimately in vision.

American University Culture and Psychology

Sarason (1981, 1982) suggested that traditional universities attract and select intellectual "rugged individualists," "assertive, ambitious prima donna types" who "go their own way and frequently clash" (Sarason, 1982, p. 222). These usually White male faculties were influenced by contingencies that rewarded short, contained studies with clear experimental controls and simple statistics, but not the local, fundamentally interpersonal activities of clinical work, excellence in teaching, or local science (see Trierweiler & Stricker, chap. 14). Faculties of influential universities teaching future practitioners felt—and often still feel—obliged primarily to ground themselves in research rather than in practice.

According to Sarason (1981), pre-war American psychology was "aclinical in orientation; at worst, it was anticlinical" (p. 831). Psychology had "no experience with what was involved in training clinical psychologists, with the creation of settings for clinical practice, and with the culture of existing settings devoted to clinical service" (p. 831). The field's strengths were its research traditions, sophistication, and skepticism consistent with its individual focus. Testing was a relatively "minor asset" (p. 831).

The economics of the development of clinical psychology has strongly influenced both its form and its bedfellows. According to Sarason (1981), after World War II, the partnership between Veterans Administration and medical centers guaranteed psychiatric and medical domination of the new profession of clinical psychology. "Basic" research dollars went into the medically dominated National Institute of Mental Health. Therefore, it seemed socially responsible to forge a tie with psychiatry, especially because the federal monies would support students and pay for expanded faculties and consultantships. With this arrangement came psychiatry's intrapsychic orientation and a quiet, not entirely uncomfortable seat for clinical psychology in the back of the bus (a bus without women and children). "Clinical psychology became part of a medically dominated mental health movement that was narrow in terms of the social order, and as imperialistic as it was vigorous" (Sarason, 1981, p. 833). This influence is felt even today with the typical licensure requirement that there be 2 years of supervised practice in an organized health-care setting. Arguably there continues to be an enormous difference in the way psychology is practiced in medically dominated settings compared with settings where psychology rules its own house.

The "Asocial" Professional Psychology

According to Sarason (1982), it was not surprising that psychology "focussed on the individual psyche, what Murray Levine calls the emphasis on 'intrapsychic supremacy' " (p. 222). The influence of the structure, organization, and traditions of the setting on daily life was thought to be minimal.

Even social psychology limited itself to the experimental study of interpersonal interactions and small groups (Leary & Maddux, 1987). As stated by Sarason (1981), "It was not social in the sense of placing these interactions in the context of a highly differentiated society with a distinctive culture and ideology that were reflected in and reinforced by governmental, political, educational, religious, and financial (profit-making) systems of institutions" (p. 832). Psychology itself has its own fundamental attribution error: vastly overestimating the power of internal forces and vastly underestimating the role of external forces in people's lives (cf. Sarason, 1982, p. 211).

Although there are certainly notable exceptions (Leary & Maddux, 1987), too little academic attention has been paid to social phenomena such that key theories in the discipline itself have developed in a way that makes them seem as an academic afterthought, peripheral, certainly not central to the science or to the realities of professional practice. There are, of course, exceptions. Sarason (1981) reported that John Dewey saw psychology in a manner consistent with this chapter and said so in his 1899 American Psychological Association (APA) presidential address. "Dewey saw clearly what psychology is blind to: The substance of psychology cannot be independent of the social order. It is not that it *should not* be independent but that it *cannot* be" (Sarason, 1981, p. 827). It is not surprising, then, that this dominant, largely individual psychology did not provide coherent theoretical conceptions to understand people in their (ecologically realistic) social contexts, let alone a central, coherent place for women's concerns or for the study of ethnic diversity. This asocial professional psychology (Sarason, 1981, p. 827) has underestimated the influence of social pathology (Albee, 1986), neglected issues of power and victimization, and minimized the importance of context—cultural and ethnic, organizational, professional, and situational—on the lives of people.

Cross-Cultural and Ethnic Psychology

In addition to the influence of the dominant individual psychologies, cross-cultural and ethnic influences on psychology have been minimized for other, more subtle reasons. The purported pursuit of universal truths, described earlier, often turned out to be an ethnocentric (and male-centered) arrogance, as if others must be generally similar to the mostly male, White, upper-middle-class professors and their student subjects. Dana (1987) asserted that "cross-cultural training has been neglected because culturally different persons are presumed to be similar to oneself and to desire the same ingredients for high-quality life-styles" (p. 12).

According to Shotter (1989, p. 135), it is the use in research of the third-person, passive voice that fails to capture the character of the important relationships between whom one studies and oneself. Therefore, this research misrepresents the others' social life as well as the ethical and political relations between what are referred to as subjects and those studying them. The lofty, scientific, third-person perch allows pronouncements to be made about the other that seem to have the truth of planetary orbits, while creating and sustaining social orders and directing attention away from certain important social and interpersonal phenomena.

It is doubtful that a valid cultural psychology can be derived unless the scientist and the people to be studied share a common language and culture, whether in a broad (e.g., Western culture) or narrow (e.g., local) sense (Smedslund, 1985). Obsolete are the historically ubiquitous culturally imperialistic attitudes that had no meaningful place in psychology for cultural difference except as defect, oddity, or regression. It follows that cultural and ethnic diversity should be both in the center of the curriculum and throughout it, not isolated in some few elective, or even required, courses on "individual differences."

As Clifford Swensen (personal communication, July 24, 1990) pointed out, religion is the most fundamental factor in many people's lives, yet it typically is ignored in discussions of diversity. He said, "The most vital movements in the third world today are fundamentalist Islam in Northern Africa, the Middle East, and part of Southeast Asia, and a fundamentalist Pentecostal Christianity in South and Central America." In the United

States, the most rapidly growing churches are the various sects, particularly Pentecostal sects, and evangelical Christianity. Psychology seldom takes these movements into account in discussions of promoting and understanding diversity, yet they form the basis by which many people interpret and cope with their world.

Moghaddam (1987) discussed the ways in which psychology has developed in a manner consistent with the cultural circumstances in the first world (United States), the second world (e.g., United Kingdom, Union of Soviet Socialist Republics, Europe), and the third world (developing countries). For example, compared with the United States, European social psychology has placed greater emphasis on cooperation and conflict, conformity, the social psychology of the psychology experiment, philosophy of science, racial and ethnic issues, and, most important, intergroup relationships. Canada has paid more attention to language variations and multiculturalism. Third-world psychology has been directed toward solving social problems. One novel element has been a multidimensional, rather than a unidimensional, conception of individualism–collectivism. In the third world, individualism and collectivism are not seen as mutually exclusive; in the first and second worlds, they are perceived as opposites (Moghaddam, 1987, pp. 917–918).

Training Context and the Professional School Movement

The same sort of contextual analysis that has been applied to traditional university professional psychology programs must also be applied to the professional school movement. The expansion of clinical psychology in traditional programs in the 1960s was fueled by Great Society grant money. As student support declined with government money, the growing availability of third-party reimbursement made the professional psychology movement possible. The somewhat older students, the increasing number of women in the field, and the massive debt for many finishing students must impact on the nature of practice and therefore on the discipline. Tuition-driven institutions with less than ideal faculty pay scales have both necessitated professional practice for many faculty and ensured that the actualities of such practice will enliven teaching. At the same time, the economics of professional school education, coupled with those of the post-Reagan era, make low-paying, socially important work choices less likely.

It is necessary to consider the social, intellectual, and political problem of specifying who the professional psychology core curriculum is actually for in the current training context. My proposal is straightforward. If statements about the core, including the National Council of Schools of Professional Psychology (NCSPP) San Antonio conference resolutions (see McHolland, chap. 21), do indeed specify the "central, innermost, and most essential parts of the professional psychology curriculum," (cf. dictionary definition of *core;* Urdang & Flexner, 1969, p. 298), it makes little sense to say that some programs, even research-oriented ones, should not have them. How could NCSPP or another comparable group say that they have identified the central, innermost, most essential, crucial, critical parts of professional psychology, but, you folks over there, you may want to do something else. If the core is the core, then it is the core. The arguments in this chapter and the San Antonio conference resolutions are for all of professional psychology.

In an ironic fashion, this position is consistent with Matarazzo's (1987) work based on an examination of the chapter headings of introductory psychology texts since the turn of the century. He convincingly argued that the boundaries of the discipline of psychology—as distinct from, for example, history or economics—have been relatively stable. Certainly, many psychologists, including myself, identify with this breadth. Still, to put forward this ecumenical construction of the one psychology is like saying that there is only one United States: much as it was at the turn of the century. Not only have times changed, but there are enormous differences among Boston; Las Vegas; Marquette, Michigan; Terre Haute, Indiana; and De Ridder, Louisiana. Furthermore, it makes a difference whether one moved there after living in five other places or has never lived anywhere else.

To support Matarazzo's (1987) inclusive construction or mine, except to increase breadth, there may be little pragmatic reason to challenge the course labels on the familiar required list or to propose that psychology's pie be divided into differently named pieces. There is sufficient flexibility that programs can usually find a way to do what they want within reasonable boundaries. What fits in these categories is ultimately arbitrated by the selection of compatible site visitors and their judgments (Fox & Barclay, 1989). The content depends on the particular course selected from within each category, on the influence of the program model, on the inherent epistemology, on the syllabus and selection of readings, and on the faculty person's orientation. The process of the teaching and the pedagogy, as well as the faculty person's teaching skill, remains central to what the students actually receive. Although the blurring of differences may be politically desirable and the course titles may be the same, Matarazzo (1987) was wrong, I think, in believing that "the same principles, processes, and core content of the discipline" are taught regardless of the specific area of application, even in "university department[s] of psychology" (p. 893).

Two further aspects of the construction of the core curriculum surround what have been called *models* and *specialties*. Models, of course, refers to those hyphenated, rhetorical phrases scientist–practitioner, scholar–practitioner, and practitioner–scholar that are written in our catalogs and understood to be essential in the accreditation process. Although there is debate about the nature of psychological science, no one from either traditional university programs or professional schools is saying that doctorate-level practitioner training should not have a scientific and scholarly aspect. We should leave behind the current confusing and divisive rhetorical practice and instead use these labels to identify the career paths, with associated priorities, for which each program prepares its students. A main-line academic PhD program preparing university researchers might call itself a scientist–scholar–practitioner program. A professional school, no less scientific, might call itself a practitioner–scholar–scientist program. Two ideas follow: First, everyone would have the same core, whereas the culture, values, and electives of a particular school would be consistent with labels. Second, APA and our students could hold us empirically accountable for our label. A program that put forward scientist training first would need to demonstrate that the majority of its students had a research career path, or changes would be necessary.

The specialty problem is less clear. The great majority of professional programs are clinical. Should the resolutions that come from this and other related conferences apply to industrial–organizational, counseling, school, health, and neuropsychology programs and so forth? In this context, for example, it becomes unclear as to how much time a core-intervention course would focus on psychotherapy. A core-assessment course with industrial–organizational or neuropsychology students would no doubt leave out personality and projective tests. There are at least three alternatives. First, each specialty could interpret the areas within its own context, giving the core a much less specific meaning than the chapters in this volume suggest. Second, these sorts of resolutions could be limited to clinical psychology, with the attendant risks of the further Balkanization of the profession. Third, more like medicine, clinical psychology could be seen as the generic basis for these specialties (e.g., clinical neuropsychology, clinical health psychology). I tilt in this direction, but I become quickly and uncomfortably aware of how central my identity as a psychotherapist is in my vision of training.

Sometimes, though, these issues seem relatively trivial and mask the larger picture. If psychology is indeed the impressive product of social forces rather than the objective and disinterested development of positivist science, then social forces—people in relationships—can free it to change and to develop a new direction.

Social Reflexivity

A fundamental characteristic of human psychological activity is *reflexivity*. Gergen (1982) paraphrased Alfred Schutz and asserted that one can step out of the ongoing flux of living and by a reflective glance examine actions and behaviors in the past tense (p. 18). This process allows a reflexive review and reconceptualization that in turn impacts on ongoing processes, which are themselves subject to further such reviews. Not only is psychology the product of scientific and professional activity, but scientific and professional activity itself is the subject matter for further scientific and professional activity that is also within the domain of psychology (e.g., the current chapter) (Smedslund, 1985). The situation is different in other professions. The study of the practice of psychology is the psychology of psychology; the study of the practice of law, for example, is the psychology of law. It is possible to delineate a number of aspects of reflexivity: personal reflexivity, personal–professional reflexivity, professional reflexivity, and cultural reflexivity.

Personal Reflexivity

Personal reflexivity is the process by which I examine my past experience with the possibility of changing my future behavior based on what I have learned. This sort of function is central to many of the activities and experiences of professional psychologists. Only dangerously narrow training on the one hand ignores this element of experience for the person of the psychologist and the person of the client or, on the other hand, says this is all one needs to know.

Personal–Professional Reflexivity

Personal–professional reflexivity is the process by which I systematically examine my personal experiences of professional practice and training with the goal of enhanced professional functioning. Common examples include the usual sorts of professional supervision, the discussion of countertransference as well as the rationale for psychotherapy for therapists in the psychodynamic tradition, and the behind-the-mirror consultation techniques of the systemic therapists. Most of us, I suspect, would describe these sorts of personal–professional reflexive experiences as being the core of our identity as psychologists.

Personal–professional reflexivity, as embodied in a systematic set of experiences, should be central to professional psychology training. In the context of a group of colleagues, students of professional psychology should bring together attitudes, knowledge, personal background and history—both intellect and affect—as well as their own reactions to practice and training experiences in what might be called the integrative or professional socialization core (for a detailed rationale, see Singer, Peterson, & Magidson, chap. 18). It may well be that such training events come to be the sentient core—that is, the set of experiences that feel most central to a program.

Currently, this aspect of training can be seen as coming about in three ways: (a) formally in the sorts of professional development or integrative seminars that some programs have; (b) informally in the various ways learning occurs by being around psychologists, fellow students, and clients in academic and clinical settings; and (c) formally through experiences such as personal therapy, certain aspects of supervision, and interpersonal groups that explicitly focus on the person of the potential psychologist. Statements about the core curriculum should specify the events in which reflexive professional socialization should occur and the boundaries of such required experiences (e.g., required therapy or not).

Similarly, there seems to be general agreement about the critical developmental elements of modeling, individualized feedback and sharing, and reflexive focus inherent in mentoring relationships as core experiences. Yet whether mentoring happens or not seems to be thought of more as a matter of individual diligence or luck rather than as something that results from systematic curricular planning.

Psychologists' views of their own core training experiences could be studied qualitatively. For example, at a recent professional development dinner for our program's faculty, we asked the faculty about the teachable, learnable experiences that made them feel like psychologists. The majority of people cited early experiences as a psychotherapist or mentoring relationships with particular people. No one mentioned course work. If we studied what experienced psychologists actually remembered from their core training and attributed to it, I suspect there would be visions of the field, perhaps a theoretical orientation, some few facts, habits of mind from mentors, active discussions and the beginnings of colleagueship, and some negative human examples. The core that arises from these kinds of questions is very different from the one that focuses on what it takes to begin competent practice or to transmit the discipline.

Professional Reflexivity

Professional reflexivity is the way the profession studies itself to learn from its own performance using a full range of methods. Typical exmples are historical examinations, such as those of Gergen (1982, 1985) or of Sarason (1981, 1982); more systematic versions of qualitative investigations, such as the one previously described; the ubiquitous APA accreditation self-study; and surveys of training practices.

A survey core, obtained when programs are polled (cf. Morrison, O'Connor, & Williams, chap. 6), reflect the state of the art. Inherently conservative, surveys delineate the degree to which programs have reflexively aspired to meet APA accreditation standards and the degree to which state-licensure statutes overlap. They measure what is, not necessarily what should be.

A variety of operational cores could be defined by asking particular questions (cf. R. J. Bent, personal communication, August 10, 1988): What would be required if we had only 1 year; or if we had to eliminate a year of training, what would go? Alternatively, we could ask finishing students to identify the six courses that were central to their development as psychologists. It could be that the answers would end up being the rediscovery of the masters degree, paraprofessional training, or social work. Indeed, it may be that the uniqueness of professional psychology training at the doctoral level is the combination of core and elective elements within a discipline.

From the perspective of reflexivity, it is clear that the training of professional psychologists should be centrally influenced by the context and demands of the professional practice situation. Although certainly psychological science does come to be applied in practice, it is equally as true that the practice—the real needs of psychologists and clients in the world outside universities—appropriately demands a particular kind of relevant and useful scientific psychology. Arguably, responsiveness to the explicit demands of professional practice is one of the cornerstones on which professional psychology and the professional school movement is based. It is only relatively recently in organized psychology that NCSPP explicitly put forward that the actual nature of practice should determine the professional core competency areas: relationship (interpersonal), assessment, intervention, research and evaluation, consultation and education, and management and supervision (including ethics) (this volume throughout; Bent & Cannon, 1987; Bourg et al., 1989). Training is to include relevant knowledge, skills, and attitudes.

Research and evaluation is both a professional competency and one way in which psychological knowledge products are developed. Consistent with the vision of Trierweiler and Stricker (see chap. 14), professionals should be seen as local clinical scientists both with an expanded array of psychological research methods and with an expanded vision of the relevance of this research to practice.

Yet another likely result of the individual focus of American psychology is that consultation and education as well as management and supervision seem superficially less central and less easy to specify and have less written about them. Certainly these processes are not inherently simpler, and professional psychologists spend substantial amounts of time in these activities. As academic administrators know, good therapists are easier to find than good teachers. A particular effort is needed to bring these areas into central focus in professional psychology education so they do not seem like add-ons.

The core as it has been discussed so far has been a product of the past and the present rather than the reflexive acknowledgment of changing professional roles and the health-care marketplace. A core for the psychologist of the future might, for example, emphasize NCSPP categories of management and supervision and consultation and education and deemphasize long-term psychotherapy and time-consuming assessment techniques.

The context of the development and implementation of a core curriculum should also be a matter of explicit scrutiny and analysis, specifically (a) the importance of national meetings on curriculum, including structure, process, organizational sponsorship, and attendance; and (b) the elements of the administration of the accreditation and licensure process. For example, the ways in which programs meet requirements are influenced by the fact that it is much easier for one to demonstrate to a licensing board or site-visit team that a course meets a particular requirement than it is to show how it was met by, say, portions of three courses and part of a practicum.

Cultural Reflexivity

On the cultural level, not only does the society influence the psychology in this reflexive manner, but psychology influences society (Gergen, 1982, pp. 18–26). Aspects of psychoanalysis and behaviorism have seeped into the culture and now influence the very phenomena that are being examined in a way that astrophysics cannot possibly influence planetary motion. Whereas some of this is unintentional, much is the intentional, ultimately positive result of the activities of professional psychologists. Primarily, this is done by impacting on the symbolic and conceptual systems, for example, bringing ideas such as repression, midlife crisis, and mental illness into our collective experience. However, it can be argued that dominant theoretical systems inadvertently can support particular potentially negative ways of making sense of experience. Perhaps behaviorism has given rise to ideas that suggest that successful functioning in relationships requires that one gain stimulus control over others' actions (Gergen, 1982, p. 32). Similarly, psychoanalysis may have encouraged a view that personal change is extremely difficult, that it takes many years to accomplish, and that an apparently passive stance is an initial prerequisite. Furthermore, developmentalists who uncritically describe the status quo position on aging inevitably support a discrediting, demeaning, and inadequate national policy (cf. Gergen, 1982, p. 170). Like a self-fulfilling prophesy, ideas such as all of these ultimately impact on public policy, education, and the core curriculum.

Social Interactional Perspective

The social interactional view argues for the primary (rather than secondary) importance of attention to dyadic and group interactions (Carson, 1983; Kiesler, 1982; Leary & Maddux, 1987). A detailed consideration of this view is outside the scope of this chapter and is discussed, in part, by Polite and Bourg (see chap. 11). Certainly, an interactional perspective on marriage and psychotherapy is increasingly included in professional psychology training. Still, the fact that NCSPP felt that it must explicitly speak of requiring the "systems view" (Bourg et al., 1989, p. 70) suggests that some programs may yet ignore or minimize the interactional perspective and that the position is gaining in importance in psychology's future.

A particular element of the social interactional view relevant to the core curriculum is pedagogy. Enormous variations in teaching quality and pedagogy among courses both between and within schools are mostly ignored in the documents produced at national conferences. Although being for good teaching is synonymous with being for apple pie, the contingencies in universities that deemphasize such classic cooking and give a secondary status to teaching continue to be influential. There should be explicit attention to the interactional elements of pedagogy in discussions of the core curriculum in a number of ways:

1. Goals and content can be vastly different even within courses of the same name.
2. The place of a course in the curriculum can change its meaning (e.g., history and systems in the first year is introductory; in the last year it can be integrative).
3. A pedagogy that emphasizes the development of critical thinking is substantially different from one that emphasizes the pouring of information from the large beaker into small ones.
4. Integration of basic science and professional training is critical. If basic science

and professional training are to be integrated in practice, they must be integrated in courses where faculty must themselves have that capability.

5. The pedagogical purpose of dissertations and other research efforts for those not aspiring to a research career should be specified (see Trierweiler & Stricker, chap. 14).

6. Course formats (lecture, seminar, field placement, special projects) influence outcome (cf. Morrison, O'Connor, & Williams, chap. 6).

7. Excellence in teaching should be a central concern of professional psychology training institutions.

Social Individual Influences

The vast number of social influences on the individual are beyond the scope of this chapter. Leary and Maddux (1987, p. 907) include two aspects when they speak of "social/dysgenic psychology" (the study of interpersonal processes in the development of dysfunctional behavior) and "social-diagnostic psychology" (the study of the interpersonal processes involved in the identification, classification, and assessment of psychological problems). Simple transpositions of the psychology of the individual have tended to confuse rather than to illuminate (cf. Sarason, 1982, p. 211). The conception of multiple levels of understanding has all too often led to justifications for staying at the individual level. It is not simply that there is a social level to understanding the individual. It is that the individual and the social exist simultaneously in an integrated manner in the lives of people.

Social Responsibility

Sarason (1986) argued that a scientific field needs a center, a sense of focus that explains, directs, organizes, and gives purpose to a field.

> In its own way it establishes a sense of community, a means whereby individual and collective effort will be governed and judged. The center not only alters the boundaries of what is known, it also points to what remains unknown. . . . The center has an implied moral quality in that it derives from a history of the field strewn with examples of immodesty in past centers that inadequately respected the significances of the unknown. (p. 900)

Gergen (1982) made a parallel point: The "valuational goals" of the scientists shape what is "found" (p. 28). Phenomena such as sexual abuse (Berson, 1989) and posttraumatic stress disorder are not "out there" (Gergen, 1982, p. 28) waiting to be discovered like some distant planet, but instead reflect the "tastes, values, needs, or motives" (Gergen, 1982, p. 28) of particular scientists.

Perhaps an aspirational core should embody the best elements of what could be created within our professional training institutions. Courses that focus on the planning, development, and public policy elements of future mental health systems might be desirable. Students might be required to donate a day per week in 1 year to work on a particularly difficult problem in professional psychology in their own communities. The values underlying the professional psychology core must reflect its highest aspirations, not just minimum standards.

To articulate our center and to give meaning to a vision of public interest, a social responsibility core should specify the principles to be embodied in all the curriculum. Consistent with the aspirations of both the NCSPP conferences in 1989 in San Juan and in 1990 in San Antonio, the social context of cultural and ethnic diversity, age, gender, and sexual preference should be an integral part of our science, practice, and curriculum. To the extent that we may be dealing with prejudice within the ranks of our own faculty and students, this aspect of the core may require a level of intervention different from that traditionally considered in curriculum changes.

Embedded in the values and attitudes underlying core curriculum, we need to bring an expanded moral and social vision to the center of professional psychology and to traditional academic psychology as well. Not only is it the right thing to do—it is the best science and the best practice.

4

ACADEMIC – SCIENTIFIC CORE CURRICULUM

Frank M. Webbe and Philip D. Farber
Florida Institute of Technology
Melbourne, Florida

Glenace E. Edwall
Baylor University
Waco, Texas

and

Keith J. Edwards
Biola University
La Mirada, California

Before the advent of applied psychology and the meteoric rise of clinical psychology following World War II, the academic – scientific curriculum was essentially the entire curriculum in psychology. The prevailing university-based psychology programs defined their own curricula with substantial variation from program to program. After the rise of applied psychology, with the need for particular applied training and other attendant issues (e.g., timing of the internship and, in some states, the movement to license psychologists), the notion of a core or germ of scientific psychology came to have an accepted meaning within the discipline, although often grudgingly (see Jones, 1987, for a partial review of this period of development). The academic – scientific core of psychology came to be seen as analogous to the mathematics and physics training in the engineering disciplines. The core was the sine qua non of psychology: that which applied psychology actually applied.

The debate as to whether there is or should be a prescribed academic – scientific core curriculum continues today in both nonapplied and applied psychology. At recent meetings of the Council of Graduate Departments of Psychology (COGDOP), for example, the discussion of the possibility of implementing common core requirements across all graduate programs in psychology provoked heated debate. Nonapplied programs are much more variable in their basic curricula than are programs subject to accreditation review from the American Psychological Association (APA) or other bodies. Considerable disagreements erupted about what the academic – scientific core of psychology does or should contain and about the associated issue of institutional autonomy. In this context, it is significant that the phrase *academic – scientific core* does not appear in the San Antonio conference resolutions, although the much less controversial phrase *knowledge base* does (see McHolland, chap. 21).

Both applied and nonapplied programs have railed against core content being delineated by accrediting bodies. Nonetheless, programs that train professionals for service delivery, particularly within the health sector and where eventual state licensing is an issue, generally accept the necessity for some consensually defined core curriculum.

Operational Academic–Scientific Core

The operational delineation of the academic–scientific core-content areas for professional training is specified in APA accreditation materials (APA, 1979) and embodied in the accumulated judgments of the Committee on Accreditation. Both now and in the past, the accreditation guidelines were created through and gain their credibility from the APA political process and the participation of esteemed psychologists in applied graduate education. Implicitly, if not explicitly, as based on their own studies of psychology, these participating psychologists determined those content areas that could be seen as core.

This operationally defined academic–scientific core includes study in biological bases of behavior, cognitive–affective bases (learning), individual differences, history and systems, social bases of behavior, and research methods and statistics (APA, 1979). Recent discussions of the scope of the accreditation process resulted in suggestions that training in ethics and professional standards, normal development, and psychological measurement be specified more directly in the academic–scientific core.

It is interesting to note that this academic–scientific core represents a mid-20th-century estimation rather than a historical appreciation of the roots of psychology. Philosophy, for example, is notably absent from this core except as covered within individual courses in the content areas. Physics, a historic contributor to psychology, also is noticeable by its absence except perhaps for the frayed remnants that remain in some areas of the biological and the learning areas. Nonetheless, APA puts forward a definition of the accreditation standards as representing an irreducible minimum of content areas beyond which groups of educators in psychology could not go without unresolvable disagreements (APA, 1982).

Academic–Scientific Core in Professional Schools Today

Rationale for the Academic–Scientific Core Curriculum in Professional Psychology

The rationale for the academic–scientific core is inherent in the interpretation of the phrase *applied psychology*. Professional psychologists apply the academic–scientific knowledge and methods of the discipline to real-world problems. The doctorate-level professional psychologist has the requisite understanding to apply nonspecific academic–scientific knowledge aptly to novel situations and to problems where manuals and textbooks are silent. This high-level ability differentiates the doctorate-level psychologist from the technician. Indeed, it has been a common observation that the critical thinking capability, developed within the framework of the academic–scientific core, is a crucial component of training for practice (Meltzoff, 1986). As long as applied training is seen in this perspective, the academic – scientific core will maintain its importance.

Pedagogy

Professional schools differ from other psychology graduate programs and from each other in the manner in which the academic – scientific core is taught. Differences exist among traditional programs, university-based professional schools, and free-standing schools in the training of the faculty assigned to teach the academic – scientific core. In traditional programs, based in departments that train other groups of students in the scientific specialties, courses are taught by active scientists who represent narrow areas of the specialties. Although this does not guarantee that survey courses, for example, will be taught well, it should ensure that the instructors remain current with the field and have specialized knowledge of some complex concepts or studies to bring to their presentations. University-based professional schools are less likely to have such specialists on their faculties. Most free-standing schools do not have such specialists on their faculties on a full-time basis, but may have them on their adjunct staff.

Regardless of faculty training and background, most professional schools appear to rely generally on the lecture method. Less frequently, laboratory courses in physiological processes, perceptual processes, animal behavior, or child development are offered. Professional psychologists, rather than active scientists in the field of study, often provide the instruction. The implications of this type of instruction for adequacy of learning have never been considered fully.

The traditional department model of active scientist-as-teacher incorporates the student-as-apprentice in the laboratory. At its best, it is characterized by excellent one-on-one training, but it is very inefficient in terms of the numbers of students who can be trained adequately within the model. In professional schools, the training model differs from the traditional department model. Students in academic – scientific core courses are trained didactically, often without hands-on experience. Knowledge and attitudes, rather than laboratory and research skills, are seen as the desirable end product of training. This type of instruction has been characteristic of professional schools for some time and is part of the identity of professional school training (Kopplin, 1986).

In training for applied practice, professional schools assume that graduates usually will not become researchers in one of the traditional scientific areas of psychology. A typical professional school goal was to train students only at the basic level of research skills and to focus more explicitly on fostering the attitude of respect for the scientific basis of the discipline and the understanding that allows them to be knowledgeable consumers of scientific information. Recently, Trierweiler and Stricker (see chap. 14) developed a much more sophisticated view of the professional psychologist as local clinical scientist. In their view, the overarching goal of much of academic – scientific core training is to develop:

> critical investigators of local (as opposed to universal) realities (a) who are knowledgeable of research, scholarship, personal experience, and scientific methodology; and (b) who are able to develop plausible, communicable formulations for understanding essentially local phenomena using theory, general world knowledge including scientific research, and, most important, their own abilities as skeptical scientific observers. (p. 104, chap. 14)

Toward this end, students are prepared with a firm foundation on which to build additional research skills, but further training is dictated by individual choice rather than program requirement. The training model and philosophy dictate the depth of the content in methodology courses and in the academic–scientific core.

Revision of the Academic–Scientific Core Curriculum

General Considerations

Any revision of the content labeled *core* can be expected to provoke considerable debate. Revisionists have two responsibilities: (a) to consider if each area that is currently included in the academic–scientific core is still crucial, and (b) to consider what, if any, new areas should be added.

In this context, one approach begins by reviewing how the academic–scientific core came into existence. A need for consistency in the training of those licensed for practice was a major driving force behind the creation of the APA accreditation office and, by extension, the construction of the academic–scientific core curriculum. The next step is to think about the extent to which the present academic–scientific core is being driven by the existing accreditation guidelines and by the continuously changing state licensing requirements as determined by the state psychology boards. A further consideration is whether these operational determiners still mirror a rational basis for the knowledge areas that are seen as crucial to applied education and practice.

There are many illustrations of emerging knowledge areas that may be considered for inclusion in the academic–scientific core. Many state boards, for example, are requiring psychologists to become knowledgeable about the myriad ways that acquired immunodeficiency syndrome (AIDS) affects psychological practice. Should AIDS-related content be included as part of the academic–scientific core? Similarly, a proposal has been put forth to include psychologists within the small group of professionals who may prescribe drugs. Should pharmacology be included in the core? Race, culture, and ethnicity are considered to be crucial in the application of psychological knowledge for therapeutic benefit. Should cultural anthropology or sociology be included as a necessary part of the core? Because religion is so often a key to the understanding of the behavior both of individuals and of groups, should religious studies form part of the core?

In the sections that follow, we propose two models or conceptualizations for revising the academic–scientific core curriculum in a responsible and responsive manner. They may be undertaken either separately or in concert.

Model 1: The Static and Dynamic Elements of the Core

On the one hand, the entity that we call psychology and that we abstract in the academic–scientific core cannot be so changeable that its identity is altered each time a new and important topic is identified. On the other hand, the academic–scientific core cannot be so fixed that it precludes change. Therefore, to ensure both continuity and the capacity for change, the academic–scientific core could comprise explicitly static and dynamic components.

In this model, the static component would not be completely static, but it would have greater inertia than the dynamic component. For example, the static component would consist of the relatively well-accepted areas that constitute the current academic–

scientific core described by the APA accreditation model. The academic–scientific core would be reviewed and evaluated either on an ad hoc basis (e.g., when sufficient dissatisfaction with the existing version reached a crescendo that could not be ignored) or on a structured schedule (e.g., every 5 years). Change would come slowly, only after much deliberation, as befits a construct as important as the core.

The dynamic component would consist of newly identified or developed areas where knowledge is very relevant to practice, such as those previously mentioned (i.e., AIDS, pharmacology, multicultural diversity, and religion). These areas would be included within the relevant content areas of the static component.

The identification of a dynamic component of the academic–scientific core would foster an agreeable attitude toward change. By providing a conceptual mechanism for change, some of the more unpleasant side effects of the current unstructured process for determining change might be eliminated. Specification of the content to be changed would be obtained through a feedback process from psychologists in practice; from state boards of psychology; and from researchers and educators in professional schools, in departments of psychology, and in other disciplines.

The dynamic component of the academic–scientific core could be seen as the precursor to change in the static component. The longer a content area is held within the dynamic portion, the more likely that it should become part of the static portion. As an illustration, issues of multicultural diversity, long included within the social bases of behavior, might become a separate content area in a modification of the static component.

Model 2: Integrating the Academic–Scientific and Professional Cores

A second approach to revision of the academic–scientific core is to integrate it with the professional core. As Peterson suggested, "The practice—the real needs of psychologists and clients in the world outside universities—appropriately demands a particular kind of relevant and useful scientific psychology" (p. 33, chap. 3). The point here is that the psychology of the 1990s is not one where there is simply a basic science and applications of it. There is also a strong and vigorous applied science of psychology. It follows that the essential elements of the academic–scientific core and the professional core could be taught in an integrated manner.

According to an integrative approach, each course in the academic–scientific core should communicate core professional relevance and vice versa. For example, in a clinical training program, the core course in biological bases of behavior should integrate elements of practice that demand understanding in biological terms. These might include eating disorders, sexual dysfunction, gender issues, and assessment of developmental disabilities. An interesting implication of such an integration is that the most qualified person to teach the restructured course may not be the laboratory scientist or the practicing professional psychologist. Rather, some retraining of either one might be necessary to accomplish the task. We would not expect the practicing professional to have engaged actively in experiments that led to current scientific advances, and we would not expect the active scientist to be experienced in the intricacies of applied practice.

As Derner and Stricker (1986) suggested, faculty in professional school roles are more subject to curricular demands and programmatic needs than the faculty in traditional university departments. Integrating the academic–scientific core and the applied core may place an additional demand on the professional school faculty. An alternative might be to develop a team-teaching approach characterized by an active scientist in tandem with an active practitioner. Although the staffing patterns of many professional schools do not lend themselves to this option, nonetheless this alternative offers great flexibility in implementing an integrative curriculum.

Integrating the academic – scientific with the applied core might be accomplished best incrementally, one professor at a time or one content area at a time. Otherwise, the entire curriculum may become so fluid that it will confuse rather than educate.

One major implication of this integration would be a move toward a curricular model that is much more content oriented than course oriented. One of the inherent drawbacks of a curriculum that is designed to satisfy accreditation guidelines and the insistence of licensing boards that a particular topic be addressed in training is that programs equate content with course. Generally, separate courses, whose titles mirror the topics judged to be important, are developed. For example, we now teach a separate course in ethics even though ethical content permeates practicum training and some didactic courses. Most curricula include a specific course in history and systems even though historical content is included in most academic – scientific core courses.

If training programs move toward an integrative model, whether alone or in concert with the static and dynamic components model, then a content-oriented, competency-based curriculum may emerge. If and when this happens, training programs and state boards must communicate better and must cooperate more in the licensing procedure so that graduates are not affected adversely. Already state boards may determine that a student who completed an APA-accredited program must take additional course work to be eligible to sit for licensure. Lack of communication and cooperation between programs and state boards would be detrimental to programs and their graduates.

Preparation for Current and Future Practice

It is our responsibility to prepare our students both for the world that they will encounter soon after graduation and for the world of the future. To accomplish this we must be able to translate our vision of future issues into the dynamism that is built into the curriculum. The issues relating to the static and dynamic portions of the academic – scientific core curriculum have an important relation to this preparation. Programs cannot rely only on the static component of the academic – scientific core to provide the underpinnings for future practice. For example, at present we can predict that the AIDS epidemic will extend into the future. How have training programs responded to this immense problem? On the basis of a brief review of course offerings and discussions with faculty at many of the National Council of Schools of Professional Psychology institutions, only a small number have responded programmatically to this issue. Clear acknowledgment of a changeable, dynamic component of the curriculum could facilitate our response to predicted demands of future practice and might foster a proactive approach toward the identification of such demands.

5

TEACHING THE CORE CURRICULUM

Marc Lubin

Illinois School of Professional Psychology
Chicago, Illinois

and

George Stricker

Derner Institute, Adelphi University
Garden City, New York

During the past few years, each of us has had students express some variation of the following: "It is nice to be going to school at a place that gives us the kind of experience that you are teaching us to provide for our patients." On a similar note, a student included in the acknowledgment section of her dissertation—which ironically was concerned with the parallel process between supervision and psychotherapy— an expression of gratitude to her program "for creating an atmosphere which fosters professional and personal growth" (Vickers, 1974, p. iii). It is exactly the nature of this learning atmosphere—in the university, in the classroom, in the supervisory session, and in the clinical session—that we address in this chapter.

Psychotherapy, the area of clinical practice that is the focus of much of professional training, is an educational experience, an attempt to teach the patient new, more comfortable, more productive, and more fulfilling ways of functioning. It must be understood that what is being taught in psychotherapy is not merely cognitive, nor is teaching concerned only with conscious material. If we recognize that psychotherapists teach affective – cognitive units and do so taking into account unconscious influences on learning, it quickly becomes apparent that neither love nor knowledge is sufficient for learning to occur.

How material is taught is as important as what is taught. Frequently, a parallel process occurs in which the student learns both what is being taught *and* the way in which it is being taught. The patient learns to emulate the therapist's calm, self-reflective manner and his or her concern for understanding rather than for judging. The therapist is able to provide these conditions in part because of the supervisor's gentle reassurance, clarity of thought, and accepting manner. The student acquires concepts to use in treatment from a classroom where free inquiry is valued and where creative thought is rewarded. Professors and students alike thrive in an institutional setting that encourages personal development and supports personal growth. At every stage of the pedagogic sequence, modeling of therapeutic, growth-enhancing behavior occurs and is transmitted in a parallel process to the other stages. The teacher, whether an administrator, a professor, a supervisor, or a therapist, models the desirable behavior. The pupil, whether a faculty member, a student, a supervisee, or a patient, identifies with the teacher, incorporates the affect as well as the content of the learning, and grows as a result of the process.

Pedagogy

Clinical Supervision

Nowhere is this pedagogic sequence as clear as in the process of clinical supervision. Regardless of the orientation, the supervisee sees a patient and then presents the case to a supervisor, who listens carefully, provides support and guidance, and helps the student to help the patient and, concurrently, to develop clinical skills. Supervision is an approach in which both teaching and demonstrating occur simultaneously. Fleming and Benedek (1966) referred to supervision as a learning alliance, and they viewed its effectiveness as maximized in a climate of trust and cooperation relatively free of neurotic conflicts on the part of both members. A similar description could apply to psychotherapy.

Appreciation of the relation between the teaching and the demonstrating functions of supervision is not restricted to any single orientation. Psychoanalysis is attuned to parallel process. Ekstein and Wallerstein (1958) considered supervision to be "analogous to the psychotherapeutic process in which we hope to help our patients" (p. 262). The more humanistic approaches also are concerned with this parallelism. Rogers (1957) discussed the need for a supervisor to model facilitative behaviors to create an atmosphere for learning in supervision, just as is needed in therapy. Conceptually, one orientation may emphasize identification and another modeling, but both require that the teaching process be consistent with the content.

Learning Environment

As the therapist is the model for the patient and the supervisor is the model for the supervisee, the administrator can be a model for the learning community that is being constructed. A community that encourages respect, openness, and mutual valuation is likely to develop faculty members who treat students in this manner, and those students will find it easier to treat patients with the empathic attunement that encourages growth. Conversely, a community that is hostile and competitive will develop a faculty that is mutually distrustful and that uses students as pawns. These students, in turn, will be more involved in using patients to prove their competence than in aiding the patients to grow. Clearly, a professional school whose expressed purpose is the training of clinical practitioners must attend to the construction of an environment that parallels the values that we hold for practice. It is through this modeling that our students can develop their skills in a manner that will ultimately benefit their patients.

Academic Instruction

Lecture format.   Core-curriculum academic instructors must recognize that doctoral students view individual lecture and discussion presentations as potential models for future professional commitments, orientations, and values. Although our students intensively pursue such models in all aspects of their education, the classroom may be where the first and most vital connections to professional models occur. At its best, in the instructor – student exchange in the classroom, students can become inspired and be guided to pursue special directions in clinical psychology. For this reason, it is useful to note briefly some prominent communicative features of the lecture and discussion formats that impact student development and identification.

The instructor's unique lecture style provides information to a student that goes far beyond the mere transmission of content. The instructor's enthusiasm and excitement about particular ideas, research, vignettes, theories, and controversies frequently signal a type and depth of interest and involvement that have the capacity to generate parallel interests in the student. Often the instructor's involvement attracts and then provides an initial foundation for student investment both in the course area and in the instructor's approach to it. In observing the affective involvement of the faculty, the student learns what matters to the teacher. The instructor's enthusiasm and passion are often more of a factor in actual student modeling than is usually recognized. Academic and clinical directions chosen by students owe much to this particular dimension of lecturing.

The student also may be drawn to the instructor by the clarity, vividness, and intellectual force evident in the lecture. The capacity to illuminate a particular area of human experience through a dramatic and organized presentation also communicates excitement. The instructor's personal integration of a range of concepts, presentation of a focused line of argumentation, and the clear and balanced display of thoughtful opinion and critical thought excite an identification process in the eager student seeking a viable model for organizing the raw data of clinical psychology.

Within this matrix of instructor enthusiasm and intellectual persuasiveness, the eager student identifies the types of knowledge bases preferred by the instructor—to be able, initially, to follow in the teacher's academic and clinical tracks. One teacher's emphasis on formal research to validate a particular theoretical position models this empirical emphasis to the student, whereas another instructor's focus on the need for clear theoretical and conceptual articulation provides the student with a different priority in approaching certain academic materials. In the lecture presentations, then, students are constantly identifying areas of instructors' affective and intellectual emphases and styles, and they use these experiences to prioritize their own interests and values.

The lecturer's balance between enthusiasm and skepticism is also carefully observed by the student. The lecturer who balances excitement and investigatory rigor models the clinician's oscillation between participation and careful and rigorous observation, a major feature of sound clinical functioning. Students can observe this same dynamic in the intellectual and affective elements of their instructor's presentations and can consider how such a balance might function in their future clinical work.

Furthermore, lecturers can demonstrate a principle of interpersonal relatedness to students. Many master teachers have noted that the effectiveness of lecture presentations of new concepts or ideas depends on the instructor's ability to relate the course material to relevant experiences in students' lives. In clinical psychology, we might call this *teaching empathy,* a process by which instructors model attention to the parallel concepts of those topics being presented and of experiential concepts in the learners. Such empathic attention, of course, is a professional requirement of the clinician in his or her role as administrator, consultant, or therapist. Effective communication dictates an awareness of the others' positions and their available and accessible learning areas.

In addition, the instructor-as-lecturer demonstrates the type of cognitive style valued in presenting a core-curriculum topic that is transferable and relevant to understanding clinical data. For example, approaches that range from clarifying and reflecting theoretical concepts to those that critique and probe such concepts can model potential assessment and intervention modalities for students. The lecturer offers personal–professional ways of organizing and understanding human experience to students through a preferred mode of organizing and presenting lecture material.

In sum, the clinical student carefully monitors the instructor's intellectual style, affective responses, and implicit valuing of different knowledge models as communicated in the lecture format. At conscious levels and less conscious levels, students begin to identify with aspects of lecturers who compel affective involvement and intellectual excitement.

Discussion format. Students are acutely sensitive to their instructor's management and investment in the discussion format because this format most directly may reveal the interpersonal style and values of the instructor. The instructor, as discussion creator, leader, and facilitator, offers a number of potential clinical models to the student. The creation of an atmosphere that values student questions, opinions, and needs for clarification models a similar clinical position vis-à-vis the client (whether an individual, group, supervisee, or organization). Therefore, instructors who carefully organize clear discussion structures in which there is both an expectation of student involvement and an accompanying assurance of safety represent the dual clinical emphasis on task focus and on spontaneous client initiative around that focus.

Implicit here is the valuing of student responses as a major foundation and guide for class discussion, a recognition that, in clinical terms, respect for the client's experience and perspective precedes the establishment of a clear intervention contract. Appropriate participation in this delicate interpersonal structure in which spontaneous and sometimes troubling issues can emerge is then modeled by the clinician-as-discussion leader, even in courses that may not be directly clinical in nature. In this context, students are intensely interested in observing how the instructor manages the tangential or highly personalized comment, the anxiety-driven question about grades, or the provocative and hostile attack on the instructor's ideas. The teacher's reactions may provide a model for parallel clinical attitudes and stance toward disruptive client behaviors and communications.

In addition, students are alert to the degree to which their instructors are respectful and facilitative of the emergence and clarification of critical questions. They gauge whether the instructor can tolerate silence or student conflict in a discussion format, and they observe the teacher's commitment to encouraging independent thought, even if it means the class must suffer through some stressful moments. The instructor's capacity to tolerate critical student comment as well as to respond constructively to student problems is profoundly significant in the student's experience of the discussion format. Through these observations, the student may begin to learn about nonjudgmental stances, constructively toned commentaries and feedback, and an intensive commitment to create fuller and richer communications between instructor and student or between psychologist and client.

Conclusion

In addition to careful attention to the creation of stimulating and supportive overall learning environments and cultures, there are some specific steps that institutions can take to improve teaching and learning: (a) Institutions should adopt faculty-evaluation criteria that explicitly address the modeling dimension of teaching and supervision; (b) syllabus formats should be developed that help focus course planning and specify how the lecture – discussion models to be used are consistent with the content objectives; (c) faculty development opportunities should be created that explicitly attend to the importance and impact of modeling in the classroom; (d) less experienced faculty should have the opportunity to find their own models among particularly gifted, master teachers and have them available for observation and supervision.

Academic instructors and clinical supervisors who train professional psychologists must recognize that students learn as much or more from the form of presentation and from classroom processes as from the course content. The interpersonal styles of faculty members come to be scrutinized intensively, and they ultimately may have more influence on students as models than as conduits for information. Faculty must aspire to attune the communicative aspects of their professional selves to the content of courses that talk about safe and growth-producing relationships.

6

NATIONAL COUNCIL OF SCHOOLS OF PROFESSIONAL PSYCHOLOGY CORE CURRICULUM SURVEY

Andrea Morrison and Lynn O'Connor

The Wright Institute
Berkeley, California

and

Barbara Williams

Spalding University
Louisville, Kentucky

The task of developing a core curriculum for clinical psychology has emerged as a central concern for educators. At the Mission Bay conference, the 1986–1987 midwinter meeting of the National Council of Schools of Professional Psychology (NCSPP), the conferees suggested that the essential knowledge base necessary for training in professional psychology must be integrated into a broad-based curriculum, combining knowledge with basic attitudes and skills in the science and practice of psychology (Bourg et al., 1989). In the Mission Bay resolutions, NCSPP members advocated the development of "a single competency-based core curriculum [that] integrates the scientific foundations and methodology of psychology with the discipline's professional foundations" (Bourg et al., 1989, p. 70). This generic core curriculum should include six competency areas: relationship, assessment, intervention, research and evaluation, consultation and teaching, and management and supervision.

In this chapter, we report the results of a survey undertaken to investigate the status among member schools of the competency-based core curricula identified at Mission Bay. The survey addressed the following questions:

1. Are the six competency areas, as represented by specified program elements, present in the core curricula of member schools?

2. Are the program elements that make up the six competency areas required or elective?
3. In what format are the program elements of the curriculum presented?
4. What is the relative emphasis given to each of the program elements?
5. Are the knowledge, attitudes, and skills components taught in an integrated manner?

Method

In the core curriculum survey, each of the six competency areas was represented and operationalized by explicit program elements. The program elements were developed from a much larger array of items derived from a review of the curricular offerings found in 15 catalogs of schools of professional psychology. These program elements consisted of specific content areas such as interviewing techniques, adult assessment, and hypothesis testing. The specific content areas might have been the equivalent of a course or might have been included within a course.

The program elements considered to be central to each of the six competency areas were addressed. Elements for Competency Area 1—relationship— were interviewing techniques, dynamics of the therapeutic relationship, culture-sensitive approaches, and ethics and the therapeutic relationship. Elements for Competency Area 2—assessment— were intelligence testing, personality testing, vocational testing, neuropsychological assessment, and child assessment (each operationalized as certain tests). Elements for Competency Area 3—intervention—were psychodynamic therapy, cognitive-behavior modification therapy, group therapy, family therapy, and crisis intervention (each operationalized as certain techniques). Elements for Competency Area 4—research and evaluation—were methodology of program evaluation, statistics, research methods and design, hypothesis testing, and program development. Elements for Competency Area 5—consultation and teaching—were occupational mental health, employee-assistance programs, stress management, and parenting and couples education. Elements for Competency Area 6—management and supervision—were techniques of supervision; administrative issues; and legal, ethical, and professional standards of practice.

A pilot survey, using the list of program elements, was constructed. The pilot survey was sent to all members of the NCSPP program-development committee, five of whom returned it with their comments. In the pilot survey, respondents were asked to report the presence of a given program element in their program; its status as a requirement, elective, or part of a special program; the format used in its presentation; and the emphasis given. Respondents were instructed to provide a numerical value for the emphasis given to each specific program element, ranging from 0, for *no emphasis,* to 5, for *high emphasis.* In addition, respondents were asked to check which, if any, of the three components (i.e., knowledge, attitudes, or skills) were present in the teaching of each program element.

The results of the pilot survey were reviewed, the core curriculum survey was revised and shortened, and the final version was sent to the 34 member schools of NCSPP. Twenty schools (59%) responded. The questionnaires were completed by either the president, the academic dean, the program director, or the director of clinical training of the responding institution.

Selected Results

Because of space limitations, only a selected subset of the data is reported here. Readers interested in a more detailed presentation of the results should contact the authors. The results, presented by competency area, are summarized in Table 1.

Table 1
Competency Areas: Representation and Emphasis in the Curriculum at NCSPP Member Institutions

Competency area	Number of schools (n = 20)	%	Mean emphasis 0 (No emphasis) 5 (High emphasis)
1. Relationship			
Interviewing techniques	20	100	4.4
Dynamics of therapeutic relationships	20	100	4.8
Culture-sensitive approaches	13	65	4.2
Ethics in therapeutic relationships	20	100	4.9
2. Assessment			
WAIS-R	18	90	4.5
MMPI	19	95	4.5
Vocational testing	3	15	0.3
Luria-Nebraska	1	5	2.8
WISC-R	15	75	4.3
3. Intervention			
Transference	19	95	4.3
Systematic desensitization	15	75	2.9
Interpersonal transactions	9	45	3.1
Assessment of family systems	8	40	3.5
Crisis-assessment procedures	10	50	2.4
4. Research and evaluation			
Method program evaluation and evaluation research	11	55	2.8
Hypothesis testing	19	95	3.9
Program development	5	25	1.8
5. Consultation and teaching			
Occupational mental health	1	5	1.0
Employee-assistance programs	0	0	0.2
Stress management	6	30	2.3
Parenting and couples education	0	0	0.8
6. Management and supervision			
Techniques of supervision	3	15	1.7
Administrative issues	0	0	0.6
Legal, ethical, and professional standards	15	75	2.8

Note. NCSPP = National Council of Schools of Professional Psychology; WAIS-R = Wechsler Adult Intelligence Scale–Revised; MMPI = Minnesota Multiphasic Personality Inventory; WISC-R = Wechsler Intelligence Scale for Children–Revised.

Competency Area 1: Relationship

All respondent schools required the study of interviewing techniques as well as study of dynamics of the therapeutic relationship. Sixty-five percent of the respondents required study of culture-sensitive approaches. All respondents required study of ethics in the therapeutic relationship. These program elements were taught in a variety of formats, including lectures, seminars, and field placements. As expected, the mean emphases for the three program elements that were required by all the respondents was very high (between 4.4 and 4.9). The mean emphasis for culture-sensitive approaches was only modestly lower (4.2).

Competency Area 2: Assessment

Intelligence testing, operationalized as the study of the Wechsler Adult Intelligence Scale-Revised, was required in 90% of the schools. Personality testing, operationalized as the study of the Minnesota Multiphasic Personality Inventory (MMPI), was required by 95% of the respondents. Only 15% required the study of vocational testing, whereas an additional 15% offered vocational testing as an elective. Neuropsychological assessment, operationalized as the study of the Luria-Nebraska Neuropsychological Battery, was required for all students by only one (5%) respondent. However, 20% of the respondents required it as part of a special program, and 45% offered it as an elective. Child assessment, operationalized as the study of the Wechsler Intelligence Scale for Children-Revised, was required by 75% and offered as an elective by the other 25%. Assessment was taught most frequently in field placements in conjunction with lectures, seminars, and special projects. Intelligence testing, personality testing, and child assessment all had high mean emphases scores (4.2 or higher). Neuropsychological assessment was in the midrange at 2.8.

Competency Area 3: Intervention

Psychodynamic intervention, operationalized as the study of transference, was required by 95% of the respondents. Cognitive-behavioral modification therapy, operationalized as the study of systematic desensitization, was required by 75% and was offered as an elective by 10% of the respondents. Group therapy, operationalized as the study of interpersonal transactions in groups, was required by 45% of the respondents and offered as an elective by an additional 35%. Family therapy, operationalized as the study of assessment and diagnosis of family systems, was required of all students by 40% of the responding schools, and it was required of students in special programs by 25% of the respondents. Crisis intervention, operationalized as the study of crisis intake and assessment procedures, was required by 50% of the respondents and offered as an elective by another 25%. The various intervention techniques were taught primarily in lectures and seminars and secondarily in field placements and in special projects.

Competency Area 4: Research and Evaluation

Program development was required by 25% of the respondents and was offered as an elective by 20%. Methodology of program evaluation was required by 55% of the respondents and was offered as an elective by 10% more. Research methods and design, operationalized as the study of hypothesis testing, was required by 95% of the respondents. Both research and evaluation were presented primarily in a lecture or seminar format; occasionally they were presented in a special project. All items in this competency had mean emphases of 3.9 or lower: Program development had an emphasis rating of 1.8; program evaluation, 2.8; and hypothesis testing, 3.9.

Competency Area 5: Consultation and Teaching

The study of occupational mental health was required by a single respondent and was offered as an elective by 35% of the respondents. The study of employee-assistance programs was not required by any respondents, but was offered as an elective by 20%. Thirty percent of the respondents indicated that stress management was a requirement for all students; at 10% of the responding programs, only students in special programs were required to study stress management. Twenty percent offered it as an elective. Parenting and couples education was not required by any respondent and was offered as an elective by 25% of the programs. These elements are presented to the students in their field placements, special projects, and lectures. The emphasis rating for these areas was relatively low, ranging from 0.2 to 2.3.

Competency Area 6: Management and Supervision

The study of techniques of supervision was required by 15% of the respondents and was offered as an elective by an additional 35%. The study of administrative issues was not required by any respondents, but was offered as an elective by 25%. Although earlier data indicated that all programs taught ethics, the study of legal, ethical, and professional standards of practice was specifically required by 75% of the respondents and was offered as an elective by one (5%). The techniques of supervision and administrative issues were presented to students primarily in field placements and special projects. Legal, ethical, and professional standards were presented to students in lectures, seminars, and special projects. In spite of their ubiquity, the techniques of supervision had an emphasis rating of 1.7; administrative issues, 0.6; legal, ethical, and professional standards of practice, 2.8.

Typically, the respondents checked all three components (knowledge, attitudes, and skills) if they taught a program element. For example, in almost every case, the respondents who reported teaching knowledge of an element also reported teaching attitudes and skills. Respondents differed, however, on the delivery of the program elements in terms of (a) requirements, (b) particular formats used, and (c) emphasis.

Discussion

The data from the core curriculum survey indicated that the six competency areas recommended by NCSPP for the training of psychologists (Bourg et al., 1989) were present in the core curricula of the member schools. However, the six areas were neither represented equally nor emphasized equally in core curricula.

With respect to emphasis, there was variation across and within the six competency areas. Across the competency areas, more program elements were offered and were required in the relationship, assessment, intervention, and research and evaluation competencies than in the consultation and teaching or the management and supervision competencies. Furthermore, there was greater consistency among respondent schools concerning program elements in the relationship, assessment, intervention, and research and evaluation competencies.

At this time, as might be expected, the newer consultation and teaching and the management and supervision competencies have received less emphasis in the core curriculum. They often were viewed by respondent schools as elective rather than required material. These emerging areas of practice offer new and creative opportunities for curriculum development.

There was considerable variation among respondent schools, vis-à-vis specific program elements, within each competency area. In the assessment competency, for example, study of the MMPI, which was strongly emphasized at most schools, was not even offered at 1 school and was only moderately emphasized at 3 schools. Vocational testing, which was not offered at most schools, was moderately emphasized at 1 school.

The variation in emphasis was greater within the consultation and teaching competency area and within the management and supervision competency area than the other competency areas. Stress management was highly emphasized by one half of the responding programs and was not emphasized at all by the others. Techniques of supervision were also moderately to highly emphasized by one half of the sample and were not emphasized at all by the remainder. Even a program element presumably as fundamental as legal, ethical, and professional standards of practice was not emphasized in slightly less than one third of the sample.

Participants at the NCSPP Mission Bay conference advocated the use of a wide variety of formats in the education and training of professional psychologists. The data from the core curriculum survey indicated that the 20 respondent schools were in fact making use of a wide variety of learning formats, that is, lectures, seminars, field placements (both at the practicum and at the internship level), and special projects.

In response to the survey questions about integration of knowledge, attitudes, and skills components, the member school respondents indicated that such integration was present in the core curricula. Schools offering students knowledge in a particular area also reported providing training in attitudes and in skills. According to this survey, the values that are critically important to responsible clinical practice have been integrated into the core curriculum.

Some caution is appropriate in generalizing from this study. Operationalizing the competency-area elements certainly makes reliable responses more likely. However, this technique necessarily invites questions about particular operations. For example, would conclusions have been different if the Rorschach instead of the MMPI had been used to define personality testing? Similarly, if program elements in community psychology and consultation had been included in the consultation and teaching area, the overall results for this area might have been noticeably different.

Data from this survey, including material not summarized here, indicated that, despite important variations in particular program elements, there was great consistency in core curriculum areas across NCSPP member schools. Thus, it appeared that the criteria established by the American Psychological Association have had the effect of standardizing content areas in programs for training clinical psychologists. This standardization did not seem to result in the development of rigid, stultified, or "carbon-copy" core curriculum program elements. Educational programs, it appears, have been able to maintain their individuality, uniqueness, and presumably their capacity for innovation.

It follows that the six competency areas identified by NCSPP appear to be useful in defining what is consensually regarded as necessary for the education of professional psychologists. This definition of the boundaries of psychology training makes it possible to determine who, in fact, has the training to function competently as a psychologist to ensure high-quality professional performance in the field.

7

FACULTY OPINIONS ON THE CORE CURRICULUM: A SURVEY

Kathi A. Borden and Cary L. Mitchell

Pepperdine University
Los Angeles, California

With the proliferation of practitioner-oriented programs in professional psychology during the past 20 years, concern has been expressed about the sufficiency of the traditional psychology curriculum. At the 1986 Mission Bay conference of the National Council of Schools of Professional Psychology (NCSPP), the resolutions advocated that the content of core-curriculum requirements for professional psychology programs be broadened so that schools would more explicitly demonstrate their coverage of competencies necessary for the successful practice of psychology. Bent and Cannon (1987) summarized six competency areas within which professional psychologists practice: relationship, assessment, intervention, research and evaluation, consultation and teaching, and management and supervision. Helping students develop knowledge, skills, and attitudes in these six competencies is at the heart of the proposed curriculum.

The competencies were identified originally by synthesizing the results of various studies and surveys (Bent & Cannon, 1987). The six competencies were later refined by program administrators at NCSPP meetings. However, ultimately, it is the faculty of the professional schools who implement the core curriculum. As stated by Derner and Stricker (1986), "the members of the faculty, including a substantial number of active practitioners, are in the best position to determine the educational and training needs of a group of students who aspire to enter the field" (p. 38). It seems crucial, therefore, to draw on faculty expertise to further develop and implement the proposed curriculum.

Method

A survey was developed to gather faculty opinions about the curricular aspects of the six competency areas identified by NCSPP at Mission Bay. After providing demographic information, faculty were asked to comment on (a) current coverage of each competency; (b) the most effective means of coverage of each competency; (c) challenges to be faced in implementing each competency; (d) each competency's role in shaping the future of the field of psychology; and (e) anticipated effects of the competency-based curriculum as a whole. Additional questions, selected as being particularly relevant to psychology training at this time, were asked about three of the competencies.

Surveys were sent to administrators of programs that are members or associate members of NCSPP, and the administrators were asked to distribute the surveys and postpaid return envelopes to their core faculty members. Of the 528 surveys sent, the actual number distributed is unknown. Completed surveys were received from 75 faculty members. Not all respondents answered every question; thus, the sample size for questions is not always 75.

The respondents were 43 men and 26 women (6 did not specify), ranging in age from 32 to 74 years ($M = 46.10$, $SD = 9.58$). Of those specifying, most (94%) held a PhD, typically obtained in clinical psychology (67%) from a Boulder-model program (72%). They taught for at least 24 different schools. Of those specifying, 61% taught full time. Many (53%) taught in free-standing programs that are not university affiliated, 44% taught in university-based programs, and 3% taught in free-standing, university-affiliated programs. The majority of respondents (56%) taught exclusively in PsyD programs, 22% in PhD programs, and 22% in both PsyD and PhD programs. Most (94%) taught courses in clinical areas.

Results

Responses are reported individually for each competency. Particular responses to the first two issues previously listed are not reported for the relationship, assessment, intervention, and research and evaluation competencies because responses indicated that most programs provided appropriate, effective levels of current coverage through courses or supervised experiences. These issues are discussed in relation to the consultation and education competency and the management and supervision competency. Along with frequency data, a sample of common and innovative responses is presented.

Relationship Competency

Challenges in implementation. The need for greater numbers of minority students and faculty was noted by 13% of the respondents. A parallel concern was to place more emphasis on understanding and on addressing the needs of minority clients and special or underserved populations (9%). Another theme mentioned by 9% of the respondents related to concerns about faculty awareness and resources in the relationship domain. The need to integrate this competency throughout the curriculum was also stressed.

Role in shaping the future. Fifteen percent of the respondents stressed the need for greater emphasis on minority groups and special populations. One respondent suggested that graduate students identify minority group "subspecialties," with required fieldwork and language study if relevant. Thirteen percent of the respondents made global statements about the need to make the relationship competency a high priority; 21% stressed the need to emphasize relationship skills and knowledge through course work or supervised clinical experience. Additional responses addressed how to integrate classroom and clinical experience and how to conduct group experiential learning activities for graduate students.

Assessment Competency

Challenges in implementation. Several discernible themes emerged. The modal concern, expressed by 17% of the respondents, was the difficulty of providing adequate assessment-training opportunities for students. Problems in generating testing referrals and locating sufficient assessment-training sites were noted. A related concern, identified by 8% of the respondents, was the ability to provide adequate experience with minority clients or special populations (e.g., children). Challenges regarding the state of the art in assessment were mentioned by 8% of the respondents including the need for a more critical approach to assessment and the need to keep pace with research developments. Other concerns, mentioned by at least 4% of the respondents, were finding sufficient numbers of faculty with expertise and interest in assessment and overcoming student disinterest or poor preparation in this area. On a more positive note, 20% of the sample reported that their schools faced no special challenges in covering assessment.

Role in shaping the future. There was little consensus about how to impact the discipline's future through the assessment competency. Global statements about the importance of assessment and the need to promote and maintain high standards were made by 21% of the respondents. One respondent noted, "[Assessment] must be emphasized to the same level as psychotherapy. After all, assessment skills are what make us unique." Another respondent lamented that "too many practicing psychologists are not [competent in assessment]." The need for assessment methods to be more cross-culturally relevant was mentioned by 7% of the respondents. Other responses ranged from a call for increased use of computers to a recommendation for a more phenomenological approach.

Intervention Competency

Challenges in implementation. The adequacy of faculty resources was identified as a special challenge by 12% of the respondents. The specific concerns included having sufficient faculty to cover all the desired intervention areas and the need to include more faculty in the supervision of students' clinical work. Another theme was the difficulty integrating various theories, research, and clinical methods relevant to intervention which 12% of the respondents mentioned. The challenge of responding to the needs of ethnic minorities and special groups was given by 5% of the respondents. Four percent of the respondents expressed concern about pressure to "separate rather than integrate" clinical from classroom work. Specific mention was also made of the usefulness of role play, personal therapy for students, and cotherapy with faculty members.

Role in shaping the future. The need to integrate intervention strategies more successfully was mentioned by 8% of the respondents. As just mentioned, the importance of addressing the needs of cultural minorities and special groups was noted by

5%. Another theme was the need to broaden the concept of intervention to include systems and organization interventions, political and legislative roles, and psychologists in the media. Other responses focused on altering our intervention models (e.g., more emphasis on short-term treatment, prevention, and methods with strong empirical support) or addressed specific professional or discipline-wide issues (e.g., more support for professional schools and dealing with the funding crisis in mental health).

Specific competency concerns. Respondents were asked whether they favored intensive training in a single theoretical orientation or modality (depth) versus exposure to several orientations or modalities (breadth). Most respondents (61%) favored breadth at the graduate school level. Moreover, there was some support for movement toward eclecticism as reflected in the comment, "We should work toward the elimination of schools of psychotherapy." A smaller number (12%) favored a depth-oriented approach. One respondent noted that "superficiality in the guise of 'breadth' is rampant." Other respondents (13%) recommended that both in-depth coverage and broad exposure should be available; several respondents suggested that in-depth specialization in a particular theoretical orientation should occur at the postdoctoral level.

Research and Evaluation Competency

Challenges in implementation. The modal challenge was that students showed low interest, poor preparation, and high levels of anxiety about research requirements (21%). One respondent suggested increasing student interest by teaching a course on influential clinical theorists with an emphasis on epistemology. A second category of challenges included faculty issues (11%), such as a lack of faculty preparation and interest, and insufficient faculty time to do research as a result of an overload of teaching and of other responsibilities. Some concern was expressed about the unequal distribution of research supervision responsibilities, which was seen as unfair but inevitable when faculty skill and interest vary greatly. A third category included pragmatic or structural concerns (15%), such as a lack of funding and incentives to do research, poor library and computer facilities, difficulty locating research subjects, the need for more clinically trained research instructors, difficulty in finding unpaid dissertation committee members, and the problem of the all-but-dissertation student. The final category of challenges was the difficulty encountered in defining the role of research in a practitioner program (16%), a problem exacerbated by the low numbers of faculty members who were trained in a practitioner model.

Role in shaping the future. The most commonly held view was that research should continue to be central to our training and that students should gain experience in doing research (28%). In contrast, others (15%) commented that training students to be critical readers of the literature ("consumers of research") who base their practice on data-based findings should be our goal. It is important to note that many respondents, including many of those who believe students should conduct research, believe that methods and content should be redefined to make research more relevant to the applied practice of psychology. Several respondents hoped that students would learn to (a) make use of well-researched clinical methods; and (b) conduct case, outcome, and program evaluation studies to evaluate their own work.

Consultation and Teaching Competency

Current and effective coverage.   Twenty-nine percent of the respondents indicated that their programs did not cover systematically consultation and teaching. However, 53% were from programs that offered some exposure. Effective teaching methods included supervised practical experience (23%), course work (16%), or a combination of the two (25%). Current and suggested methods of coverage that were unique included providing (student) speakers to the community, connecting with campus organizations to consult, and having students develop a course to be critiqued.

Challenges in implementation.   The modal challenge (16%) was finding time for additional courses in an already crowded curriculum. Eleven percent were concerned about being able to find opportunities for student practice. Some felt this competency should be omitted (5%), and others felt that students were not interested in this competency (3%). Although many faculty viewed coverage of this competency as ideal, their enthusiasm was tempered by the inability to reconcile the difficulty of expanding an already crowded curriculum.

Management and Supervision Competency

Current and effective coverage.   Twenty-five percent of the respondents taught in programs in which the management and supervision competency was not taught systematically, although 23% taught in programs where elective or required courses were offered. Three percent of the respondents came from programs where a hierarchical system of having senior students supervise more junior students was used. Effective teaching methods included courses (23%), supervised experience (8%), or both (25%). Some felt this should be omitted from the curriculum (7%).

The modal concern about the inclusion of this competency was the lack of room in the curriculum (15%). Other concerns were difficulty finding opportunities for supervised experience (5%) and difficulty finding qualified supervisors (5%). Several (8%) respondents simply stated that this competency did not belong in the curriculum. As one respondent stated, "It is difficult to teach supervisory skill until students have reached [an advanced level of clinical skill]."

Role in shaping the future.   Nine percent of the respondents would like to see courses, practica, or some combination offered in the management and supervision competency. Five percent would like this to be a specialized elective track. Other respondents suggested omitting this from the curriculum; still others focused on the importance of this competency for enabling psychologists to direct programs, avoid malpractice suits, and avoid managed health care.

Specific competency concerns.   The faculty was asked whether the curriculum should address specifically the skills needed to establish and maintain a private practice. The responses to survey items reveal strong disagreement among respondents. Thirteen (17%) respondents said yes, cover this quite specifically through course work and other experiences. Twelve (16%) said no, we should not address this in the curriculum. A typical negative response was "We need to focus on how (societal) needs can best be met; professional psychology programs do themselves and the public a

Table 1
Frequency of Responses to Questions About the Impact of the
Competency-Based Core Curriculum in Professional Psychology

| | Direction of impact | | |
Affected factor	Increase	Remain the same	Decrease
Revelance of curriculum	41	24	3
Competence of graduates	53	13	3
Ability of graduates to become licensed	30	36	1
Number of malpractice suits	3	33	27
Student satisfaction with programs	38	16	12
Faculty satisfaction with programs	28	26	13
Length of doctoral program	35	30	2
Cost of doctoral program	45	19	2
Number of electives taken	20	26	20

disservice by focusing on private practice." An additional 11% said that workshops or colloquia taught outside of the general curriculum would be acceptable. Although not advocating for a separate course, 15% of the respondents stated that issues of private practice could be covered as part of a course on ethics (7%) or various delivery systems (8%). Clearly, there is a need for further discussion of the role of private practice training in the core curriculum.

Anticipated Effects of the Competency-Based Core Curriculum

As is seen in Table 1, the majority of respondents projected the impact of the professional core competencies in the curriculum to be quite positive. Most faculty stated that the proposed core will increase the relevance of the curriculum and that student and, to a lesser extent, faculty satisfaction will increase. Most encouraging is the belief of the vast majority of respondents that the core curriculum will increase the competence of program graduates. Respondents also believed that the ability of graduates to become licensed will increase and the number of malpractice suits will decrease. On a more cautious note, the majority of respondents believed that both the length and the cost of programs will increase when the core is implemented.

Conclusion

As perceived by the faculty, most programs in professional psychology adequately covered the relationship, assessment, intervention, and research and evaluation competencies. Challenges in implementation included the need for greater attention to issues of diversity; the need to provide increased quantity and quality of assessment-training opportunities; difficulty knowing how and when to integrate diverse intervention methods, theories, and research; and the need to find models of research more relevant to professional psychology training and practice.

The consultation and teaching competency and the management and supervision competency were not seen as consistently covered. Several faculty members expressed confusion about the intended content in these competencies. As one respondent commented, "[Consultation and teaching, and management and supervision] are poorly defined above and in previous NCSPP reports." A common source of confusion was the grouping of these competencies. For example, in the consultation and teaching competency, 59% of the respondents addressed one component (e.g., consultation) or the other (e.g., teaching) or addressed the two components as entirely separate competencies. The same was true for the management and supervision competency (61%). In addition, some faculty experienced difficulty dividing supervision and teaching into two separate competencies, suggesting that the skills involved in these two professional roles may be functionally related. More work is needed to define the content of these competencies for faculty. The authors of several chapters in this volume address this concern.

The vast majority of respondents believed that the competency-based core curriculum, as specified by NCSPP, will improve professional psychology education. However, faculty believed that the trade-off for better prepared graduates will be longer, more costly programs. Although some concern was raised about these latter effects, it is clear that the faculty endorsed much of this curriculum and have much to contribute to its implementation.

8

INNOVATIONS IN CURRICULUM: THE USE OF PERSONAL COMPUTERS IN TRAINING PROFESSIONAL PSYCHOLOGISTS

Kjell Erik Rudestam
The Fielding Institute
Santa Barbara, California

We are witnessing the dawning of the electronic age in higher education, and there is no reason to believe that graduate psychology will be left behind. Most graduate students these days are aware that word processors can simplify the task of writing papers and dissertations. Most departments have access to a new generation of powerful computers for data storage and analysis. Anyone returning to formal education after a hiatus of several years cannot help but be impressed and overwhelmed by the way in which computer-search strategies have replaced card catalogs in research libraries. Yet few psychology programs are taking advantage of the full range of educational services that personal computers are now able to offer, and indications are clear that these services will expand dramatically in the near future. In this chapter, I summarize and briefly describe applications of this technology to the training of professional psychologists.

Electronic Seminars

Several universities, such as the New School for Social Research (New York), the New York Institute of Technology (Old Westbury, NY), and Nova University (Fort Lauderale, FL), have struggled with the dilemma of serving students whose geographic inaccessibility or scheduling conflicts prevent them from attending classes on a regular basis (Meeks, 1987). One solution has been to offer the same course work both as an on-campus course and as a teleconferencing course. A teleconferencing course is not the same as the packaged video presentations that sometimes substitute for the live presence of an instructor. It is on-line mentoring that makes use of computer conferencing systems, personal modems, and on-line data bases.

In the Fielding Institute Psychology Program, which serves 450 midlife, midcareer doctoral students who reside throughout the United States and Canada, one function of computer conferencing is to offer seminars electronically. Students throughout the system enroll to take a seminar in one of the curricular areas offered by the program. The seminar has a set starting and ending date and lasts about 4 months. The faculty member guiding the seminar communicates the course requirements on an electronic bulletin board that is accessible to all faculty and students within the system no matter where they reside. A typical seminar requirement might consist of preparing responses to and discussing 8 to 10 questions on the topic. A seminar on legal and ethical bases of behavior might require answers to the following questions: "What are the legal, ethical, practical, and moral backgrounds to the question of 'informed consent,' and what are their ramifications for practice in today's social and legal climate?"

One question is transmitted by the faculty mentor every few weeks. The students then prepare answers by going to the library, reading, and researching the topic. Each student prepares and transmits an answer to the question to the bulletin board. In this way, every student in the seminar is able to read every other student's response. The course also requires the students to discuss each other's answers, so that the seminar becomes an engaging and scholarly discussion. Because a new question is presented on a regular basis, the seminar can cover a range of topics. Of course, the faculty member also is able to present on-line input to the students. Moreover, other students in the program who have not registered for the seminar are able to look in on and even download (i.e., audit the seminar), but may not participate in the dialogue without being enrolled formally.

A primary advantage of electronic seminars is that they allow students to cover material at their own pace and timing. Students seem to be particularly motivated because their work is also viewed by their peers. This method allows time for research and thoughtful reflection, the full use of group resources, easy dissemination of written materials, and a permanent record of the proceedings and of each student's contributions. Interestingly, students who are relatively inactive in the traditional classroom environment have more opportunity to participate in electronic seminars. Furthermore, it is not possible for the seminar to be dominated by a small number of students, which is often the case in face-to-face meetings.

Communication Network

The electronic network at the Fielding Institute initially was introduced to provide a cost-effective and rapid means of communication and information sharing with the faculty – student community rather than to conduct distance learning seminars. Each user in the network has an electronic mailbox, which enables that person instantaneously to send messages to or receive messages from the Fielding Institute offices, faculty, students, and alumni who are users. The system is operated using U.S. Sprint's SprintMail Service. The content and features, however, are determined by Fielding Institute's needs and are frequently updated. Any brand of computer will operate within the system, and the only additions that are required are a modem and a communications software program. It takes very little computer knowledge and typing ability to plug into and use the system. However, we do retain a strong in-house support and training system to help faculty and students overcome difficulties and increase their facility with using the network.

A host of communication functions are now available to our students and faculty by means of personal computer:

1. Notice boards provide schedules for seminars and residential sessions, faculty and student rosters, faculty assessments, course requirements, minutes from faculty committee meetings, reading lists, dissertation topics, and instant access to other needed information.
2. The entire academic community can contribute to and has access to common data bases of test instruments, articles, internship sites, jobs, and so forth.
3. Faculty and students can review a paper, critique a thesis or dissertation draft, or engage in supervision. They also use the network to solicit support and advice, deal with crises, and quell rumors.
4. There is the opportunity for individuals in different locations to involve themselves in joint projects, such as sharing resources regarding research topics or clinical approaches. We are currently exploring the use of the system for conducting multisite research.
5. The network makes it possible for faculty to discuss major policy changes without waiting for a scheduled face-to-face meeting. It is also easy to solicit student input before making important program decisions. Faculty committee meetings are regularly conducted through electronic conferencing.
6. It is not uncommon for faculty and students to engage in informal discussion on a variety of provocative topics from their offices at work or at home.

There is also, of course, potential for intercommunity networking and discussion among academic groups at different institutions. The National Council of Schools of Professional Psychology has committed itself to establishing a learning resource center, including information on interactive computer technologies. A next step might be to have such resources available electronically. It would not be difficult for programs throughout the country that share common goals to communicate with one another in this manner. In some instances, electronic communication could be used to conduct low-cost meetings, thereby eliminating travel expenses. It would also go a long way toward eliminating "telephone tag."

Other Applications of the Personal Computer

There are other, less ambitious applications of computer technology that can be recommended to graduate students in professional psychology programs. First, on-line data bases can be used for research and curriculum development. As libraries become transformed into electronic data banks, they become increasingly accessible from the personal computer in the home or the office. Both Compuserve and Dialog, commercially available information services, access major data banks that contain *Psychological Abstracts* and reference to virtually every important psychology journal and book. These systems make it possible to conduct an electronic search based on key words, obtain a list of relevant references on any psychological topic, and even create a personal journal library. *PsychNet* now has the full texts of most psychology journal articles available overnight by electronic mail.

Second, the personal computer has tremendous implications for self-learning and data analysis. Software is currently available to help master decision rules in psychodiagnostics using the revised third edition of the *Diagnostic and Statistical Manual of*

Mental Disorders (DSM-III-R; American Psychiatric Association, 1987). As personal computers have become increasingly powerful, most major statistical procedures can now be accomplished without a major investment in research consultants or mainframes. Statistical Package for the Social Sciences (SPSS) is available currently at a number of levels of complexity for the personal computer user, as are programs for determining sample size and power, revising manuscripts and papers into American Psychological Association format, producing professional quality tables and graphs, checking spelling and grammar, searching text, and developing bibliographies.

Just several years down the road, an enormous array of opportunities will emanate from developing information technology in higher education. The amount of information in libraries and data bases is doubling every 8 years, creating a pressing need for better systems of information management and use for scholars and researchers. At Fielding Institute, we envision an adult learning community in which electronic communication will integrate textual and numerical data and voice and visual information into a single medium and a single message. In response to a portion of a student's dissertation, for example, a faculty member could send one message that included typed bibliographical references, a reproduction of a diagram from a book, and a spoken response to the student's work. Through this communication network, students, faculty, alumni, and visiting scholars would be able to participate in a rich series of on-line seminars on topics related to the training and development of professional psychologists.

9

CORE CURRICULAR CHANGE: BARRIERS AND STRATEGIES FOR ACHIEVING MEANINGFUL CHANGE

W. Gary Cannon

California School of Professional Psychology
Fresno, California

and

James D. McHolland

Illinois and Minnesota Schools of Professional Psychology
Chicago, Illinois

Leaders of professional schools have a responsibility to prepare students of today for careers of tomorrow. Ongoing social and cultural changes, as well as a broadened vision of career settings and client populations, require constant reevaluation of curricular relevance. Computer literacy largely has replaced the foreign-language requirement as a doctoral research tool. Slide rules have disappeared in favor, first, of hand-held calculators, now computers. As emerging areas of study such as hospital practice, mental health administration, community public policy, neuropsychology, health psychology, minority mental health, and forensics are added to the curriculum, some previously sacred curricular components must fall by the wayside. Changes in faculty and administration induce curricular change because each new group seems driven to improve on what they find.

A rigidly inflexible curriculum is anathema to a discipline, profession, and social structure that are in constant flux. Commenting on his own preparation as a psychologist, Mink (1982) stated:

> *What was lacking was the awareness of the kinds of changes psychology was about to undergo or was already undergoing and the political and social influences in society that were changing the larger context in which we operate. We were not good in predicting trends then and we aren't much better now though prediction and control is what we are supposed to be about. In any case, the changes that are challenging us now require flexibility, the capacity to analyze problems, an array of methodological skills which we can*

apply selectively, and confidence in our competence to add to changing circumstances while maintaining a sense of continuity with the core of concepts and techniques that make up the enduring content of psychology. (p. 36)

Although flexibility may be required, it is seldom present. In the foreword to Mayhew and Ford's (1971) *Changing the Curriculum*, Godwin repeated the story of a distinguished educator who some years ago accepted the academic deanship of a bustling state college. The president of the college said to him, "You will have a free hand in this job—make whatever changes you see fit to make. Just don't monkey around with the curriculum" (p. xi). In contrast, in the preface, Mayhew and Ford (1971) asserted, "The college curriculum can be considerably more than an aggregate of courses offered as professional interests dictate. The curriculum should be based on human needs and structured to make educational sense to students" (p. xiii).

How then does one achieve change in academia? After a thorough review of the curricula of 22 schools of professional psychology, Kopplin (1986) noted that the American Psychological Association (APA) criteria for accreditation appeared to be the principle influence in shaping these curricula. In a study of clinical training programs from 1964 to 1965 and from 1968 to 1969, Simmons (1971) indicated that the 1964 APA Chicago conference (Hoch et al., 1966) had a profound effect on the content of curricula in professional psychology. Therefore, it may be realistic to hope that the San Antonio core-curriculum conference, as well as the other focused midwinter meetings of the National Council of Schools of Professional Psychology (NCSPP), will stimulate change in the professional school curriculum.

Barriers to Change

There are many barriers to change, some of which are justified. To some degree, change in and of itself is not inherently of any particular value, and it even may be destructive. The nature, extent, direction, and timing of change are all-important. In his classic description of field forces and field theory, Lewin (1951) suggested that behavior tends to be stable because there are approximately the same number of driving forces as there are restraining forces so that behavior is held in a state of equilibrium. Obviously, the amount of flexibility or rigidity that is desirable, as well as achievable, depends on many different factors. In the following sections, we discuss the factors that influence curricular change.

Organizational Settings

Curricular change may be facilitated or impeded by the organizational structure of the institution in which change is desired. Fox and Barclay (1989), in a report based on the 1987 NCSPP Mission Bay conference, the 1987 Association of Psychology Internship Centers Gainesville conference, and the 1987 Salt Lake City, Utah conference, indicated that there is an emerging consensus that university-based education is a preferable training model for professional psychologists. If indeed there is such a consensus, it is not because such settings facilitate curricular change. If university departments, university-affiliated professional schools, and independent professional schools are compared, it appears that it is most difficult to achieve curricular change in university departments because of the complex organizational structure of universities and the frequent necessity for university-wide review processes. Concerns held not only by other departments in the same school but also by departments within other schools must often be addressed.

Samuels, Hatcher, and Cannon (1988), for example, described the development and ultimate failure of the doctor of mental health degree in the University of California system. This new degree was to combine aspects of the education and training of social workers, psychiatrists, and clinical psychologists to create a more ideally trained mental health practitioner. In tracing the history of the doctor of mental health degree, Hatcher detailed the many battles fought to obtain permission to offer the new program, described the unraveling of the program, and attributed its ultimate demise to a battle lost in a struggle with the anthropology department at the University of California, Berkeley.

In describing the university environment, Mink (1982) said, "Ironically the challenge of the future is responded to in many institutions with a reclamation of the past and a concomitant emphasis on fundamental courses and distribution requirements" (p. 35). Albee (1970) cited Bennis's observation that "changing a university is about as easy as reorganizing a cemetery!" (p. 1072). When it comes to flexibility and self-determination, independent schools of professional psychology appear to have an organizational advantage compared with university-affiliated professional schools and university departments.

Philosophical Considerations and Personality Style

In addition to the impact of various organizational settings on curricular change, philosophical considerations and, in particular, personality styles play a major role in the ease with which change is accomplished in an organization. It is not lost on psychologists that some personality types abhor change, whereas others welcome and embrace it. For these reasons, the introduction of change in a discipline, profession, or curriculum is often fraught with resistance.

An example from the discipline of medicine illustrates this point. In the mid-1800s the medical profession was in the early stages of development much as psychology is today. John Elliotson, an English physician, a professor of the practice of medicine, and later a senior physician at the university college hospital in London, played a primary role in the establishment of the hospital connection to the medical school (Boring, 1957). The value of such an arrangement is obvious to us today, but in the mid-1800s the connection between the medical school and the hospital was opposed vigorously by some of Elliotson's more conservative colleagues. Similarly, Elliotson's attempt to introduce the use of the stethoscope, which had been invented on the continent, into medical practice and into training was met with ardent resistance (Boring, 1957). One argument was that the introduction of this instrument between the physician and the patient would lead to a less caring and a less humanistic approach to practice. Of course, many people would later contend that this is precisely what has happened to the profession of medicine, that is, technology and mechanization have led to a cold and unfeeling profession. Despite this, few of us would argue that the stethoscope or other modern innovations never should have been adopted.

In our own profession, the tension between innovation and change on the one hand and resistance to change on the other is illustrated by the debate about prescription privileges for psychologists. Some encouraged such prescription privileges and argued that modification of professional school curricula is the first step toward a legislative endorsement (Burns, DeLeon, Chemtob, Welch, & Samuels, 1988). Others countered that medication is detrimental to therapy, and psychologists have no business considering such an option.

Shaping or Being Shaped by the Future

Higher education responds to the needs of society; thus, the birth of clinical psychology and, later, the professional school movement itself. Educational institutions can respond to societal needs in one or more ways: (a) resisting change, being dragged, kicking and screaming, into the future; (b) coevolving and adapting with societal change; or (c) initiating change that anticipates the future.

As we look toward the 21st century, obvious emerging societal needs demand our attention. The data regarding our aging and our multiculturally changing society are compelling. The significant role for health and organizational psychology specialities cannot be ignored. Changes in family structure and stability have highlighted an urgent need for child and family treatments.

In addition to data-driven change, two alternative strategies for shaping change remain: first, divining the more remote future by "guessing ahead"; and, second, shaping the future. Professional schools should be bold by responding humanely to current and emerging societal needs and, through planning, building the future we wish for ourselves, our society, and our profession.

Strategies for Achieving Curricular Change

The informed support and willingness of the faculties of professional training programs are required to implement significant change in the core curriculum. In this section we suggest some specific and general approaches for achieving change.

Linkages Between National Training Conferences and School Faculties

If faculty in their home institutions are to act on the information generated and on the resolutions approved by national training conferences, there must be systematic linkages both before and after meetings. Preconference discussions with faculty about the critical training issues based on relevant papers both brings the issues to the attention of the faculty and allows their opinions and concerns to be represented in the national discussion. If faculty are not involved systematically before the conference, they are likely to have little interest in its outcomes and conclusions. Involved faculty will participate more readily in change if the changes are not imposed by department chairs, deans, or provosts.

As a representative organization based on schools, NCSPP is particularly well organized to develop these sorts of linkages between its national training conferences and local faculties. Because at the annual conferences the institutional representatives themselves have had the opportunity to develop working relationships with their counterparts during a period of many years, the likelihood of productive and influential outcomes is greatly increased.

Promotion of Curricular Change

The administration must provide educational leadership for establishing a forum wherein all the faculty (not only the curriculum committee) consider the nature and scope of the curriculum for training professional psychologists. Ideally, these discussions should take place during a 3- to 4-month period to increase awareness of the scope and the significance of the following issues:

1. Regardless of the intended career application, what should the core curriculum of professional psychology be?
2. What is unique about our program's core curriculum?
3. How are considerations of diversity and gender integrated into the curriculum?
4. How does the present core curriculum differ from what was emphasized 10 years ago?
5. How do we want to impact the profession in the next 10 years through curriculum? Specifically, what kind of psychologist do we want to train in the next 10 years and beyond?
6. What specific barriers to curricular change exist?
7. What strategies can be used to facilitate curricular change?
8. How best can the curriculum of psychology be taught?

Incentives for Curricular Change

The desire to be part of one of the best training programs in psychology motivates faculty toward considering change. Furthermore, faculty will recognize the opportunity to be part of a national consortium that moves together to create significant change in how professional psychologists are trained. The professional psychology movement itself is an excellent example of how dramatic changes in the training of psychologists can occur. On a more personal level, rewards and recognition for contributions leading to significant curricular change, words of acknowledgment and encouragement, and expressed appreciation for attitudes conducive to change may provide incentives. In addition, underwriting expenses for faculty presentations at state and national psychology conferences will provide greater exposure to the common goals of professional schools.

Accountability

Discussion of local curricular change without an identified goal is as effective as target practice without a target. Discussions should consider explicitly the processes by which the changes identified in national conference resolutions can be achieved. To ensure specific action consistent with the national resolutions, administrative leaders should facilitate time-limited discussions on the core curriculum as well as provide the structure of deadlines to ensure accountability.

NCSPP itself should require a mechanism whereby member schools report annually on their success in responding to NCSPP resolutions.

Competition

Some curriculum changes will occur because training programs will not want to lose a competitive edge in the marketplace. This will be true for university-based and for free-standing training programs alike. Competition occurs in two arenas: (a) the recruitment of students, and (b) the employment of graduates in the mental health marketplace. It is anticipated that, for example, the growth of health maintenance organizations (HMOs) and preferred provider organizations (PPOs) will reduce the client base currently available to private practitioners of psychology. Therefore, programs that are recognized for preparing their graduates to adjust to changes in the marketplace and to changes in required skills will do well competitively. Programs that refuse to change when change is required not only will lose the competitive advantage, but may indeed have their own survival brought into jeopardy.

Allowing Change

Sometimes it is not the faculty who resist the change; rather it is the administration of the university, the dean of the training program, or the students. The recent move of an eastern professional school of psychology from one university to another appears to be an example of administrative resistance to change. Within our member schools, department chairpersons, deans, provosts, and presidents must be articulate and frequent in their statements of support for regular curriculum review and for necessary change. Students can be a factor in blocking curricular change if the importance of the change is unclear. Faculty or administrative ambivalence can be exploited to split "the powers that be."

Curricular change involves the whole system of the training program, including the faculty, students, and administration. To the extent that all three sectors can be involved in change, the impact on the system will be more agreeable. As is true in a family system, one person or several are in charge of the training program system and can allow change, discourage it, suspend it indefinitely, or foster it. We hope that the leadership of professional school programs is in the hands of mature, healthy, rational, considerate people who will allow constructive change, not thwart it.

PART II
THE PROFESSIONAL
CORE COMPETENCY AREAS

10

THE PROFESSIONAL CORE COMPETENCY AREAS

Russell J. Bent
Wright State University
Dayton, Ohio

The participants at the Mission Bay conference, the 1986 – 1987 midwinter meeting of the National Council of Schools of Professional Psychology (NCSPP; Bourg et al., 1987) supported an emphasis on key functional competencies of psychologists that would define a single, unified core or foundation for professional psychology programs. The chapters in Part II of this volume were, in earlier versions, the preconference papers at the San Antonio conference on the core curriculum, NCSPP's 1989 – 1990 midwinter meeting. They build on and refine the work begun at Mission Bay.

It is critically important that the idea of the competency areas should serve as a flexible guide for curriculum development. The curriculum should be sufficiently stable and explicit to define psychology as a profession. At the same time, it should be flexible enough to allow for diversity, growth, creativity, and organized development of new competencies and truly advanced applications. We also need to assure ourselves and the public that all practitioners have fundamental competencies, thereby ensuring a connectedness and a source of integration among all professional psychologists.

The competencies discussed in the next six chapters were based on a review of expert opinion, a review of empirical work, an analysis of current and future practice skills (Bent & Cannon, 1987), and a model for a developing knowledge base (Jones, 1987). The Mission Bay conferees moved to integrate skills and knowledge with attitudes or values. The result was the six key functional competencies elaborated in this section: relationship, assessment, intervention, research and evaluation, consultation and education, and management and supervision. The complexity of contemporary practice requires that professional psychology curricula include more than individual assessment, psychotherapy, research, and aspects of the psychology discipline knowledge base.

The competencies are fundamental clusters of integrated knowledge, skills, and attitudes that are used in practice applications by the professional psychologist. The competencies, at a basic or foundation level, constitute a single, unified core curriculum for all professional applications. The competencies are unified further in the mature role functioning of the professional psychologist, gaining more breadth and depth with added training and experience.

Knowledge, skills, and attitudes do not stand alone, but merge into competencies that are invariably complex blends. Seldom is any activity predominantly knowledge, skill, or attitude, except in early education and training. For example, research has a strong knowledge base, but the productive researcher must also acquire related skills and integrate proper attitudes. The competencies, observable throughout the various activities of psychological practice, are capable of being evaluated.

San Antonio Conference

As chairperson of the San Antonio conference professional core competency section, I put forward preliminary descriptions of the six competency areas to each of the authors who prepared a preconference paper. A major task for the San Antonio conferees was the development of a useful, consensual definition for each competency area, which would serve to guide further curriculum development. Each definition had to allow flexibility and creativity while preserving a sense of commonality. The global definitions were to serve as roots for strong, diverse growth. Each program would specify its own detailed definition of the competency areas in relation to its mission and its definition of the psychologist graduate, the eventual practitioner.

The chapters in this section address the basic or core level of each competency. The chapters represent particular specifications and elaborations of each competency area and, therefore, are intended to be aspirational rather than prescriptive. In the form of preconference drafts, they were designed to stimulate and provide a basis for conference deliberations. For the complete conference definition of each competency, the reader should refer to the conference resolutions.

In addressing the competencies, the Mission Bay resolutions include two important points. First, the term *client* should be used in a broad sense to include individuals, couples, families, groups, organizations, and communities. Second, diversity should be addressed explicitly in all competencies (see Davis-Russell, Forbes, Bascuas, & Duran, chap. 20).

Although the conference resolutions provide much more detail, the six professional core competency areas can be defined briefly as follows:

1. *Relationship* is the capacity to develop and maintain a constructive working alliance with clients.
2. *Assessment* is an ongoing, interactive, and inclusive process that serves to describe, conceptualize, characterize, and predict relevant aspects of a client.
3. *Intervention* involves activities that promote, restore, sustain, or enhance positive functioning and a sense of well-being in clients through preventive, developmental, or remedial services.
4. *Research and evaluation* involve a systematic mode of inquiry involving problem identification and the acquisition, organization, and interpretation of information pertaining to psychological phenomena. Professional psychologists systematically acquire and organize information about psychological phenomena and often engage in the general practice of science.
5. *Consultation* is a planned, collaborative interaction that is an explicit intervention process based on principles and procedures found within psychology and related disciplines in which the professional psychologist does not have direct control of the actual change process. *Education* is the directed facilitation by the pro-

fessional psychologist for the growth of knowledge, skills, and attitudes in the learner.

6.   *Management* comprises those activities that direct, organize, or control the services that psychologists and others offer or render to the public. *Supervision* is a form of management blended with teaching in the context of a relationship directed toward the enhancement of the competence of the supervisee.

Perspectives on the Professional Core Competencies

The competencies can be defined at varied levels. The levels vary in generality (focus), complexity, and experience. The foundation or core level should be generic to all programs, should be the most general, and should require the least professional experience. The more focused or special proficiency level should be differentiated, drawing on foundation experience. Finally, the specialty level should be the most focused (including a focus as a generalist), and the psychologist should be very experienced with the capacity to conduct a complex practice.

An overview of the generality, complexity, and experience manifest in the competencies at different levels of graduate psychology training is given in Table 1.

Much of what is basic and is included in the professional core in all our current specialties could be taught in 2 years of foundation-level teaching. If postdoctoral training and experience with advanced certification were to become necessary to qualify specialties through a national system of certification, programs would need to prepare students with a solid foundation and with one or more special proficiency areas, leading to later career specialization.

New specialty certification is emerging. For example, boards for forensic psychology, neuropsychology, and marriage and family psychology have joined the American Board of Professional Psychology, and others are in negotiating positions. Appropriately, professional psychologists are no longer satisfied with decades-old specialty areas. Therefore, educational programs must be more flexible and responsive in preparing candidates for the established, the new, and the emerging specialties. In moving toward curricular reform, programs should be able to ensure an adequate foundation for general or specialty practice while educating students in one or more areas of special

Table 1
Competencies at Different Levels of Graduate Psychology Training

Year	Competency
1 and 2	Foundation work
3	Special proficiencies
4 (internship)	Constructive balance of general and focused practice
Postdoctoral training, continuing education, experience, and practice style	Specialty, including general practice

proficiency (emphasis) in preparation for the option of specialization at the postdoctoral level. Programs should have the curricular flexibility to relate to the new and the emerging specialties. At the same time, the new and the emerging specialties should have more flexibility to relate to curricular innovations in the educational programs.

A major argument for a competency-based curriculum is that the competencies can be operationally defined in a manner that allows for explicit evaluation. The NCSPP 1991–1992 midwinter conference will focus on the relation between the competency-based curriculum and methods of evaluation. Such evaluation will contribute to program development, quality assurance of programs, and quality assurance of graduates.

Challenge of Curricular Reform

Undoubtedly, adoption of a core competency curriculum will necessitate some changes in the way we currently think about psychology training curricula. We need to think creatively about finding ways to meet the challenges before us.

Perhaps the time has come to move more concertedly toward a full-calendar-year program. Such a format would allow for reasonable curriculum expansion and the development of full-service, program-administered service centers. Program hours and continuity may be increased without adding to the total number of years required to complete the program.

There must be more flexibility and creativity in our curricula. Think of the ideal curriculum as one that embodies the teaching of the competencies by integrating scientific and professional knowledge, skills, and attitudes. Often too little of the practitioner perspective is incorporated into classroom work; too little discipline-based or scientific perspective is incorporated into field experience. There must be more balance.

The competencies should not be considered solely as the province of single courses, but rather as being distributed among a number of courses; as being taught in supervised practice, and as developing through the program's culture, through role modeling, through relationships among students, and so on.

The curriculum is more than formal classroom work. Almost 40% of the curriculum involves fieldwork under supervision. Modeling by faculty and by supervisors, relationships developed while studying with peers, the professional socialization of the student, attitude and value development, and much more constitute the curriculum.

The ideal curriculum should reflect about 60% foundation-level activities and 40% special proficiency or special emphasis activities. Most of Year 1 should be foundational; Year 2 should be a mix of foundation concerns and special proficiency pursuits; and Year 3 should emphasize special proficiency material. Some specialization may begin at the internship level, but specialization should be completed at the postdoctoral stage.

There seems to be little question that curriculum development requires more detailed, cooperative planning among faculty. In our program at Wright State University, the curriculum committee has been restructured to include the coordinator of each competency area. Each coordinator, in turn, heads a subcommittee of faculty who have major teaching responsibility in that particular competency. The structure has been very productive thus far.

We should not believe that graduates are "finished products." Rather, when students receive their doctorates they are professionals who are reasonably prepared to embark on lifelong development as practicing psychologists. Much will happen, perhaps most, as careers develop. Remember, from the acorn . . . .

The challenge of the core professional curriculum, the competency-based curriculum, is clear. The rewards appear to be worth the effort involved in instituting curriculum reform. The excitement of creative change permeated the San Antonio conference. The following chapters on the competency areas reflect the creative potential of these new directions.

11

RELATIONSHIP COMPETENCY

Kenneth Polite

Biola University
La Mirada, California

and

Edward Bourg

California School of Professional Psychology
Berkeley/Alameda, California

"Relationship is the capacity to develop and maintain a constructive working alliance with clients" (McHolland, chap. 21, p. 162). The relationship competency is the foundation and the prerequisite for all the other competencies in professional psychology. In this context, the relationship competency includes psychological knowledge relevant to relationships, the necessary skills, and relational attitudes appropriate to the professional psychologist. Assessment, intervention, research and evaluation, consultation and education, management and supervision, and other functions of the professional psychologist rely on the basic ability to establish, understand, and maintain an authentic and appropriate relationship.

The paramount importance of relationship cuts across both theoretical orientations and professional specializations. Although psychodynamic and client-centered orientations perhaps have been more explicit about the central role of the relationship competency (Messer, 1988; Pinsof, 1988; Rogers, 1965), cognitive and behavioral interventions also are reliant on the relationship context in which services are offered (Arkowitz & Hannah, 1989). In addition, systemic theories focus primary attention on the patterns of relationships, although the nature of the therapist's role varies. From all major perspectives then, the quality of the relationship between the psychologist and the individual, family, or group with whom he or she is working remains central.

Similarly, although the clinical and counseling specialities in psychology traditionally have stressed the importance of interpersonal skills, the relationship competency is equally critical in other traditional (e.g., school and organizational psychology) and emerging (e.g., forensic, health, and geriatric psychology) specialities. As a case in point, in a recent consultation on the development of an organizational psychology program, a distinguished psychologist, formerly on the faculty of a school of management, advised that the only sine qua non of the core curriculum should be explicit attention to the self as instrument (R. Tannenbaum, personal communication, March 15, 1987).

Professional psychologists spend a substantial proportion of their working lives dealing with relationship issues: problems between parents and children, between spouses, among family members, and among work groups. Professional psychologists themselves work in a context of relationships. The services they provide, the activities in which they participate, and the research they produce all are strongly influenced by the relationship context (see Peterson, chap. 3). Relationships are a central focus of the psychological knowledge on which professionals depend.

Following the conceptualization adopted by the members of the National Council of Schools of Professional Psychology (NCSPP) at the Mission Bay conference (Bourg et al., 1989), we discuss the central elements of the relationship competency by exploring the relevant knowledge, skills, and attitudes that we see as essential for the professional psychologist.

Knowledge

The knowledge base pertaining to relationship that is necessary for professional competence encompasses three domains: (a) expert knowledge of a relevant portion of the psychological data base, (b) knowledge of self, and (c) knowledge of others.

The Psychological Data Base

To say that a student must possess expert knowledge of a relevant portion of the psychological data base is a necessarily broad statement because a substantial percentage of psychological knowledge is relevant to relationships. The portion of the data base that is relevant for a particular type of psychologist may vary with particular subfields (e.g., clinical psychology compared with neuropsychology). However, all psychologists need to have some acquaintance with the theory and the research regarding interpersonal relationships if they hope to use their relationship skills effectively.

Arguably, much of the psychological knowledge, including theory and research, implicitly or explicitly deals with what goes on in relationships (e.g., Carson, 1983; Kiesler, 1982; Leary & Maddux, 1987). For example, there seems to be wide agreement from a variety of perspectives that problematic and dysfunctional early relationships have a strong negative impact on the developing person. Leary and Maddux (1987) suggested that knowledge about relationships may well provide a viable interface between social psychology and clinical and counseling psychology. Furthermore, professional psychology is increasingly attentive to the impact of differential power and domination on relationships as well as to the social, cultural, and ethnic context in which they occur (see Edwall & Newton, chap. 19; Davis-Russell, Forbes, Bascuas, & Duran, chap. 20).

In another sense, to establish effective professional relationships with particular clients who have particular needs, psychologists must have expert knowledge of specified areas of psychology (e.g., developmental to serve children, forensic for the courts). In fact, psychology is unique among the mental health disciplines because it grounds interventions on a broad-based science of psychology. A key element in establishing effective professional relationships is the respect and trust of the client. People seek the services of a psychologist in part because of the general knowledge psychologists possess about human functioning and because of the specific knowledge (certain) psychologists have about a wide variety of human situations (e.g., family patterns, neuropsychological assessments, and psychological sequelae of physical illness.

Knowledge of Self

Emphasis on the science of psychology (and of related disciplines) should not lead us to neglect knowledge of self—the second domain of the knowledge essential for effective professional functioning in a field that necessarily must remain an art as well as a science. Singer, Peterson, and Magidson (see chap. 18) also discuss issues pertaining to knowledge of the self in clinical training. Our knowledge of ourselves (motivations, limitations, peculiarities, and so on) greatly hinders or enhances our ability to relate to others and, hence, our professional effectiveness.

The role of self-knowledge in establishing effective professional relationships cuts across theoretical orientations. From a psychodynamic perspective, self-knowledge is critical in dealing effectively with transference and countertransference issues. Rogers (1965) and his followers emphasized the importance of self-awareness in client-centered work. Family systems practitioners stressed the importance of understanding one's own family of origin to deal successfully with the complex kaleidoscope of family patterns. Effective behavioral interventions are dependent on the quality of the relationship between the psychologist and the client. The importance of self-knowledge in the training of professional psychologists is evidenced by the many NCSPP programs that require or highly recommend individual or group therapy for students (Kopplin, 1986).

Knowledge of Others

The third relevant knowledge domain for professional competence is knowledge of others. The well-trained psychologist does not attempt to work with others without first gaining some knowledge of the larger context in which the client functions. The context includes microsystems (e.g., individual personality differences, gender differences, and family dynamics) and macrosystems (e.g., work environments and national norms). In addition, knowledge of differing life-styles is a crucial prerequisite to effective therapist–client relationships. How can professional psychologists work successfully with evangelicals, gays, Blacks, or Hispanics without knowledge of their cultures and values?

Skills

The previous discussion of knowledge of the self and of others demonstrates the intimate link between knowledge and skills emphasized in the Mission Bay resolutions on the basic competencies of professional psychologists (Bourg et al., 1987; Bourg et al., 1989). The skills central to the relationship competency include, but are not limited to, the ability to (a) communicate empathy, (b) engage others, (c) set others at ease, (d) establish rapport, and (e) communicate a sense of respect.

These skills have been investigated under the rubric of interpersonal skills and the therapist (Kurtz, Marshall, & Banspach, 1985; Mahon & Altmann, 1977). Kurtz et al. (1985) undertook a review and analysis of the research during a 12-year period on relationship-skills training. Although they discussed the growing view that relationship skills are not important to treatment outcomes, in the final analysis they asserted that "the assumption generally prevails that the counselor's level of functioning on interpersonal dimensions is related to constructive client change" (Kurtz et al., 1985, p. 250). Although Kurtz et al. (1985) referenced a wide array of labels used to talk about relationship skills, they observed that virtually every skill typology they investigated either implicitly or explicitly included one or more of what Rogers (1965) called the core facilitative conditions: empathy, genuineness, and positive regard.

This observation notwithstanding, Stiles, Shapiro, and Elliott (1986) argued that the quest for a core of personal characteristics and behaviors located in the therapist that can account for therapeutic change has faded. Rather, they suggested that there may be more hope of finding an explanation for clinical effectiveness in clients' behaviors and attitudes (e.g., involvement in therapy, exploration of internal frame of reference.). In addition, Stiles et al. (1986) suggested that the concept of therapeutic alliance may prove more fruitful as an explanatory concept undergirding positive therapeutic change. Drawing on the work of Bordin (1979), Stiles et al. (1986) described the therapeutic alliance as consisting of three aspects: (a) the emotional bonding between client and therapist, (b) the quality of involvement in the therapeutic task, and (c) the degree of agreement between client and therapist on the goals of therapy. Whether one adheres to the traditional yet empirically unvalidated position that therapeutic change is inextricably linked with empathy and other therapist variables, or whether one adopts the more empirically promising position that therapeutic change is linked to the nature of the alliance between therapist and client (with primary importance on how the client perceives the therapist), one cannot escape the conclusion that training in relationship skills is an essential part of the core curriculum.

Drawing on sociolinguistic and related research, Higginbotham, West, and Forsyth (1988) provided helpful considerations that can augment any program in relationship-skills training. Although a full explication of their hypotheses cannot be included here, we refer briefly to one of their ideas that has implications for relationship-skills training, which is sensitive to issues of diversity. They argued that students should be trained in what they call conversational cooperation. This refers to initial clinical encounters that are characterized by students detecting and analyzing uncomfortable moments in the conversation, restraining from making judgmental inferences, and looking for background commonality between themselves and the client, while not probing too deeply into intimate areas. Without establishing conversational cooperation, one runs the risk of misinterpretation and distortion of the therapeutic relationship. Gumprez (1982) and Erickson and Schultz (1982) provided multiple examples of how therapeutic encounters can go awry if students are not trained to relate to people of different cultural backgrounds.

Attitudes

The inclusion of some type of relationship-skills training in the core curriculum of virtually every member organization of NCSPP attests to the centrality of the relationship competency. In addition to knowledge and skills, and equally important, the relationship competency involves attitudes, aptitudes, and values. In his review of psychoanalytic perspectives on the therapist–client relationship, Messer (1988) reminded us that Freud, as early as 1912, underscored the importance of attitude in therapists' work with clients. However, Stricker and Callan (1987) noted that the role of attitudes has been neglected in discussions about the education and training of professional psychologists.

At the Mission Bay conference (Bourg et al., 1987; Bourg et al., 1989), the NCSPP participants emphasized this important dimension. To underscore the critical importance of including a direct focus on values and on attitudes in training professional psychologists, NCSPP adopted the following resolution (Mission Bay Conference Resolutions for Professional Psychology Programs, 1987):

> 1. *In order to function most effectively in varied professional roles, a professional psychologist should demonstrate certain personal characteristics and attitudes, including but not limited to the following:*
>   a. *Intellectual curiosity and flexibility.*
>   b. *Scientific skepticism.*
>   c. *Openmindedness.*
>   d. *Psychological health.*
>   e. *Belief in the capacity for change in human attitudes and behaviors.*
>   f. *Appreciation of individual and cultural diversity.*
>   g. *Interest in providing human services.*
>   h. *Personal integrity and honesty.*
>   i. *Capacity for developing interpersonal skills (empathy, respect for others, personal relatedness).*
>   j. *Self-awareness.*
> *(pp. 26–27)*

Inherent in this resolution is the implicit belief that attitudes have an impact on effectiveness because they influence the psychologist's ability to relate. The relationship competency and appropriate professional attitudes and values are necessarily intertwined. Consistent with our earlier discussion of the knowledge and skills that are basic for psychologists to relate effectively, it is clear that intellectual curiosity, flexibility, scientific skepticism, open-mindedness, and appreciation of individual and cultural diversity are important, essentially interpersonal attitudes for the professional psychologist.

Conclusion

Although there are a multitude of approaches that have been developed to teach relationship skills, we believe that the entering student must have a foundation of initial relational ability on which to base the development of the more complex relationship skills necessary for effective functioning as a psychologist. Most professional schools require an interview with prospective applicants precisely to determine students' aptitude for basic interpersonal skills (Stricker, 1986). Because selection procedures are not infallible, however, student retention and advancement policies must include an explicit focus on interpersonal and relationship competence. Indeed a central element of the broader clinical competency review procedures in place in a number of professional programs includes explicit assessment of relationship issues, such as the ability to establish a productive relationship and the capacity for self-examination in an interpersonal context.

We have a responsibility to our students and to the public to ensure that our graduates are competent to relate to others. Although our faculty can provide modeling, role playing, didactic material, and practical experience, ultimately it is the students' responsibility to develop their own relationship capacities. If students are unsuccessful in doing so, the faculty has the responsibility to counsel those people out of the profession.

We have argued that the relationship competency is central to professional psychology. The values implicit here go beyond relationships with clients to illuminate student – faculty interactions, the nature of collegiality, and the importance of connection to local communities. Embedded in this position is a broader philosophical vision that positive relationships are the foundation of caring and productive human communities.

12

ASSESSMENT COMPETENCY

Steven N. Gold and Frank De Piano

Nova University
Fort Lauderdale, Florida

"Assessment is an ongoing, interactive, and inclusive process that serves to describe, conceptualize, characterize, and predict relevant aspects of a client" (McHolland, chap. 21, p. 163). It is unique among the major components of the core curriculum that constitute the foundation of the functioning and identity of the professional psychologist. Once the cardinal skill of the practicing psychologist, assessment has taken a progressively less central role in defining the profession. During the past three decades, assessment has become the target of intense scrutiny and dissatisfaction from within psychology as well as from outside the profession.

A core curriculum in assessment must provide students with the comprehension, knowledge, and skills to meet current societal assessment needs and prepare students to meet the future needs of a rapidly evolving society. To accomplish these goals, the construction of a core curriculum in assessment must be based on and responsive to a systematic review of the criticisms of traditional psychological assessment.

Historical Context: Criticisms of Assessment

The degree to which psychological assessment is considered a valued skill in the profession of clinical psychology has fluctuated substantially in recent decades. The emergence of psychology as an applied profession is intimately linked to the advent of intelligence testing early in this century and to the growth of personality testing in the 1950s. Throughout the first half of this century, the perceived efficacy and real successes of psychological testing led psychologists and the general public to hold its practice in high esteem.

In the early 1960s, however, the value, validity, and desirability of psychological assessment came under serious attack by factions within the profession and external to it (Holt, 1967). Popular works (e.g., Black, 1963; Gross, 1962; Whyte, 1956) criticized psychological testing on the grounds that it was intrusive, controlling, invalid, and antithetical to democratic principles, limiting the individual's opportunities for educational and career advancement. In 1965, spurred by these arguments and by the public indignation that they aroused, special congressional committees investigated the charge that psychological testing constituted an unwarranted invasion of privacy. Psychologists were concerned that Congress might place severe restrictions on the practice of psychological assessment (Messick, 1965). The threat of governmental controls prompted the devotion of an entire edition of the *American Psychologist* to the congressional inquiries and to the issues that they raised (Brayfield, 1965).

At the same time, the status of assessment among practicing psychologists was rapidly waning. Before World War II, the clinical psychologist's role consisted primarily of psychological testing and evaluation. After the war, psychologists gained widespread access to the practice of psychotherapy. Increasingly, clinical psychologists considered psychotherapy as their primary professional activity, rather than psychological assessment. In this process, clinical psychologists wanted to expand their professional identity beyond the former role of psychodiagnostic assistant, subservient to the psychiatric therapist.

In this climate, behavioral psychologists and humanistic psychologists stood on common ground in finding fault with psychodiagnostic testing. Each faction rejected the diagnostically oriented medical model of psychopathology on which psychological assessment had been based. Social learning theorists argued that diagnosis was unreliable and perpetuated psychological problems through the effect of social labeling (Ullman & Krasner, 1969). Humanistic psychologists found psychodiagnostic assessment to be excessively abstract and removed from experience, reductionistic, artificial, excessively intellectualized, and judgmental (Sugarman, 1978). Behaviorists and humanists agreed that assessment focused too heavily on client deficits to the relative exclusion of competencies and strengths (Goldfried & D'Zurilla, 1969; Maslow, 1962). They asserted that this emphasis severely limited the potential for effective intervention by omitting identification and evaluation of those client capabilities that could most readily provide the basis for problem resolution.

A sampling of attitudes and behaviors of members of the profession during this period reflected the changing climate and practices in assessment. Repeated canvasing of psychologists working in a range of clinical settings (e.g., inpatient facilities, outpatient clinics, counseling centers) confirmed a steady decrease in the proportion of time devoted to assessment from 44% in 1959 (Sundberg, 1960, cited in Lubin & Lubin, 1972), to 28% in 1969 (Lubin & Lubin, 1972), to 22% in 1982 (Lubin, Larsen, Matarazzo, & Seever, 1986). Despite this decline, among employers advertising clinical positions in the American Psychological Association Employment Bulletin in 1971–1972, 91% considered testing skills a condition of employment, 84% required familiarity with projective techniques, and 89% sought applicants with both projective and objective testing skills (Levy & Hayward, 1975).

Conceptual Framework for Assessment Training

Restructuring the Outmoded Model

Considering its 30-year history of adverse criticism and decline in status, it may seem incongruous that assessment retains a fairly central place in the training of psychologists and that practitioners continue to value it as highly as they do. In fact, it has been argued that assessment does not maintain its status as a result of its effectiveness, but merely because it constitutes a function and a marketable skill unique to the profession (Breger, 1968).

We contend that there are multiple, sound, and substantive reasons for the persistent vitality of assessment in training and in applied settings. First, and probably most important, the nature of assessment has changed dramatically, concurrent with and in many respects in response to the criticisms. Much of the critical literature finds fault with an increasingly outdated model that equates assessment with

1.   testing
2.   of an individual person
3.   conducted as a prelude to treatment
4.   for the primary purpose of formulating a diagnosis.

Such a model is easy to discredit, primarily because it is outmoded.

The advent of the *Diagnostic and Statistical Manual of Mental Disorders* (DSM-III; American Psychiatric Association, 1980) and its subsequent revisions, which replaced the impressionistic description of earlier diagnostic systems with specific criteria for diagnostic classification, has greatly reduced the relevancy and utility of test data in clarifying diagnosis. The diagnostic criteria of recent versions of the DSM-III lend themselves more readily to interview data and to behavioral observations than to test data. The development and dissemination of behavioral assessment approaches, which are often more compatible with interviewing and monitoring techniques than with the administration of standardized tests, have diminished the need for routine formalized pretreatment testing.

If the function of psychological testing is conceived narrowly as an aid to pretreatment diagnosis, it becomes at best uneconomical and at worst superfluous. Assessment in many treatment cases is best construed as an inherent, relatively informal, and ongoing component of treatment. Nevertheless, it is likely that the formalized, structured, detailed training psychologists receive in testing and assessment provides them with the ability to conduct informal assessment during treatment with a much greater level of sophistication and efficacy than therapists from other disciplines. In this sense, training in assessment provides psychologists with a disciplined approach to conceptualizing and hypothesizing about a given client.

Expanding the Dimensions of Assessment

As the need for formalized pretreatment testing has diminished, the demand for psychological testing and assessment skills in other contexts has expanded. Educational, legal, medical, business, and other professionals have turned increasingly to psychologists for assessment of individuals, groups, systems, and programs. Extensive assessment training, particularly in testing, equips psychologists with the ability to conduct assessments in a wide range of fields with relatively quick and accurate evaluations of a range of aspects of functioning (e.g., intelligence, academic achievement, personality style, behavioral predispositions, attitudes, interests, neuropsychological impairment). In these contexts, psychological assessors will assume a consultative role vis-à-vis other professionals. Consequently, other professionals will expect psychologists to address the types of questions that require familiarity with areas beyond the traditional diagnostic and treatment concerns of the clinician. As they develop expertise in responding to the assessment needs of other professionals, psychological assessors will have to become conversant with the concerns, norms, and knowledge bases of those professionals.

A core curriculum in assessment must orient doctoral candidates toward this wide potential range of demands. Students must become conversant with a broad-based model of assessment encompassing a range of approaches and instruments. In addition, effective consultative skills must be developed as an integral component of the assessment enterprise. Perhaps most important, the core curriculum must impart a conceptual framework for assessment that is extensive and flexible enough to accommodate a wide spectrum of needs evolving from disciplines with concerns that may be at times far afield from the traditional province of clinicians.

A model capable of serving this extended range of purposes must recognize several concepts explicitly:

1. A competent professional psychologist draws on diverse methods of evaluation, determining which methods are best suited to the task at hand, rather than relying solely or primarily on formalized testing as an automatic response to situations requiring assessment.

2. The appropriate subject of evaluation in many instances is not an individual person but a couple, family, organization, or system at some other level of organization.

3. The skills required for assessment can and should be applied to many situations other than pretreatment evaluation, including, for example, treatment outcome, program evaluation, and problems occurring in a broad spectrum of nonclinical settings.

4. The primary purpose of psychological assessment is to provide an understanding that informs a practical plan of action rather than producing a diagnostic classification as an end in itself. In many situations, it is more pertinent to identify strengths or competencies that can be built on than to detect deficits for categorization.

In the past, core-assessment curricula were organized around particular tests or types of tests. Training in psychological evaluation tended to focus almost exclusively on the technical aspects of administration, scoring, and interpretation of particular instruments. The recent history of psychological assessment underscores two crucial reasons why a curricular shift toward greater stress on the conceptual foundation of assessment is imperative. First, without such a foundation, the probability of naive and inappropriate application of specific assessment techniques is increased drastically. Second, in a field moving in new and unanticipated directions, grounding instruction in the mastery of the use of specific techniques and instruments increases the risk of overemphasizing skills highly vulnerable to obsolescence, while failing to provide the fundamental understanding of assessment needed to comprehend new emerging procedures.

Assessment as a Generic Process

A core curriculum in assessment that is designed to prepare students for sophisticated, effective, ethical, professional functioning in a wide range of possible settings and contexts must be structured around the concept of assessment as a generic process. Within such a framework, the execution of particular assessment techniques is conceived of as only one component of a much more extensive enterprise. This curriculum should explore in detail a number of discrete steps in the assessment process that traditionally have been neglected or addressed tangentially. These include, for example the following:

1. Formulation of a referral question. This aspect of the assessment process did not require extensive attention when evaluations were conducted routinely in mental health settings as an aid to diagnosis. As the composition and range of consumers of psychological assessment services has expanded, this step has become more critical. At the outset, it is crucial that time be spent clarifying with the referral source exactly what questions he or she hopes will be answered through the assessment process. This requires refined consultative interviewing skills on the part of the psychologist to help the referring agent clarify and articulate what he or she expects to discover or to be able to decide on the basis of the assessment. Only with an explicitly formulated referral question can the psychologist determine what types of instruments and techniques are appropriate, what information he or she needs to collect, and what issues need to be addressed by the findings of the evaluation. In short, the more time and care that is spent in this initial step, the easier and more effective the remainder of the process will be.

2. Selection of methods. Inherent in this model is the assumption that there are multiple legitimate methods including, but not limited to, testing for obtaining relevant information. In the past, the equation of assessment with testing too often failed to acknowledge the central function of interviewing and of behavioral assessment in the evaluation process. As a consequence of equating assessment with formalized testing, traditional models failed to provide workable methods of evaluating couples, families, organizations, and systems.

    We believe that assessment will and must undergo a transition analogous to the change that has been occurring in intervention: movement away from parochialism toward eclecticism. In an eclectic approach, questions such as which types of assessment technique are best (e.g., behavioral vs. traditional testing, self-report vs. observational data, projective vs. objective testing) come to appear meaningless. Various techniques come to be seen as different tools, each of which has an appropriate range of purposes. The relevant question becomes not which technique is superior but which combination of methods is best suited to the task at hand; that is, which set of techniques is most likely to provide information that can most fully and accurately answer the referral questions.

3. Information collection and processing. This step in the process encompasses the actual execution of assessment techniques (e.g., test administration, behavioral monitoring) and summarization of the collected data (e.g., scoring tests responses, graphing behavioral observations). It is more important that students have a conceptual foundation in each major type of assessment technique (e.g., clinical interviewing, intelligence testing, projective testing, objective testing, behavioral assessment) than mastery of many specific techniques. Full comprehension of a class of techniques likely can be achieved only through hands-on experience. In this regard, it is probably important that the core curriculum provide students with mastery of one technique that is representative of each type of assessment procedures. Familiarity with the conceptual model of a class of assessment techniques and with a specific technique exemplifying that class provides students with a knowledge and skill base from which other techniques in that class can be assimilated through subsequent course work, supervised clinical work, or self-instructional materials.

4. Generation and integration of interpretive hypotheses. A distinction that often receives insufficient explicit attention in assessment training, and which students find difficult to grasp fully, is the difference between the raw data yielded by evaluative procedures and the interpretive conclusion drawn from those data. In most instances, the data themselves (e.g., test scores, statements made in an interview, behavioral observations) have little value or meaning especially from the viewpoint of the consumer (i.e., the examinee or the referral source). Data must be interpreted into meaningful conclusions.

   Data attain meaning only when their interpretative implications, in relation to a theory or a body of empirical data, are formulated. These implications rarely constitute facts or certainties but are almost inevitably conjectures and statements of probability derived from knowledge of a given response's possible theoretical significance, empirical correlates, or likelihood of repetition in situations outside the assessment setting. An interpretive conjecture derived from any single datum carries a fairly high level of uncertainty. It is only when multiple interpretations from various sources are combined to support, contradict, embellish, and modify each other that a reasonably high degree of accuracy can be achieved. The more completely these concepts are understood, the less likely students are to formulate erroneous conclusions as a result of uncritical acceptance of cookbook interpretive manuals, computer-generated interpretive narratives, or other materials that may blur the distinction between data and their possible meanings.

5. Dissemination of findings. Ultimately, the value of an assessment rests on the ability to communicate information, oral or written, to the examinee or the referral agent in a manner in which it can be understood and used effectively. This requires the identification, development, and exercise of skills, primarily of a consultative nature, not often explicitly recognized as components of the assessment process. The psychologist must be able to translate findings into jargon-free terminology, phrase them in a way that will minimize the possibility of misinterpretation, and provide adequate responses to questions posed by the referring agent. This often entails assisting in the formulation of a constructive action plan.

Conclusion

The extensive knowledge base and multiple skills that make up the assessment process cannot be conveyed adequately through the core curriculum alone. At the onset of training, assessment should be introduced as a generic process that is more extensive than the method for gathering and processing information. Excessive attention to methodology, to the relative exclusion of the broader framework of the assessment process, is likely to lead to unsophisticated, inappropriate, and inept application of those methods learned. The resulting poor level of practice may well be largely responsible for the criticisms of assessment.

The majority of the material taught in the core curriculum of many professional psychology programs may continue to focus on specific assessment procedures. However, understanding this material in the explicit context of the total assessment process will help ensure that the methods taught will be applied in an appropriate, responsible, competent, and ethical manner. Moreover, the flexibility of application of the generic model compared with extensive instruction in particular assessment techniques will prepare students to respond more competently to the changing market for psychological assessment services.

13

INTERVENTION COMPETENCY

Russell J. Bent
Wright State University
Dayton, Ohio

and

Richard Cox
Forest Institute
Springfield, Missouri

"The intervention competency is conceptualized as activities that promote, restore, sustain, and/or enhance positive functioning and a sense of well-being in clients through preventive, developmental, and/or remedial services" (McHolland, chap. 21, p. 163–164). The conferees at the 1986–1987 midwinter meeting of the National Council of Schools of Professional Psychology (NCSPP), the Mission Bay conference, had little difficulty agreeing that intervention should be a competency area in the curricula in professional programs in psychology. It is significant that intervention, not psychotherapy, was the designated curriculum competency area. This advance in curriculum conceptualization represented the recognition that intervention is an increasingly broad, complex area that includes more than the psychotherapies. The Mission Bay conferees explicitly directed that intervention should include theory and technique related to systems (couples, families, groups, and organizations) as well as to individuals (Bourg et al., 1987). As is implicit in all the competencies, the emphasis in intervention on demonstration of skills necessitates an experiential learning and evaluation component, not only classroom lecture and paper-and-pencil examinations.

The conceptualization of intervention developed at Mission Bay was reaffirmed and expanded at the NCSPP 1989–1990 midwinter meeting, the San Antonio core-curriculum conference. In addition to the Mission Bay formulation, the San Antonio conferees resolved that:

> *The intervention competency relies especially on the following knowledge base: theories of individual and systems change, including the functioning and change of sociopolitical structures; theories and strategies of intervention; methods of evaluation and quality assurance; professional ethical principles and standards of practice. Along with the information derived from psychotherapy research, the knowledge and methods appropriate to the understanding of self and the self–other relationship, as well as to the significance of power and authority, are particularly relevant. (McHolland, chap. 21, p. 164)*

We believe that the future of all psychological intervention depends on outcome effectiveness, reasonable accessibility, and cost-effectiveness. Because no single model or theory is effective for all persons and practitioners, we propose a systematic, eclectic approach to learning and practice. Our formulation of the intervention competency includes both established and innovative components.

Individual Intervention

Psychotherapy (or counseling) for individuals is an essential part of the core. The psychotherapy core component should be rooted in an eclectic model, presenting major theoretical approaches such as psychodynamic, interpersonal, systemic, experiential, and cognitive-behavioral as positive viewpoints, all of which contribute to understanding clients and to change. Advanced study or special proficiencies are related to, but not an intrinsic part of, the core. Areas such as health psychology, addictions, women's issues, and forensic applications may be taught from either an eclectic or a specific theoretical orientation.

The individual psychotherapy core might reasonably be built on a human problem-resolution model. In this formulation, the unifying concepts are a respect for empirical research findings related to intervention and an attempt to apply such findings, attending to strategies, techniques, and outcome more than to theory. The Mission Bay vision for all competencies is relevant here: (a) the importance of the scientific component, (b) the value system of scientific self-criticism, and (c) the recognition of the limitations of each approach.

Most individual psychotherapy models are based on models developed for long-term treatment. We believe that long-term treatment approaches are not consistent with public and private utilization patterns, client satisfaction, or outcome. Therefore, we propose that instruction in long-term approaches be reserved for a special proficiency level. As such, they would not be seen as the usual approach for the majority of clients but rather the exception. Focused, more active psychotherapeutic service strategies should be taught at the core level.

Systems Intervention

For many years, individual psychotherapy and assessment (a battery approach) have been the primary activities of clinical psychology. A NCSPP curriculum survey (Kopplin, 1986) indicated that 45% of the responding schools did not offer, much less require, a course in group, couples, or family psychotherapy. The Mission Bay conference resolution supporting the inclusion of couples, families, groups, and organizations in the intervention area presented a challenge in curricular reform (Bourg et al., 1987). Since that conference, it is our impression that many programs have begun to include systems larger than the dyad in the intervention curriculum.

The systems approach is an essential part of the intervention core. Clients should be viewed as embedded in a pluralistic, multicultural context. The curriculum should provide students with a base from which to approach couples, single parents, families or units of significant others, groups, organizations, communities, and international configurations. Programs may develop special proficiencies in couples and families or in organizational psychology, for example, based on the same generic or core curriculum and later may develop specialization programs in these areas. This conceptualization has profound implications for curricular reform.

Broadening the Intervention Core

Programmatic or systematic approaches to intervention should be included in the core. Psychotherapy usually involves individualized service planning (a basic knowledge and skill). Programmatic approaches extend this basic planning ability to the design of regularized service delivery systems and programs. Examples include pain-reduction programs, eating-disorder programs, organizational team-building programs, and so forth. These powerful intervention programs have applications in many contexts. They lend themselves to the use of nondoctoral personnel and contractually packaged programs. In a general contractor role, instead of in the historic employee role in psychiatric settings, the psychologist must apply the management competencies proposed by Bent, Schindler, and Dobbins (chap. 16). It is anticipated that future training in intervention will prepare the psychologist to be the most well-rounded and fully equipped human service provider in society.

The intervention curriculum should include biomedical technology and psychopharmacological components. Psychologists should be expected to have a basic understanding of medical technology such as biofeedback, CAT (computerized axial tomography) scan, MRI (magnetic resonance imaging), EMG (electromyography), EEG (electroencephalography), PET (positron emission tomography), and the ever-increasing armamentarium of diagnostic and treatment modalities using biomedical technology.

A fundamental appreciation of psychopharmacotherapy is now taught in many programs; all programs should include this component. Some psychologists are advocating for limited prescription rights and for training in the administration of pharmacological agents. Demonstration programs have been proposed. This could be an option for a special proficiency area, even though it is fraught with practical and political problems.

The intervention core should include training in developing productive relationships with community helping networks. Collegial planning with related professionals, evaluation of the effectiveness in meeting the needs of referring parties, and referral networking are fundamental to modern practice.

A computer component is suggested as a foundation requirement. Familiarity with computer-assisted information retrieval, including suggested psychotherapeutic methods, manualization of psychotherapy approaches, computer-assisted therapy, and computer assessment techniques, will be increasingly important in the intervention area.

It is important to broaden the concept of client or patient. We prefer client to patient because client implies participation, choice, and coactivity on the part of the service provider and the service recipient in a way that is consistent with an emphasis on context and the systems approach. A client may be an individual, a group, an organization—any service partner. One may use the term *patient* in certain situations, for example, in explicitly medical circumstances, but it is difficult to think of a marriage or an organization as a patient.

The introductory core should introduce the concept of change in terms of wellness. Perhaps the national image that best suits psychology as a profession is helping "the worried well" and building wellness or effectiveness in people's lives. Within this framework, client rather than patient is more compatible with perspectives emphasizing wellness, human effectiveness, and development. The student should learn to assume the role of human resources expert, able to deal with current and emerging configurations of the human dilemma. We must appeal beyond our well-established territory in the diagnosis and illness terrain and not use only concepts from psychopathology.

Prevention is related to wellness. We contend that prevention methods of intervention should assume a central role in future curricula. The realm of the psychologist should include normal everyday problems, developmental issues, and conflicts inherent in life situations in addition to or in place of work in the illness context. The prevention approach shows particular promise when there is an emphasis on the development of effective life-styles that relate to stress reduction, enhanced productivity, and the prevention of psychological and physical disability.

The other five competency areas (i.e., relationship, assessment, research and evaluation, consultation and education, and management and supervision) relate to and integrate with the intervention competency. The relationship competency, in particular, is a central and critical component of intervention. Focused, early teaching of the relationship competency allows early and coherent integration with the intervention competency.

There is a consensus that differing intervention methods and orientations may lead to client improvement based on spontaneous remission, common therapeutic factors, special techniques, and placebo effects (Lambert, 1986). Spontaneous remission depends in large part on the context of the client's life. A systems intervention may enhance life variables, for example, involving a family in therapy or developing a surrogate family. The common therapeutic factors should be greatly enhanced by special attention given to the interpersonal relationship competency, critical to forming and maintaining the positive therapeutic transaction. Special techniques should build a reasonable base, especially an introduction to group and family approaches, and teach a limited, varied number of psychotherapy techniques from a transtheoretical perspective. The placebo effect may be enhanced by proper therapy role induction, by education, and by more careful attention to client expectancy variables through reasonable goal-attainment "contracting."

In summary, a comprehensive and broad vision of the intervention competency explicitly should include the following:

1. A respect for the positive aspects of all major approaches, which should reflect an openness to varied viewpoints and methods.
2. An appreciation of a systematic, eclectic approach.
3. The learning of an array of varied, specific psychotherapeutic techniques from a transtheoretical viewpoint, including individual psychotherapy and interventions with systems such as couples, families, groups, and organizations.
4. A problem-resolution model.
5. A focused service strategy at the basic level and long-term approaches at the special proficiency level.
6. More use of the programmatic approach.
7. An understanding of basic biomedical technology.
8. Inclusion of a foundation in psychopharmacotherapy.
9. Mutual planning skills with community helping networks.
10. An introduction to computer information retrieval.
11. A broad view of the client that includes serving the client in many locations.
12. A human effectiveness perspective as well as an illness or a diagnostic model.

13. A prevention approach coupled with an effective life-style component.
14. Fundamental reliance on and training in establishing a positive therapeutic relationship.
15. Sensitivity to context and to diversity, especially multicultural and gender issues.

Pedagogy

Each program should establish the intervention core curriculum consistent with its (a) definition of professional psychology, (b) special proficiency areas, (c) resources, (d) methods of evaluating competency, and (e) career patterns of graduates.

Questions to be answered include the following: Where, when, how, and by whom should the core be taught? What resources should be used? We have no simple answers. Because each program has its own array of resources and emphases, particular approaches to the intervention core, quite reasonably, should vary. Although a generally defined foundation is essential, each program should teach it in a manner that is consistent with its goals and its training model.

The intervention core curriculum necessarily includes fieldwork and simulated laboratory work under supervision. Increasingly, supervised practice should occur in program-sponsored and controlled psychology service systems (centers) where training can be more specific and can be controlled by the program itself. Development of these training resources is very important in meeting the specific curriculum requirements.

We believe that programs should move to year-round curricula, that include a minimum of 1,200 hours of supervised experience. These hours should total about 2 days a week for a 40-week practicum in a practice placement. In addition, the first-year skill and knowledge development, with laboratory hands-on training, should include technical learning using video, manualization, simulated situations, and small-group methods. The internship should follow extensive course work often as an extension of the curriculum itself or as a closely coordinated experience with regional, cooperative internship programs that have a continuing relation with the predoctoral program.

We suggest a reduction in formal, academic, lecture-format teaching, so that single content or course areas can extend across quarters, semesters, or trimesters. Areas to be taught, particularly in competency areas, should be organized in logical clusters early in the curriculum. Workshop formats, practice tutorial methods, and independent learning should be used more extensively. Examples of methods that make teaching more effective and less labor intensive include more technical support for teaching, such as computer-assisted programs for testing and for planning skills; observation of actual practice; immediate feedback; and supervision.

Based on a general curriculum-design format, the model presented in Table 1 is one approach to teaching the intervention competency core. Each teaching sequence should be about 10 class meetings (25–30 hr) plus laboratory or practicum experience. Starting at the second-year level and continuing at the third-year level, special areas of proficiency or focus should be offered. These areas may contribute to a generalist application or may narrowly relate to special applications.

Table 1
One Approach to Teaching the Intervention Competency Core

Year/quarter	Teaching sequence
1	
Fall	Introduction to intervention
Winter	Basic individual psychotherapy 1
Spring	Systems intervention 1: couples and family
Summer	Systems intervention 2: groups and organizations
2	
Fall	Psychopharmacotherapy, biomedical and computer technology, physical interventions
Winter	Basic individual psychotherapy 2
Spring	Programmatic approaches
Summer	Intervention: special proficiency level

Note. Basic laboratory and intensive observation and simulation methods should be incorporated throughout the first year. In the second year, the student is in a supervised practice field placement for two days per week.

Conclusion

This perspective on intervention goes far beyond traditional formulations. Once limited to the psychotherapy of individuals, the focus of intervention has been broadened to include the entire array of human systems. Initially, intervention was seen as a psychotherapeutic process designed to cure the mentally ill. Now, more globally defined, intervention is the advancement and the support of positive development or change and the enhancement of effectiveness. Every less-than-productive human situation or enterprise could profit from positive psychological intervention.

Psychologists of the future need broad-based, multidimensional intervention skills. To impart this new, comprehensive vision of intervention, programs need to initiate curricular reform. The psychologist of the future must be able to "pull the logs out of the stream" and in addition be able to move upstream to prevent a log jam from occurring. It is our belief that the training inherent in this expanded view of the intervention competency will enable the psychologist of the future to do both.

14

RESEARCH AND EVALUATION COMPETENCY: TRAINING THE LOCAL CLINICAL SCIENTIST

Steven J. Trierweiler

Antioch New England Graduate School
Keene, New Hampshire

and

George Stricker

Derner Institute, Adelphi University
Garden City, New York

Consistent with many of the ideas in this chapter, the San Antonio conference resolution on the research and evaluation competency began as follows:

Psychological science is a systematic mode of inquiry involving problem identification and the acquisition, organization, and interpretation of information pertaining to psychological phenomena. It strives to make that information consensually verifiable, replicable, and universally communicable. Professional psychologists systematically acquire and organize information about psychological phenomena, and often engage in the general practice of science. Nonetheless, it is recognized that, because of the particular conditions that frequently limit inquiry in the local contexts of professional psychological practice (e.g., nonrepeatability of phenomena in time, privacy, etc.), the scientific goals of consensual verifiability, replicability, and universal communicability are attainable more in principle than in practice. Despite these practical realities, we endorse a view of the professional psychologist as a local clinical scientist: an investigator of local psychological phenomena who engages in the rigorous, critical, and disciplined thought engendered in striving toward scientific goals. Therefore, research training in professional psychology should be viewed as an essential tool for developing and enhancing critical thinking in students, and it should be integrated throughout the curriculum. All of our graduates are expected to function as local clinical scientists; some of our graduates may engage more directly in the application of research methodology in roles such as program evaluator. The application or diffusion of research results into practice is an important

The authors thank Roger L. Peterson, Russell J. Bent, and Donna K. Nagata for helpful comments on earlier versions of this chapter.

process that should be enhanced and encouraged through research training. (McHolland, chap. 21, p. 164)

In this chapter, we discuss the place of research training in the professional psychology curriculum. We address two classes of concerns. First, we pay heed to traditional concerns about the professional's ability to generate, interpret, and integrate scientific findings into professional practice. Second, we attempt, in preliminary fashion, to develop an image of the professional psychologist as a local clinical scientist, an individual whose task is to develop localized descriptions of clinical case phenomena that are scientifically accurate and that facilitate decisions about the relevance (fit) of various theoretical and research findings to that case.

The chapter is divided into four sections: the notion of local clinical scientific inquiry, research training goals, knowledge base in scientific and research methodology and practice, and pedagogy. Our intention is not to develop a definitive argument for any given proposition but rather to raise issues for discussion in the professional community.

What is Local Clinical Scientific Inquiry?

Our vision of the local clinical scientist is captured by the image of a professional investigator who enters the typically ambiguous clinical situation (an open system) equipped with both technical skills and capacities for localized inquiry. The ultimate goal is veridical assessment of the situation and effective problem solving within the boundaries of accepted professional practice. In professional psychology, a local clinical scientist rarely finds the professional knowledge and technical skill base completely adequate to the task; therefore, skills in local investigation and in problem solving (thinking on one's feet) assume unusual importance.

We propose that the needs of this investigator guide the development of the scientific research methods curriculum in professional psychology programs as well as the development of other parts of the curriculum. The overarching goal of such training is to develop critical investigators of local (as opposed to universal) realities (a) who are knowledgeable of research, scholarship, personal experience, and scientific methodology; and (b) who are able to develop plausible, communicable formulations for understanding essentially local phenomena using theory, general world knowledge including scientific research, and, most important, their own abilities as skeptical scientific observers.

Although largely compatible with traditional scientific methodological training, this view calls for differing educational practices because it emphasizes (a) being a generalist of knowledge and method as opposed to a specialist; (b) focusing on local realities in which data are gathered as they apply to a particular case and may be limited in the extent to which they generalize to other cases; and (c) developing an active inquiring mind as opposed to concentrating on technical expertise with scientific methods. In effect, methodological training neither can be put aside, nor can it simply continue to echo traditional university training. Rather, it must be explicitly integrated with the interests of the active professional.

The idea that clinical inquiry differs from standard scientific inquiry is not new to discussions of professional psychology training. As stated at the Boulder conference,

> *Much of the time, thinking in a practical, clinical setting requires suspension of highly critical, analytical concern over constructs, especially where immediate problems of human welfare are involved. The clinical psychologist ordinarily functions in a social setting in which abstract ideas cannot be debated at all times, but where practical decisions must be reached by a number of persons with differing backgrounds and skills. Realization of the need for adaptability should, in the long run, free the clinical psychologist from feelings of guilt over the "unscientific" demands of clinical reality, if at the same time he has had the opportunity to learn how to analyze personality concepts in terms of their systematic implications. There cannot be overindoctrination in the scientific attitude. There can be an illusory oversimplification of the problems faced by the clinical psychologist who is also a scientist. (Raimy, 1950, p. 86)*

Nonetheless, we believe that the implications of such thinking largely have been undeveloped, and a significant difference in emphasis is needed in modern practitioner training.

Historically, training has emphasized skills necessary for scientific knowledge production, whereas scientific skills related to local clinical analysis have received relatively less explicit attention. In contrast to traditional training models, we propose that professional psychology programs develop and expand the early insight that the professional psychologist is a local clinical scientist (e.g., Shakow, 1976). We take as self-evident the need to continue also to train clinicians who will be devoted to the production of scientific psychological knowledge. The major difference between the traditional training model and the model we propose is that, in our model, the capacities necessary for local clinical science and scientific knowledge production do not need to be developed fully in the same individuals.

We also differ from the Boulder formulation because we do not agree with the grim implication that scientific "adaptability" to local circumstances requires "suspension of highly critical, analytic concern [in response to the] 'unscientific' demands of clinical reality" (Raimy, 1950, p. 86). Indeed, the essence of the training problem is to help students conceptualize clinical judgment and decision making in such a way that critical analysis of the local evidence, required to establish a fit between clinical theory, data, and action, is in the foreground of the clinician's concerns. We can accomplish this if we conceptualize research training explicitly as training in critical thinking and as a means to instill scientific attitudes. In the following section, we propose goals for research training that reflect this position.

Goals of Research Training

General Goals

Professional psychology programs should include research training that enables students to develop (a) a basic understanding and respect for the scientific bases of the discipline; (b) methodological knowledge designed to make them good consumers of scientific knowledge products; (c) enough basic skill in conducting research to be able to design and execute competent projects in professional and in some cases academic contexts with the support of properly trained consultants (e.g., statisticians).

Critical Thinking

Research training should be viewed as a major tool for developing and enhancing critical thinking skills in students. Because the logic and method of science transcend substantive areas and deal with the nature, generation, and verification of knowledge, research courses offer a unique opportunity to develop skills in observation, logic, and the generation of plausible inference.

In particular, students should be able to use empirical evidence to illuminate a problem or question while remaining cognizant of the limits of certainty inherent in different types of clinical and scientific data and scholarship. Furthermore, students should have the theoretical skills that are necessary to generate and to select among alternative possible views of a situation based on the best available empirical evidence. To these ends, a research curriculum should recognize explicitly that professional psychologists operate in open systems as opposed to the conditions of closure sought in controlled research settings. Open systems require inquiry skills commensurate with the realities of such systems.

Attitudes and Judgment Skills

Research training should provide a means for developing and manifesting various desirable attitudes and judgment skills related to professional inquiry and problem solving. These include (a) openness and receptivity to the multiple ways of looking at a problem (as opposed to dogmatism) and the various strengths and limitations of these approaches; (b) respect for empirical support (either local support or support offered in the scientific literature) for a particular viewpoint tempered by a healthy skepticism about the certainty such support affords and the appropriateness of its application to particular circumstances; (c) a sense of professional knowledge, responsibility, and authority (professional voice) with respect to the conduct of an inquiry that facilitates timely decision making and action while explicitly eschewing professional arrogance; (d) explicit recognition of one's own biases and predilections and how these might serve to limit an inquiry in deleterious ways; (e) explicit recognition of the interplay between ethics and scientific inquiry especially with respect to special issues that arise in local circumstances; and (f) explicit recognition of the need for collegial input and feedback in any inquiry however routine.

Knowledge Base in Scientific and Research Methodology and Practice

The discussion thus far provides a set of overarching goals for a research curriculum in professional psychology. There are, of course, more substantive objectives related to the demonstration of knowledge and skills in scientific methodology. Although many of these should be explicitly addressed in a science and research curriculum, it is obvious that they are also important to other aspects of the curriculum as well. These objectives are as follows:

1.   The acquisition of basic knowledge of philosophy of science and the various ways it has impacted scientific psychology, especially in this century. This should in-

clude explicit recognition of scientific knowledge production as a social and political process.

2. The acquisition of basic knowledge of applied statistics and measurement theory as fundamental tools for the study of scientific constructs in populations. There should be explicit recognition of the issues and assumptions involved in applying aggregated findings to the individual case and in generalizing from individuals to populations.

3. The acquisition of basic knowledge of the logic of research design ranging from its most highly controlled level in laboratory experimentation to approximations of this control in quasiexperiments and field studies. The emphasis should be on how different research designs yield greater or lesser levels of certainty or plausibility with respect to a particular empirical result and how this may or may not afford equivalent certainty about conclusions that are drawn based on that result. In addition to encouraging the application of this logic to help solve local problems, efforts should be made to extend this logic to clinical contexts where prospects of experimental control are limited. For example, students should be taught to use knowledge of statistics and research design (the scientific imagination) as a means to enhance realistic judgment and decision making, although definitive research projects may be impossible to execute in local contexts.

4. The acquisition of basic knowledge of qualitative research methods with particular emphasis on the nature of reliability and validity in the collection and interpretation of qualitative data. Professional psychologists operate far more as anthropologists than as experimental researchers (open systems, specific cases, limited samples, and so on). Qualitative data have a special place in the generation of accurate and complete localized descriptions of phenomena, in grounded hypothesis generation, and ultimately in locally relevant explanation. Thus, skills in qualitative investigation—which include observation, research (as opposed to clinical) interviewing, summarizing and bounding qualitative data collection and analysis, and generating and reporting conclusions that follow from the data—are highly germane to daily practice. Formal training in the logic of qualitative approaches and their relationship to traditional quantitative approaches is central to a local clinical science.

5. The acquisition of basic knowledge of applications of various research approaches to social systems as well as to individuals. These include evaluation research approaches, survey approaches, sociological approaches, and the like. Many of the most widely used research methods logically are most compatible with the study of social systems (e.g., multiple regression). Professional psychologists need to understand how the study of social systems impacts the study of individuals and vice versa. In addition, it is important that the professional psychologist be able to design and execute applied research projects of this type in local settings for both program-evaluation and program-development purposes.

6. The acquisition of basic knowledge of one's personal epistemology, including personal biases, theoretical predilections, the nature of the "evidence" that leads one to develop particular beliefs about the nature of clinical phenomena and the place of scientific research in this matrix of professional beliefs. Scientific research is a major arena for public legitimation of professional psychology, but it is only a small portion of the personal fund of knowledge used in everyday practice, even among those who explicitly try to ground all action in scientific approaches (e.g., behaviorists). Professional psychologists need to be aware of the source and le-

gitimacy of the knowledge they use be it from science and scholarly sources, from a respected colleague or mentor, from institutional culture, or from compelling personal experience. Awareness of how one ascribes credibility to an idea lays the foundation for critical self-examination informed by evidence.

7. The acquisition of solid skills in professional writing, with particular emphasis on the research report where empirical or scholarly data (broadly defined) are used both to answer a specific question and to inform reasonable extrapolations to other contexts. Good written communication captures the essence of critical thinking skills; therefore, it is an essential tool for educating the local clinical scientist.

Pedagogy: Toward a Realistic View of Local Clinical Science

Traditional Concept of Scientific Inquiry

The major challenge in meeting these goals is the development of a pedagogy that links all aspects of scientific research training to the concept of local clinical scientific inquiry. This requires some changes in ideas about what scientific inquiry is and what it can become.

There are powerful identity issues involved in the relation between science and practice (Stricker & Keisner, 1985a). Although professional psychologists benefit from research instruction, traditional research training has been at the center of professional psychology's disaffection with scientist–practitioner training, attempts to deny this notwithstanding (e.g., Barlow, Hayes, & Nelson, 1984). A major reason for this dissatisfaction is the failure of professional psychology to develop a research pedagogy that is uniquely geared to the needs of professional inquiry.

Without discounting the power of clinical applications of scientifically derived concepts (e.g., behaviorist, cognitive, interpersonal), it is clear that scientific training in professional psychology has been as much training in a critical-empirical attitude as in scientific techniques, although this is seldom openly discussed in the literature. Unfortunately, this attitude, subordinate to the publication traditions of university science, often has failed to grasp the significance of the many different approaches to local clinical phenomena.

One outcome of a narrow view of science is that some psychologists—through personal backgrounds, interests, training programs, and so forth—have tended to identify with the scientist role by conceptualizing their work in terms of phenomena that are tractable in traditional scientific research contexts. Other psychologists, in contrast, have remained ambivalent about science, bemoaned its narrowness and apparent irrelevance, and pursued specialties and theoretical orientations that often suit personal taste as much as the realities of clinical phenomena. (How often have you heard psychologists note how competent or incompetent they are at statistics and research design, as if this, in itself, determines their adequacy or inadequacy as clinician–scientists? How often has a shrugging off of scientific work been the basis for following other theoretical traditions, usually those espoused by wealthy urban clinicians?)

Goal of Local Clinical Science

We believe that a professional environment in which some psychologists view themselves as more scientific than others is indefensible. Therefore, we propose that training programs develop methods to invest psychologists with a clear, shared sense of how science, in all its variety of manifestations, operates in day-to-day professional activities, a shared sense that defines science as a tool for all rather than as a source of prestige for a few. This objective should have higher priority than the success one has as a practitioner of university science. The curricular goals, previously described, are a step in this direction.

The key question is whether the professional psychologist enters the clinical situation thinking as a scientist, informed by general knowledge while receptive to important specifics, interested in discovering how theory fits observation, and vice versa. To discuss whether one published one's dissertation, performed a multivariate analysis, or found research alienating or irrelevant to clinical practice simply misses the point. Rather than asserting one's theoretical preferences, the local scientist must be responsible and creative in identifying empirical linkages between local realities and theory that could stand the test of critical scrutiny by colleagues. In addition, he or she must be aware of and responsive to the fallibility of any particular approach to the situation.

A pedagogy that addresses these concerns necessitates changing our commonly held ideas of what scientific training is designed to accomplish. Instead of concentrating on knowledge generation, we should emphasize how knowledge is produced in a variety of contexts. In so doing, we must accept the possibility that much of the scientific training we have received is inadequate. We need to design new ways of translating scientific thinking into approaches to professional inquiry. We must develop rules of evidence to be applied in local clinical contexts. We should return to an emphasis on how and why scientific methodologies work and eliminate the cookbook mentality that makes science seem irrelevant to clinical concerns. Finally, we must recognize that science cannot account completely for the array of unique situations we confront clinically however good we become at identifying the underlying order of things. We are not repeating the cliché that clinical work is art, but clinical work does require an approach to science that is ecologically compatible with the reality of clinical practice. Professional psychologists with this approach to science can assume their proper place within psychology as scientific investigators of the local conditions of human psychological dysfunction. If professional psychologists do not have to rely solely on academic scientists as scientific models, they will no longer have to struggle to ensure their professional legitimacy.

Pedagogy for Local Clinical Science

The design of a research pedagogy must move beyond the mere teaching of methodological tenets to the explicit unpacking of their implications for critical thinking and practice. Issues in research and in clinical practice often are akin to each other. Table 1 presents some specific examples of the types of critical questions raised by various research concerns. Material from experimental, qualitative, and evaluation research and from applied logic are presented to emphasize that local clinical science requires a broad concept of inquiry. Our objective is to show how the critical logic of research

Table 1
Some Examples of How Methodological Concerns Raise Important
Critical Questions for the Local Clinical Scientist

Research concept	Methodological concern	Critical questions for the local clinical scientist
From experimental research: Some threats to validity[a]		
History	A confounding event occurring during an experiment	Are results of intervention due to some intervening effect unrelated to treatment, such as a job change or a change in marital status?
Statistical regression	Subjects in an extreme group will often change toward the mean simply as a result of a statistical artifact related to unreliability of measurement	Interventions virtually always deal with extreme groups. Is the initial presenting pattern statistically extreme for this client or for the populations the client "represents?" If so, what changes can be expected in the next "measurement/observation"?
Selection	Experimental subjects from a select group (e.g., volunteers) may limit the extent to which we can generalize the observed results to an unselected group	Clients who seek treatment are a select group; those seeking a specific type of intervention are even more select. Are observed effects due to special characteristics of these clients? Which characteristics and to what extent? How would the effectiveness of an intervention look in an unselected sample?
Experimenter expectancy	Experimenters can communicate a confounding expectation to subjects to behave in a manner confirming the hypothesis of the experiment	Has the psychologist communicated an expectation to the client that may yield results consistent with that expectation? For example, it is not unusual to note differences in symbolism that appear in the dreams of clients in psychotherapy with therapists of different orientations
From qualitative research[b]		
Bounding data collection and analysis	Because qualitative data often require extensive summarization and coding, researchers must set boundaries around the analysis that are logically related to the research questions	Professional psychologists commerce with an unbounded field of information potentially relevant to an intervention. What are the most pertinent sources of data and how can they be systematically summarized? What and how do particular sources of data support inferences drawn about a case?
Research interviewing	A focus on the subjective realities of research participants requires skills in thorough interviewing about particular issues: furthermore, it requires an understanding of language usage in local contexts	Are the particulars of clients' subjective experience being investigated as framed within local language communities without distortion from premature translation of information into theoretical formulations? Are applications of theory adequately translated at the local level and supported by local evidence?
From evaluation research[c]		
Leverage of an evaluation question	Evaluation researchers attend to the extent to which projects yield results that will be useful to the system studied	Are the major issues being investigated in a way that can make a difference to the clients? Are values, theories, or methods being applied that are not consistent with the realities of local circumstances?
From applied logic[d]		
Conditions under which a statement can be accepted at face vales	Logicians ask under what conditions a statement can be accepted as true. (e.g., statements that refer to material directly observed by an informant carry greater credibility than those that suggest an interpretation)	"The newspaper reports that candidate X views the national debt as a disgrace" is a credible statement about the report and less credible about candidate X's views. Psychologists largely deal with abstract reports of this sort. Are the credibility and meaning of various reports being assessed realistically? Is application of theory consistent with the most logically sound information available?

[a]Based on Cook & Campbell (1979). [b]Based on Miles & Huberman (1984) and Mishler (1986). [c]Based on Cronbach (1982). [d]Based on Dauer (1989).

methodology extends, in interesting ways, to a greater appreciation of the process of psychological intervention.

Research methodology.   The complicating confounds that trouble the experimental researcher are parallel to the complicating conditions of treatment that trouble the clinician. Both researcher and clinician are concerned with observation and control, but the demands and expectations for precision in these efforts differ depending on the circumstances. Our approach encourages an integration of the scientist identity with that of the practitioner. The clinician, faced with a difficult set of heterogeneous problems, cannot use the researcher's solutions (e.g., randomization and averaging). Instead the clinician is encouraged to develop explicit means of responding to that which, under traditional circumstances, is considered to be beyond control. We only have begun to tap this potential in our pedagogy and in our conceptualization of the professional enterprise.

Applied statistics.   More than 30 years ago, Meehl (1954) concluded his influential book comparing clinical and statistical prediction with a chapter entitled "The Unavoidability of Statistics." He did not mean that a clinician could not exist without performing analyses of variance. Rather he was alluding to the need for the clinician to validate clinical hypotheses and the role of statistics in providing confirmation or disconfirmation of hunches. Furthermore, however much we attempt to individualize our approach, population effects will be manifest in treatment as we move from individual to individual; choosing to remain ignorant of them can be equivalent to dishonesty.

Meehl and Rosen (1955) pointed to a fundamental manifestation of population effects in their discussion of base rates, defined in the most simple way as the frequency with which an event occurs naturally. The population realities summarized in a base rate ensure, for example, that a diagnostician who can predict the occurrence of suicide with 75% accuracy in a select group in which suicide occurs 60% of the time, will gain a reputation as a genius, whereas the same diagnostician, working with the same rate of accuracy in an unselected group in which suicide occurs 1% of the time, will contribute little and stop receiving referrals very quickly. Such considerations are seldom part of our conversations about colleagues we admire or of our assessments of our own efforts. Yet base rates are crucial in much professional decision making, and they are most important within a local frame of reference.

For years, the practical implications of these statistical facts have been lost in the fog that has existed on the boundary between the science and the practice of psychology. We are suggesting that professional psychology mount an effort to develop formally and to transmit to clinicians practical skills in collecting or at least intuiting local base-rate information, in assessing the ways population characteristics are and are not manifested in individuals, and in facing directly the gambler's problem (assessing this individual in this situation at this time) endemic to a local clinical science.

Psychological measurement.   In a more recent methodological development, Lamiell (1987) and Lamiell and Trierweiler (1986) discussed the problem of measurement of the individual without reference to populations. Although the technical argument is beyond the scope of this chapter, suffice it to say that such measurement is seen to derive meaning from a dialectical reference to what might have been but was not (interactive measurement) rather than from reference to a population norm (normative measurement). This is a major step beyond the interminable idiographic-nomothetic debate because this "idiothetic" approach provides a logic whereby data and generalizations from that data are derived within the meaning frame of the subjects, a position clearly compatible with the needs of the local clinical scientist. Students find this work compatible with their clinical work and inspiring because it encourages looking beyond the information given to the limits of an individual's or social unit's frame of meaning. We need to develop ways to help students bring such conceptual and research tools to bear on the assessment and decision-making problems of professional practice.

Future development of the research and evaluation curriculum. Obviously much needs to be done to move us beyond these preliminary suggestions to the generation of explicit investigatory strategies for the local clinical scientist. Several areas for future development of the research curriculum are as follows:

1. More work bridging the gap between basic research and clinical efforts is needed (e.g., Stricker & Keisner, 1985b) and full-time professionals need to be involved in developing these translations using the groundwork laid by research clinicians. In so doing, researchers and clinicians need to collaborate in generating models for the proper diffusion of research into practice; a local clinical science involves knowledgeable application in local contexts as well as skills in inquiry.

2. Views of science that explicitly recognize the problems of clinical inquiry need to be incorporated into training. Particularly promising heuristically is the realist view in philosophy of science (e.g., Harré, 1986; Manicas & Secord, 1983) that directly addresses the relation between experimental and interpretive approaches to scientific inquiry.

3. More explicit adaptations of the kind of thinking found in anthropology, history, and so forth (e.g., Lincoln & Guba, 1985) are needed. Feminist scholars have taken the lead in the productive adaptation of such approaches in ways compatible with a local clinical science (e.g., Belenky, Clinchy, Goldberger, & Tarule, 1986).

4. As suggested in Table 1, the principles of logic, properly translated, could provide tools for critically analyzing the type of direct and indirect data that are common in professional practice (e.g., Bakan, 1956; Dauer, 1989).

5. As has been long recognized (e.g., Raimy, 1950; Shakow, 1976), participant observation and other self-as-tool skills (see Singer, Peterson, & Magidson, chap. 18) need to be conceptualized in the research–scientific context.

We believe that if professionals come to see themselves overtly and practically as local clinical scientists, many of the identity issues still being acted out in professional circles between academic and professional psychologists (see Stricker & Keisner, 1985a) will lose their force, and the mutually respectful dialogue envisioned for the profession from its onset may be realized.

Conclusion

We recognize that some aspects of our proposal are controversial, and our formulation requires further development and refinement. It is a mistake to interpret our approach as encouraging a loosening of standards of rigor in the profession. We do not suggest that, for example, clinicians accept increasing dependence on impressionistic data and call it science. Rather, we propose the opposite: Clinicians should be responsible for critically evaluating the source of their inevitable impressions in a manner available to the critical scrutiny of colleagues. Certainly, this is a difficult task, and it is improbable that any of us have accomplished it definitively in our thinking about our work.

Our primary objective is to set an agenda for research and evaluation competency curriculum development within the context of the practitioner training model. Although some research curriculum revisions have been undertaken, their documentation and overarching conceptualization have been minimal. We hope that the presentation of this preliminary material is a step toward remedying the situation and the beginning of a brighter relation between profession and science.

15

CONSULTATION AND EDUCATION COMPETENCY

Robert J. Illback

Spalding University
Louisville, Kentucky

Charles A. Maher

Rutgers University
New Brunswick, New Jersey

and

David Kopplin

Baylor University
Waco, Texas

Professional psychologists engage in psychological consultation and educational activities in a variety of settings to address problems experienced by individuals, groups, or organizations. Psychologists working in community mental health centers regularly consult with crisis-intervention agencies, public schools, social services, and day-care settings on individual or program problems. In medical settings, psychologists are involved with life-style training and stress-management programs. Psychologists in schools consult with teachers and parents about the developmental needs of children, conduct psychological skills training groups with at-risk students, and teach high school psychology courses. Increasingly, psychologists consult with business and industry on topics such as health promotion, peak performance, employee-assistance programs, worker satisfaction and productivity, leadership, and organizational development. Many professional psychologists teach undergraduate-level and graduate-level psychology courses at colleges and universities. In addition, they provide in-service education to staff members or colleagues through workshops and lectures. Consultation and teaching activities will continue to expand as the field of professional psychology becomes more diverse, relevant in an increasing array of settings, and at the same time more specialized.

Although consultation and education activities constitute a substantial portion of the practice of professional psychology, professional training programs traditionally have not placed great emphasis on explicit training in this area (Bourg et al., 1987). In this chapter, we describe the knowledge base, applied skills, and professional attitudes required for consultation and education as well as training components that facilitate thorough preparation for them.

Background and Rationale

Psychological consultation and education activities are rooted in the history of psychology as evidenced by the early emergence of the American Psychological Association's divisions (numbered in the order that they were created): Teaching of Psychology Division (2) and Consulting Psychology Division (13). Psychologists have long been involved with developing and applying knowledge in areas such as normative human learning and development, positive and healthy psychological functioning, and promotion of humane and responsive societal institutions and organizations. There is a strong base within each of the various schools of thought in systematic psychology (e.g., behavioral, humanistic) for this orientation.

The advent of the community mental health movement in the 1960s (Rappaport, 1977) served to increase the involvement of professional psychologists in consultation and education activities. Interventions with a broader range of effectiveness were sought given the inherent limitations of individual therapy, concerns about its overall efficacy, and the severe shortage of trained mental health personnel to address societal mental health needs. Aided by the Community Mental Health Centers Act of 1963 (Rappaport, 1977), these concerns gave rise to a new direction in psychology, with an emphasis on promoting human welfare through prevention programming, "giving psychology away," and strengthening the community context. Rather than viewing human problems as amenable only to traditional individual-level intervention, community psychologists, with an ecological orientation, focused on strengthening the individual and the setting in which problem behavior emerged.

As prevention and intervention programs (e.g., coping-skills training) designed to attenuate psychopathology and disturbance evolved, problems began to be defined more broadly to include underused resources and missed opportunities. Thus, professional psychologists broadened the emphasis from a traditional clinical focus to include a broad array of problems and possibilities in human services, business and industry, government, and other settings. Examples of emergent areas for practice in which consultation and education competencies are preeminent include sports psychology, social skills training, behavioral medicine, community-based treatment, substance-abuse education, workplace literacy, and management-skills training.

Definition and Description of Consultation and Education

Consultation

Consultation refers to the planned collaborative interaction between the professional psychologist [consultant] and one or more clients or colleagues [consultees], in relation to an identified problem area or program. Psychological consultation is an explicit intervention process that is based on principles and procedures found within psychology and related disciplines, in which the professional psychologist has no *direct* control of the actual change process. Psychological consultation focuses on the needs of individuals, groups, programs, or organizations. (McHolland, chap. 21, p. 165)

The task of the consultant is to assist the consultees in problem identification and resolution through facilitative social influence processes, many of which are parallel to psychotherapy. The key distinction between the consultant and the psychotherapist is that the consultant has no direct control of the actual change process among the ultimate consumers of the services.

Although consultants draw from various theoretical orientations and strategic approaches, consultation is essentially a problem-solving process with identifiable components. Usually consultants begin by defining and clarifying the problem situation with the consultees. Then they conduct an analysis of the problem in context, including characteristics of the setting and historical factors that may be contributing to problem maintenance. Consultants facilitate consideration of a range of alternative strategies that can lead to problem amelioration or resolution and help consultees to evaluate and decide among these. After the consultation itself has been conceptualized, consultants and consultees determine their respective roles in implementation and in monitoring progress, periodically meet to review the implementation process, and ultimately make determinations about the success of the chosen strategy.

Education

"Education is the directed facilitation by the professional psychologist for the growth of knowledge, skills, and attitudes in the learner" (McHolland, chap. 21, p. 165). Education involves social influence and problem solving, but it may involve less collaborative interaction around a particular problem focus or goal than consultation. Education is a more foundational process: Its objective is the transmission of information and skills to others (e.g., clients, supervisees, staff members, other consultees). Formal education occurs within the context of sound instructional design in which the learner's needs and goals are identified, appropriate instructional methods and materials are used in delivery, and attainment of learning objectives is assessed.

Knowledge, Skills, and Attitudes

There are specific competencies that professional psychology training programs should incorporate to prepare trainees adequately for consultation and education. The content knowledge, skills, and attitudes considered essential to competence in consultation and education are now discussed.

Knowledge

The core of basic knowledge related to consultation and education is derived both from psychology and from related disciplines (e.g., education, systems science). The key areas of knowledge with which all professional psychologists should be familiar are as follows:

1. Historical development of the community mental health and community psychology movements, including concepts of primary and secondary prevention, "giv-

ing psychology away," strengthening the competency of individuals and settings, and consultation and education roles of professional psychologists.

2. Conceptualizations of human behavior that emphasize ecological-transactional perspectives and their application.

3. Theoretical and empirical knowledge base for consultation processes found within psychology, including behavioral theory, mental health, organization development, and related consultation approaches.

4. Principles and procedures of sound instructional design, technology, and the teaching and learning relationships found within psychology and education.

5. Group, social, and organizational psychology concepts, including group dynamics, interpersonal relationships, organizational theory, systems analysis, program planning and evaluation, and models of planned organizational change.

6. Foundation knowledge about organizational design and features (e.g., political, economic, legal) of a broad array of service-delivery systems within which professional psychologists may consult, such as health services, education, corrections and justice, governmental and regulatory agencies, social services, and business and industry.

7. Needs and characteristics of high-risk populations or those for whom nontraditional services may be more appropriate, such as minority groups, the long-term mentally ill, and developmentally disabled persons.

Skills

Core skill competencies in consultation and education for all professional psychologists include the following:

1. Establishing the consulting relationship by gaining entry into the setting, negotiating about the purposes of consultation, and delineating the process that will follow.

2. Capitalizing on the consultation relationship through effective interpersonal skills such as listening, paraphrasing, empathy and genuineness, persuasive communication, and elicitation of consultee involvement (cf. Polite & Bourg, chap. 11).

3. Gathering data about the nature and severity of problems and formulating hypotheses about the factors that are contributing to the problem through qualitative and quantitative means (e.g., interviewing, observation, surveys; cf. Trierweiler & Stricker, chap. 14).

4. Conducting a contextual analysis of the problem, arriving at a problem conceptualization, and framing this for the consultee.

5. Agreeing on a course of action to address the problem and establishing a strategic plan for the change process.

6. Facilitating collaborative interaction through teams and work groups within the setting to implement system interventions, manage conflict, and improve long-term maintenance of change.

7. Balancing the needs, wants, and interests of various client or consultee systems and negotiating mutually acceptable and workable solutions.

8. Assessing intervention effects and determining whether revision is required.

9. Conducting a needs analysis of knowledge and skill deficits of learners to serve as the basis for an instructional program.

10. Selecting appropriate methods (e.g., didactic, experiential) and materials to facilitate the transmission of information and the development of requisite knowledge and skills of learners.
11. Conducting and evaluating instruction using sound principles of instructional design, such as lesson planning, sequencing and pacing the presentation, varying instructional approaches, involving learners in discussion, and seeking feedback.

Attitudes

Core attitudinal competencies in consultation and education for all professional psychologists include the following:

1. Tolerating ambiguity and inadequate data in making decisions about interventions.
2. Making a personal commitment to precepts of psychology in the public interest, in social responsibility, and in service to one's community.
3. Believing in the ability of organizations, institutions, and other social systems to change through collaborative planning and systematic intervention.
4. Recognizing and advocating the psychological and civil rights of individuals and groups in society, particularly those who are most vulnerable, and seeking their empowerment.
5. Considering the diverse and often contradictory demands of multiple-client systems without being judgmental or arbitrary.
6. Being sensitive to and appreciative of multicultural diversity and communicating this attitude to others.
7. Maintaining equanimity and personal integrity in high-stress, conflict situations.
8. Engaging in sophisticated reasoning about complex ethical dilemmas and using specific ethical principles in seeking their resolution.
9. Respecting and communicating the fundamental worth and dignity of learners, clients, and consultees.
10. Demonstrating enthusiasm for learning, capacity for psychological growth, intellectual curiosity, openness to experience, and appreciation for empiricism.

Recommendation for a Model Curriculum

We propose the following program components as one approach to the inclusion of consultation and education competencies in the training-program curriculum:

Formal Course Work

The training curriculum should include a course, taught no later than the second full year of training, that provides a comprehensive overview of consultation and education. The course, entitled "Consultation and Education," "Consultation Processes," or "Psychological Consultation," should incorporate both didactic and experiential components including both a systematic review of the knowledge base previously described and planned training experiences in consultation skills, systems analysis, and teaching. Specifically, experiential components of the course should include practice in consultation interviewing and in microteaching, and it should require the completion of a small consultation project in an organizational or community setting.

Consultation and Education Skills Portfolio

Before the internship experience, the student should be required to submit a description of a program or project in consultation or education that he or she has conceptualized and performed in an organizational or community setting under the supervision of a professional psychologist, preferably in the context of a practicum placement. The project description should be sufficiently detailed to demonstrate knowledge, skill, and attitudinal proficiencies, including a discussion of the presenting problem, a theoretical and conceptual analysis of the situation, the rationale for the change strategies that were used, and methods and materials developed to implement the change. Whenever possible, audiotapes or videotapes of consultation or teaching experiences should accompany the program description.

Because a secondary purpose of the project is to instill through modeling a commitment to community service, faculty should be involved in assigning and coordinating these projects. Examples of acceptable projects include consultation with community agencies (e.g., schools, day-care centers, neighborhood services, programs for the elderly), involvement with prevention programs (e.g., crisis hot lines), consultation with businesses, institutions, or agencies (e.g., health promotion, organizational development), or an extended teaching experience (e.g., parenting classes, social skills training).

Internship Level

A full range of consultation and education experiences should be included in the training of each intern. This component should be specified in the student's internship plan, with goals and activities delineated. Activities should be individualized based on the unique needs of the intern and of the setting. At a minimum, the intern should be expected to complete at least one systematic consultation program continuing during an extended period of time and to provide training for other staff members using appropriate instructional methods.

Conclusion

As a field, professional psychology has gone forward beyond its historical emphasis on research, assessment, and intervention. Every bit as stimulating, challenging, and complex as these traditional areas, consultation and education increasingly are becoming staple activities of professional psychologists. Coherent, systematic training in consultation and education should be a central element in the preparation of the professional psychologist both for today and for the future.

16

MANAGEMENT AND SUPERVISION COMPETENCY

Russell J. Bent, Nancy Schindler,
and James E. Dobbins
Wright State University
Dayton, Ohio

Management and supervision are included within a single competency area because they share many characteristics in common. In psychological applications, "management consists of those activities that direct, organize, or control the services of psychologists and others offered or rendered to the public. . . . Supervision is a form of management blended with teaching in the context of relationship directed to the enhancement of competence in the supervisee" (McHolland, chap. 21, p. 165). In supervision, the focus is on individuals or on small units.

Often management and supervision are used interchangeably. Although the two terms are closely related, we use them with differing emphases. Management, a broader concept than supervision, involves more activities, particularly resource development. The control in supervision is often more detailed, direct, explicit, and individualized than the control in management. One manages an organization, whereas one supervises a person.

Management

Management strategies and issues are intrinsic to the practice of psychology. Management involves individuals, groups, and organizations. Individual case management, managing a practice, or managing a pain center are examples of the management activities of psychologists.

The management of psychological practice is influenced by internal and external factors. The internal influence is exerted by the profession itself (e.g., standards of practice and ethical guidelines). The external influence comes from sources such as legislation, general management activity, federal policy, or third-party insurance-payment procedures. The management of psychological practice is influenced by the complex interplay between the internal and external forces inherent in a pluralistic society.

Stromberg et al. (1988), in *The Psychologist's Legal Handbook*, observed about psychologists:

> *Little in their training directed their attention toward the commercial, legal, or managerial aspects of practice. For many, it came as a rude awakening to find themselves in a profession where the necessary survival skills are managerial as well as clinical. Psychologists today need more than the abilities to provide effective therapy and to inspire confidence in referral sources. (p. i)*

In contrast to current educational practice, psychologists-in-training should receive instruction in management to deal effectively with the diversity of practice and the impact of internal and external influences.

Management of the Professional Self

Perhaps the best introduction to the importance of management principles and methods is gained by addressing the management of the professional self. The hallmark of well-trained professionals is that they adhere to and practice within the profession's established consensual standards and guidelines. Their vision of appropriate professional behavior is organized and activated by sources of influence within the profession itself.

Before entering the professional training program, students are not bound by specified professional obligations. On entering the psychology training environment, students should clearly understand that they are members-in-training of a profession and are obliged to conform to the consensual standards of that profession. Through introductory teaching and perhaps through a formal ceremony, students should pledge allegiance to the profession's standards, particularly the ethical standards. In each program, a sanctioning ethics committee with student membership should be established to ensure compliance throughout all aspects of the program.

Professional persons are expected to meet obligations, to be sensitive to others, and to conduct their personal life in a reasonable manner. In addition to the management of one's professional behavior according to consensual guidelines, students are expected to manage time, to prioritize obligations, and to develop a life-style commensurate with their professional training. Small-group teaching should help develop awareness of burnout patterns, stress patterns, stress management, principles of time management, professional goal setting, and personal organization to meet training and, later, professional requirements.

Case Management

Case management is the management of clients. In our formulation, therapy techniques or the therapeutic relationship are not the focus of case management. Rather, case management is concerned with the basic practical, ethical, legal, interdisciplinary, and interagency considerations involved in dealing with clients. In the complex service considerations with which psychologists deal briefly, effective service often demands effective case management. Knowledge of client – agency expectancies, networking with community resources, individualized service planning, documentation, and so forth is critical to client service. Competent case management necessitates knowledge of the legal issues that underlie informed consent, clear contracting, confidentiality, privileged communication, and fee setting.

Professional Issues

Professional management relies, to a large extent, on standards and guidelines formally established by the profession. The student should be knowledgeable about the history of the applied psychology movement and contemporary issues in the field including the professional school movement, the accreditation process, specialty designation, licensure, and certification. The history and current status of standards of practice, customary practices, ethical case presentations, advanced certification for the diplomate, and designation issues need coverage. There should be ongoing attention to contemporary professional issues related to self-regulation.

Professional identification and socialization should be reinforced by recommending student membership in professional organizations. Student participation at local, state, and national levels should be encouraged. Particularly by modeling direct participation in professional organizations, faculty can help students become involved in psychology organization work.

Service-Delivery Systems

The management competency should include the study of service-delivery systems, particularly a consideration of the major forms of practice, that is, the independent office, the group practice, the corporate practice, and the employee assistance program (EAP). Instruction should attend to the general parameters common to all service-delivery systems: a population to be served, a way of engaging that population, services to be rendered for particular goals, a designation of clients served and providers tô serve them, resources including sources of revenue, information-system requirements, legal-legislative and professional requirements, quality control, accountability methods, and an organized way of interrelating the management of all of these features.

Service-delivery systems manage these parameters in different ways. Hospitals, school systems, community agencies, and vocational rehabilitation agencies, for example, have service-delivery systems that have both enhanced and limited the activities of professional psychologists. Managed care, health maintenance organizations (HMOs), preferred provider organizations (PPOs), major federal programs (e.g., Medicare, Medicaid, CHAMPUS), and psychologist-managed care systems such as Biodyne and General Psychological Services should be examined in a delivery-system context.

Psychological practice initially was rooted in public agencies. In recent years, the private sector has emerged as a major influence on the provision of psychological services. Public agency and the public are not synonymous. The majority of the nation's population receiving personal and health services are not served through public agencies; yet the profession often has been biased against forms of service that might impact the general public. "Money making," "entrepreneurial," and other such epithets have been used to describe professionals who serve clients outside of public agencies. Other than corporate group health insurance support and government insurance-like systems, little attention has been directed to ways of delivering psychological services to the vast majority of persons in the nation. We do not propose to diminish our responsibility to respond to the poor or to the disadvantaged. However, we should work toward developing more creative ways to serve persons or organizations of moderate or sufficient means in those many aspects of functioning that make up the daily fabric of our national life. For this reason, modern methods of marketing and of managing services should be introduced in the curriculum.

Ethnic diversity is greater than ever; approximately 21% of the U.S. population is Black, Hispanic, or a member of other non-White racial groups (New York Public Library, 1989, p. 676). In some urban areas, the minority is now the majority. There are particular opportunities for creativity in program development, financing, and administration of psychological services for ethnically diverse groups. Programs should attend to these issues throughout the curriculum.

The process of quality assurance, particularly as it relates to maintaining quality of service and to the management of service provision, needs to be taught early. The use of management-information systems and documented review, with an associated attitude of receptivity toward professional review, are important to learn at the entry level.

Management by Board

Most public and private agencies are managed by boards drawn from the community that determine policy and oversee programs and services. Therefore, it is important to establish the value of participating in a community's political fabric as a means of influencing its human service policy. An awareness of and basic skill development in this level of organizational management should start early in the program. Participation in school or university governance, management of the program's psychological service center, and some observation of community boards in action contribute to this important competency.

Supervision

Perhaps the most neglected area of a psychologist's education and training is learning how to be supervised and how to supervise others. Because about one half of a professional psychologist's formal training involves learning through supervision, this area is critically important.

Psychologists are supervised through laboratory experiences, practica, internships, and postdoctoral practice. Most psychologists who work in organized settings assume the responsibility of supervising others, including nonpsychologist staff and assistants. Psychologists in independent practice often employ assistants and office staff who require supervision. Therefore, supervision is an important foundation competency for one's own training, for the training of others, and for service provision.

Developmental Approach to the Teaching of Supervision

We suggest a developmental approach to teach the knowledge, skills, and attitudes involved in supervision. This approach is based on the assumption that at each level of training, including prepractice, practicum, predoctoral internship, and postdoctoral residency, students have progressively more varied needs related to supervision. A practicum student's supervision may attend to basic interviewing strategies, whereas a third-year student might focus on the personal complexities of being a therapist and of developing a professional identity. The role of the supervisor may change from being a teacher or mentor to being a consultant or an administrator. Each developmental level has different data sources and requires varied sorts of supervisory involvement. As supervision training progresses, a student might move from being a supervisee to observation of supervision to discussion of the supervisory process to supervised experience in supervision.

The first stage of training in supervision begins early in practicum and should focus on being a good supervisee. Good supervisees typically are characterized as active learners who are open to supervision, well prepared, able to use time efficiently, nondefensive, organized, willing to take risks, aware of their limitations, and so on. This role induction should come through a variety of didactic and experiential activities. Participation at this level should include writing clear learning goals, reacting to the supervisory process, and participating with advanced students in some supervisory sessions. Later practicum may include training in the supervision of some specific skills, such as the mechanics of test administration.

At later stages of the practicum, before the internship, teaching also should involve all or part of a course or an intensive workshop experience devoted to the provision of supervision. At this level of training, the student has had experience being supervised and often has supervised others in restricted skill-building activities. Preinternship teaching should include a review of the supervision literature, a review of supervision models and methods, and an overview of the technical resources available for supervision. Most of the training in supervision should occur during the predoctoral internship when each trainee should experience a full range of supervisory activities as both a supervisee and a supervisor under supervision.

Attitudinal and Cultural Issues

Whereas the teaching of supervision has received limited attention, attitudinal and cultural issues in supervision have received little or no consideration. Value differences, power relationships, problematic interactions, and issues of gender, culture, and ethnicity need to be recognized and addressed insofar as our limited knowledge permits. Certainly we need a more systematic consideration of all of these dimensions as they influence both the therapeutic relationship and the supervisory relationship. Supported by knowledge about minorities and cultural issues, we must develop a conceptualization of what prejudice is and how it impacts our therapeutic and supervisory work.

The supervisor needs to develop a paradigm for understanding individual differences in the context of the supervision process. The conceptualization by Marden and Meyer (1978) may be helpful in viewing interpersonal transactions between dominant and nondominant cultures. When dominant and nondominant cultural matches occur in therapeutic or supervisory transactions, special attention must be accorded cultural, ethnic, gender, or other individual differences.

Supervisors also must be aware of their own strengths and limitations in regard to issues of cultural diversity. Although the argument sometimes still is made that therapy is a value-free interaction, supervision and management of cases involve exchanges that go beyond therapeutic considerations, and these must be viewed in the context of the cultural backgrounds of the participants.

Most supervisors have not taken course work in issues of cultural diversity and perhaps may not feel competent to handle such issues. Although a culturally diverse faculty can alleviate this problem to some degree, a word of caution is offered. Faculty from nondominant cultures should not be pigeonholed into the role of supervising those cases that make supervisors from the dominant culture feel uncomfortable. Rather, supervisors from nondominant cultures should serve as consultants to supervisors from the dominant culture so that the latter group can learn and ultimately model appropriate supervisory activities.

Including supervision as a foundation competency area serves to expand and to integrate theory, practice, and research. It adds a significant dimension to the curriculum and to the improved training of the professional psychologist.

PART III
BROADENING THE
CORE CURRICULUM

17

BROADENING THE CORE CURRICULUM

Glenace E. Edwall

Baylor University
Waco, Texas

On the most direct level, the chapters in this section advocate an expansion of the traditional content to include material relevant to the self of the professional psychologist, to experience, to women, and to ethnic diversity. On a more general level, all of the following chapters are based on a broadened conceptualization of the core curriculum, beyond definitions by content, beyond traditional university science, and beyond the frame provided by the competencies put forward earlier in this book.

According to Singer, Peterson, and Magidson (chap. 18), beyond any particular substantive content in the core curriculum there should be "systematic attention to the nature of the relationship between the self of the student and the work of professional psychology" (p. 133). As a core process, they suggest that reflexivity, the ability to reflect on actions and behaviors in the past (Gergen, 1982, p. 18; Smedslund, 1985), must be in the center of training in professional psychology.

Newton and I (chap. 19) make the case for a broadened psychological epistemology based on the contributions of feminist scholarship. Then we critically examine the core structure of professional training curricula, experiences, and processes from the perspective of women.

Finally, Davis-Russell, Forbes, Bascuas, and Duran (chap. 20) discuss the necessity of understanding current psychological paradigms and of adopting a new one to evaluate effectively and to generate knowledge pertaining to ethnic diversity.

At the National Council of Schools of Professional Psychology (NCSPP) midwinter 1989 – 1990 conference on the core curriculum, my brief talk and the material represented in the preconference version of these chapters were the focus of the first afternoon. The morning session had been marked by a lively discussion of the general attitudes that do or ought to inform clinical training and practica. In the afternoon session, participants were asked to make immediate application of the principles they had just enunciated, along with ideas found in this section, by considering how the core curriculum could better reflect the experience of women and minorities and how the psychologist's awareness and use of self could be integrated productively with these issues. A number of striking conference resolutions evolved from this afternoon's work: an affirmation of multiple ways of knowing, the fundamental value of diversity and inclusiveness, the necessity of education of the person and the professional self, preparation for multiple roles, the centrality of relationships in the clinical enterprise, and the importance of the responsible use of power and authority (McHolland, chap. 21). These conversations also prepared the way for detailed discussion of the competency areas, which were the final focus of the conference.

In this book, this part has a different but parallel intention. These chapters continue to provide the intellectual background for the same innovative general resolutions that appear in Part IV. At the same time, even after the thoughtful delineation of the competency areas in Part II, it remains critical that a broadened vision of the core curriculum informs future discussions of professional psychology training.

My remarks, originally a short introduction for the afternoon's deliberations, are less an academic piece than a personal way of bringing together my experience of my self as a psychologist, some concerns of women, and issues surrounding minorities and diversity.

I appreciate Roger Peterson's reminding us this morning (chap. 1) of the relational basis of what we are doing here at a conference on the core curriculum in professional psychology. Like many of you, I have appreciated NCSPP as a place where I am more free to be who I am than in most other organizational contexts. I would like to take advantage of the freedom proffered by the context to comment, largely metaphorically, on the experience of diversity and its incorporation into the larger fabric of our profession and our institutions.

While I was working on my part of the paper that Nancy Newton and I wrote for this conference, I was teaching an undergraduate course about the psychology of women, an experience that always heightens my awareness of language, and especially of the metaphors that structure our discussions (this class is my biannual respite from football talk). In the writings of women that we read in this course, I was struck by the prevalence of images taken from traditional women's handiwork, especially weaving, embroidery, and quilting. I was surprised at the power of these images for the young women in the class and the more amazed as I realized that most of them, like me, had little direct experience with thread and needle beyond sewing an occasional button.

The quilt metaphor has been especially personally powerful for me, and our talk in this class enriched my understanding of some particular experiences in which quilts marked a deepening of my awareness, a healing of my pain, or an expansion of my joy. Two of these experiences happened in the summers of 1988 and 1989, during which, because I am no fool, I left my sweltering Texas home and fled to Minneapolis. The first of these was an experience by now common to hundreds of thousands of Americans: I viewed the quilts assembled by the NAMES project, each lovingly made to represent the life and death of one person with acquired immunodeficiency syndrome (AIDS). The stadium in Minneapolis, which is more typically filled with noise and action, was still and quiet as hundreds of friends and relatives of people with AIDS walked the rows of quilts. The quilts themselves varied almost unimaginably. Some were beautiful in a classic sense, especially those modeled on traditional quilt patterns. Others, like Alexander Calder sculptures, stretched the very limits of the definition of quilt; they were banners, posters, collages, even portraits. Some were, to my taste, straightforwardly ugly, gaudy, brash. Many served to heighten my awareness of the range of symbolism that exists within my own culture but to which I am not privy.

As diverse as the quilts were the expressions of grief on the part of us as onlookers as we moved along the walkways. There was some, although little, wailing; many quiet tears; persons both known and unknown to one another touching one another's hands, shoulders, faces in gestures of understanding and support; and even some laughter as a characteristic of or experience with a loved one was recalled.

The experience was heightened—at times, almost to the point of surreality—for me by a division of my consciousness that I could not shake and that I later discovered was common to many viewers. The whole and the individual parts switched back and forth repeatedly as figure and ground, virtually every time I turned a corner, until any given quilt tugged at our grief and rage at the enormity of the AIDS tragedy. At the same time, the display as a whole seemed alive as a representation of any particular one whose life and death was commemorated. It recalled for me my first viewing of Maya Yang Lin's Vietnam Memorial, but the vastness of the quilt display made this merger of the particular and the whole even more potent.

The second Minneapolis summer experience was, if less intense, far happier. Two of my friends, who had made a quilt for the NAMES project, are quilt collectors and designers, and they, along with another couple, organized a show of antique quilts that occupied a hidden little corner gallery of the Minneapolis Institute of Arts for several weeks. I went in several times during my stay. I was drawn again to the connection in the show between the effort and artistry of each quilt and the corporate meaning of the tradition of women's work that they represented. The same interplay of the small and hidden with the larger often existed within a quilt as well, with the discovery of patterns, symbols, or even messages worked into individual pieces. I remembered my grandmother and, even more, stories about a great-grandmother and the quilts both of them made. Neither would be likely thought of as artistic; their quilts were pieced from scraps of fabric and from the "still good" parts of old clothes. I took out one of these quilts recently and tried to see how many pieces I could identify. All sorts of images returned, from favorite play clothes to the hated starched white collars my mother favored. I felt, as I suppose is obvious, deeply connected to both sorts of memories and to the persons attached to them.

I will try not to reify this metaphor any further because I risk killing it both for myself and for any of you who may have responded to it. I also fear pursuing the metaphor into a dangerous romanticism, inasmuch as all of us are aware, and some in this room are aware in a very direct fashion, of the hard economic and political realities in which issues of diversity reside and of the exclusionary pain that still lurks around and behind each question, each discussion. Yet I suppose that if there is any point to my little morality tale, it is that sometimes, in the middle of the most tragic expressions of natural and human cruelty, there is the possibility of new recognition (in my religious tradition, of epiphany) that this is not all there is, that this is not the end of the story. Nevertheless, the recognition comes in unexpected places and often from persons overlooked in our ordinary routines. There is a moral imperative to respond more fully and more appropriately to diversity for the sake of the other, but there is also the inescapable fact that we must also do it for ourselves: Our sisters and brothers, like pieces of the quilt in their various arrangements, are the basis of our ever-new experience of meaning and of beauty.

18

THE SELF, THE STUDENT, AND THE CORE CURRICULUM: LEARNING FROM THE INSIDE OUT

David L. Singer and Roger L. Peterson
Antioch New England Graduate School
Keene, New Hampshire

and

Ethel Magidson
Massachusetts School of Professional Psychology
Dedham, Massachusetts

Consistent with the resolutions adopted at the San Antonio conference, the 1989–1990 midwinter meeting of the National Council of Schools of Professional Psychology (NCSPP), in this chapter we elaborate the position that, whatever the substantive content of the core curriculum, it is critical during training to provide systematic attention to the nature of the relation between the self of the student and the work of professional psychology. This position rests on the acknowledgment of reflexivity, a fundamental characteristic of both human psychological activity and the discipline of psychology, which is the process through which one may step out of the ongoing flux of living and, with a "reflective glance" (Gergen, 1982, p. 18), examine actions and behaviors (including doing psychology) in the past tense (Smedslund, 1985). This is the observing ego function in psychoanalytic theory.

Personal–professional reflexivity is the process through which one systematically examines personal experiences of professional activities and training (see Peterson, chap. 3), potentially integrating them into the larger context of the self: the examination of self-in-role.

There have long been those who advocated attention to the education of the self about the self in clinical training. The original notion, psychoanalytic in origin, was that clinicians must become cognizant of the ways in which their own biases, needs, and countertransferences (i.e., the propensity to perceive and react to clients in ways that stem from the psychologist's internal processes rather than from the characteristics of the current situation or other people involved) might affect their clinical work. Personal

133

therapy, process-oriented supervision, and training groups are some of the vehicles that training programs have typically promoted as ways of achieving this goal.

This focus on the self, primarily in the clinical context, seems narrow today, particularly in view of the varied roles filled by professional psychologists, of our current understanding of the processes of professional education and adult development, and of our awareness of the social meaning, role, and power of psychology as both a profession and a science. These issues have been particularly well articulated by social constructivist theory and feminist theorists. However, even with the limited goals and methods previously described, education about the self in professional psychology typically has been either attended to haphazardly or neglected and seen as peripheral, secondary to, and less worthy of systematic thought, systematic inclusion in the curriculum, and academic credit than content or technique-oriented courses. Our experience is that in times when resources are in short supply, the pieces of professional training programs relevant to the self of the student tend to be cut back first.

In our view, however, the education of the self should be at the very center of the core curriculum in professional psychology, providing its backbone. This is especially so for our discipline, addressing as it does the understanding and change of human behavior and experience. It is also true from the perspective of our obligations to all three of our profession's constituencies: our students, our profession, and the general public.

In what follows we further articulate what we mean by education about the self, indicating why we believe it is central to professional preparation and offering some suggestions for enhancing the relation between the self of the student and the work of professional psychology. We also describe some techniques for integrating education about the self into the professional psychology curriculum and explore some of the dilemmas that arise in this practice. Essentially we are talking about enhancing the process of professional socialization in its broadest and richest sense.

Concept of Role

A key linking concept is the notion of role: in its organizational sense, denoting the work tasks one is authorized to perform and for which one is held accountable; in its social sense, reflecting relationships (e.g., parent, friend, consultant, therapist); and in its sociopsychological sense, describing the informal, often unconscious, socioemotional functions individuals may come to serve (e.g., clown, nurturer, scapegoat, conscience, rebel) in families, groups, and organizations at a given time.

Another key concept is *self-in-role:* This refers to the way in which differing professional and organizational tasks, roles, and dynamics foster the expression or suppression of differing aspects or facets of the self—what is stimulated in us by our activities and contexts—for better or worse (Lawrence & Miller, 1976). We do not experience ourselves the same way in all circumstances and with all people. Understanding the evocative pull of differing ways of and contexts for being a psychologist is important learning for the emergent professional psychologist.

Task of Professional Education

We are pleased with the operational definition of the task of training in professional psychology as preparation for effective role functioning adopted at the San Antonio conference. Indeed the six content areas identified by the earlier Mission Bay conferees as central to the core curriculum in professional psychology can be thought of as identifying an array of roles (interventionist, consultant, assessor, supervisor, researcher, and so on) potentially pursued by the professional psychologist (Bent & Jones, 1987).

Given this frame, several things follow. First, professional education must encompass teaching not only the substantive knowledge and theory in the field and the technical skills involved in their application but also appropriate attitudes. More important, it must involve working with students so that they become aware of the different ways in which they can take up the profession and use their training to forge an initial career structure. These and other related matters can be grouped under the rubric of professional socialization.

Professional Socialization and the Self

Earning a doctorate and joining the profession of psychology is a complex socialization process that involves much more than the acquisition of knowledge, concepts, attitudes, and skills (Singer, 1982). It involves making choices about the kind of psychologist one wishes to be and the activities in which one wishes to engage. Furthermore, it involves joining a culture with its own norms and values and developing a set of attitudes about oneself, one's clients, one's colleagues, and one's profession (Clark, 1973). Aspects of one's profession tend to become internalized parts of one's identity; one begins to think and to see the world as other members of the profession do, to adopt its key values, and to use the language and jargon of the field.

To become members of a committed, effective, socially responsible profession, emergent professional psychologists must be able to assume the various roles available within the field with technical, interpersonal, and organizational competence. They must do so in a manner relatively unburdened by ambivalence about their profession or by unresolved issues from the past that intrude counterproductively on professional functioning. Each psychologist must be enlivened by curiosity, a need to serve, and a need for excellence that derive from and are linked to central aspects of the self and key elements of one's history.

To survive and flourish, the student ultimately needs to assume the identity and roles of a psychologist in a way that is both "viable and suitable" (Levinson, Darrow, Klein, Levinson, & McKee, 1978), working well enough in the outside world and being satisfying enough for the self. Each of the roles available to professional psychologists carries with it different challenges, meanings, attendant relationships, sources of anxiety, and potential satisfactions. Each requires overlapping yet somewhat distinct skills and talents. It is thus important that as a central part of their educational and training process students examine how each of these roles affects them (i.e., what it stimulates in them) and how their selves and personal styles impact on their work.

Adult development is an important context within which professional socialization occurs. Occupation, or career, is a central element in the life structure of most professional men (Levinson, 1977; Levinson et al., 1978; Levinson & Gooden, 1985) and women (Carlsen, 1988; Mogul, 1979). Evolution of one's life structure will also often involve recurring shifts in the personal meaning and importance of one's work throughout one's life. Key and valuable parts of any professional's current self—values, aspirations, talents, identifications with key figures, and developmental tasks—need to be expressed in work and professional life at any stage in one's ongoing adult development.

Other aspects of adult development also affect students' experience of professional training. Some will be starting a doctoral program in their 20s; others in their late 30s or early 40s. Some will be using graduate school as a means of exploring possibilities for new ways of being in the context of a transitional period in their development; others will be using the same program to consolidate and build a new and stable life structure as the result of just having gone through a developmental transition or crisis (Singer, 1982).

In addition, joining a doctoral program involves major shifts that can be both stressful and demoralizing (Seashore, 1975). Adult students, especially, in essence enroll their families and some significant others in the program when they join, often inadvertently abandoning others for years. For those who enter a program as midcareer adults, there are shifts in status as they become junior practicum trainees rather than the senior, masters-level staff they used to be. There is also the experience of being de-skilled when one continually is working in domains where one has beginning rather than advanced skills. Without support, it is likely that high levels of emotional distress and casualties will emerge; with support, more students are likely to survive and thrive (Gopelrud, 1980). How can self-awareness and understanding of these developmental experiences be incorporated into students' training to help them navigate these waters and learn about themselves in the process?

There is also the matter of finding one's voice (Taylor, 1986, 1987): becoming able to participate in the clinical and academic dialectic or conversations through which knowledge is socially constructed (Gergen, 1985). This often poses problems for those—especially women—for whom differentiation is difficult and for whom a reworking of issues of status, competence, and authority turns out to be a necessary, although unanticipated, aspect of the return to graduate school. Taylor (1986) observed that the very processes of taking a point of view (standing fully and alone in the center of our subjectivity), articulating a point of view (occupying center stage), and giving voice to this point of view (taking the ball and running with it) run directly counter to stereotypical female socialization and indeed to the socialization of many men as well. Looked at another way, however, this is but one manifestation of the task of becoming senior— becoming a doctorate-level psychologist—faced by all professional psychology students. How may we work with students to help the self speak with the voice of authenticity as well as clinical and scientific authority by the time they graduate?

: Responsible Use of Our Power as Professionals

The power of the psychologist to influence the terms, if not the reality of the clinical encounter, has been commented on astutely by many writers (e.g., Guggenbuhl-Craig, 1971; Strupp, 1972). Our clients come to us in times of need and dependency, we control the settings in which we meet with them, and we are socially sanctioned as experts. Whether we take responsibility for this power in the relationship, it is there, and one may use it for good or for ill. This is also true in scientific psychology, although less intuitively obvious. The issues of what is discovered, what remains hidden from view, and the context in which knowledge is understood are profoundly influenced by the nature of the questions asked by the investigator, the methods used, and the framework within which the results are described and interpreted (Gergen, 1985; see also Peterson, chap.

3; Edwall & Newton, chap. 19). How can we work with students so that they may not only become aware of these issues of power, but also struggle with the moral, ethical, and political dilemmas posed?

Methodology for Education About the Self

There is little in the literature or in the clinical training lore to guide us in attending to the relation and fit between students' self and their experiences in professional roles during professional training. We propose that education of the self in professional psychology education involves several interrelated dimensions. First, there is the technology: examined experience of self-in-role. Second, there is the question of program cul-: ture. Third, there are issues of curriculum design. Finally, there is the question of faculty organization and structure.

Examination of self-in-role experience first and foremost requires that internal experience be considered a valid source of data. In this sense it is learning from the inside out. It also includes the process that Taylor (1987) termed "carrying the question." Examination of self-in-role involves taking the various experiences one has had, in the various roles within which one has had them, and continually asking questions such as: What does this say about me? What was stimulated in me by this situation? How may I best understand the parts of me—the behavioral patterns, the feelings, and the images— evoked by this experience? Why did I choose this course of action as opposed to others that were available? What can I learn from it about myself as a student and as a psychologist? What does it tell me about my vulnerabilities, blind spots, unfinished family-of-origin business, preferred roles and activities, and functioning in work groups as both leader and follower? What does it tell me about my own adult development at this point? How do my developmental needs as I am coming to understand them inform the choices I will be making in the program and when I graduate? How does all of this relate to what I am studying in course work?

Questions and Issues

Integrating the exploration of self-in-role into the core curriculum requires times and places where people come together to address the kinds of questions we have listed as well as an organizational environment that supports and values this activity. In our experience, one effective approach to structuring such work and setting a supportive cultural tone is to provide a credited, ongoing small-group professional socialization seminar, one of whose primary tasks is to work with students exploring experiences involved in or stimulated by (a) entering the program or leaving it, as the case may be; (b) joining and being a trainee in a practicum or internship setting; (c) the academic material and clinical techniques to which they are being exposed; (d) clinical work on practicum or internship; (e) functioning as part of a small work group or staff group—including the seminar itself—in which many if not most psychologists function these days whether in private or public settings; and (f) ethical dilemmas that arise in clinical or organizational settings; and so forth.

Antioch New England Graduate School's 2.5 hour per week "Professional Seminar," in which students participate in various configurations throughout their program, is one such event. Another is "Stress and Transition in Adult Development," a required weekend workshop at Antioch New England for entering psychology doctoral students. Taught by a team of core faculty and advanced students, this workshop is described by entering students as one of the high points of their first year. It provides didactic input, offers modeling by faculty and advanced students who explore their own experiences in the program in fishbowl format, and includes small-group discussion sessions in which the newly entering students explore their experiences of joining the program, returning to graduate school in midcareer, and so forth.

Of course, examination of experience of self-in-role may be encouraged as part of the discussion in any more traditional course or seminar.

The shared vision of the faculty as a work group collectively responsible for students' education rather than a collection of independently practicing educators is another requisite element. There needs to be a collective understanding of what the central tasks of professional training are all about and collaborative work surrounding whatever professional socialization vehicles have been devised so that they may be integrated effectively with the more typical courses and seminars.

Those faculty teaching professional socialization seminars themselves need a supportive professional socialization group for sharing dilemmas in working with students. In regular meetings, they can examine their experiences in their roles, learn more about themselves in the resulting discussion, enhance their skills as professional socialization group leaders, and keep tabs on students and their progress.

Finally, there is the need for a culture that promotes and values this venture and supports the notion that we all should be "carrying some questions" about ourselves in our various roles from which we will be learning (cf. Taylor, 1987). Without support from the program culture, specific curricular innovations will be relatively meaningless.

Certainly these proposals raise many questions. How does one make a cultural innovation? How can ownership of this task by faculty be secured? How can faculty be trained to provide leadership with students in the kind of work described here both in more traditional courses and in the small-group professional socialization seminars as previously described? Can faculty work with students in an intimate small-group seminar where a "holding environment" (Winnicott, 1965) needs to be created for exploration of self-in-role experience and also evaluate their performance without compromising either the learning or the evaluation? What is the boundary between professional socialization work—or exploration of self-in-role—and psychotherapy? These are thorny questions on which easy agreement is unlikely. Our own experience, however, prompts us to take a rather clear stand on several of these issues.

First, although what transpires in a professional socialization seminar and a therapy group might overlap at any given moment, the basic difference is the task that is being pursued. Clarity around task makes leader choices a bit easier in any group (Singer, Astrachan, Klein, & Gould, 1975). In the professional socialization seminar, the task is to help students become more effective and more actualized in their roles as psychologists and to better understand their role dilemmas. By contrast, in psychotherapy we attempt to reduce emotional distress, enhance functioning, and enhance personal actualization in a much broader sphere. Even a formulation as simple as this makes it easier, at least in principle, to decide what is in bounds and what should be out of bounds in a professional seminar. Unless it is relevant to one's functioning as a psychologist, material is not appropriate to the group; if it is relevant, then it is appropriate.

Second, we believe that evaluation is inherent in any training situation and, to the extent that this is so, it needs to be completely acknowledged and placed in full view. An evaluation-rich environment is ultimately the safest environment; one knows where one stands. Students quickly learn whether they can trust an instructor, with what issues, and on what levels. In our view, to avoid evaluating students' capacity to function effectively in their professional roles and to learn from examined experience is to abdicate one of our key responsibilities as educators. Currently, most licensing laws are not competency based, so it falls to us to make these often difficult judgments. If we will not, who can or will?

Conclusion

In summary, effective and responsible education demands that future generations of professional psychologists themselves know what their chosen profession, their daily work roles and activities, and their clients are likely to evoke on a personal level. Furthermore, they must also be taught how to learn continually in these domains. Only with this knowledge may they choose wisely, consistent with their own personal well-being, among the many paths open to them, avoid responding to their clients in counterproductive if not destructive ways, become caring and collaborative colleagues, and pursue inquiry with full awareness of the social, political, and psychological consequences of their work.

Some educational techniques and structures for pursuing these goals have already been developed. We hope that the resolutions adopted at the NCSPP San Antonio core-curriculum conference will foster further thought, effort, and innovation in this direction.

19

WOMEN AND THE CORE CURRICULUM

Glenace E. Edwall

Baylor University
Waco, Texas

and

Nancy Newton

Chicago School of Professional Psyhchology
Chicago, Illinois

The roles and contribution of women in psychology have dramatically expanded during the past 15 years, a period coincident with the development and growth of the professional school movement. The theoretical and practical issues relevant to training created by this change are diverse, substantial, and fundamental. They will be examined by the National Council of Schools of Professional Psychology at its midwinter 1990–1991 meeting, entitled "Women in Psychology." In this chapter, we anticipate some of the issues that will structure the more complete discussions, while focusing specifically on those that have immediate implications for the core curriculum and the process of training. We consider, first, issues relevant to the academic content of psychology, and then we discuss issues that have a major impact on the structure of professional training curricula, experiences, and processes.

Women and the Content of Psychology

Although one might readily assume that incorporating women into a discipline requires little adaptation on the part of the discipline, the actual experience has been quite different (Harding & Hintikka, 1983; D. Smith, 1987). Women's relation to psychology is analogous to a traditional quilt that women pieced together from bits of fabric and the still good parts of old clothes (cf. Edwall, chap. 17). Formalized in feminist critiques and reformulations, previous work and ideas are by no means discarded but wrested from their original contexts, scrutinized with an eye to potential use, and then combined with new material to create a functional product different in form from what had previously existed. Feminist understandings of and contributions to the core meaning of the discipline of psychology have displayed this sort of conservatorship: The traditional ways of thinking and working have been dismantled while saving the most useful components to be reused in new contexts and for new purposes. The new contexts and purposes articulated by women in psychology open fundamental and critical questions regarding the nature of the discipline. Seen in the new frame provided by the quilt's increasingly complex pattern, structure, and design, the answers both to contemporary questions and to those previously raised take on new and broader meanings.

We illustrate some of the revisionary process by briefly considering contributions of feminist scholarship to questions of the metatheory of psychology and to specific theoretical issues.

Metatheoretical Contributions

Philosophers and various social scientists interested in placing women and women's experiences into the discourse of psychology have noted that fundamental categories seem to change and shift with each consideration. We do not attempt to redefine such basic categories as epistemology or ontology along the lines of this discussion, but we will comment on some of the most important issues that have been raised.

First, there must be new ways of conceptualizing means of knowing in order to incorporate the perspective of the knower who has been placed outside the canons of knowledge and of the processes of knowing. Miller (1976, 1986), for example, illustrated clearly the different realities known to "dominants" and to "subordinates" and the different epistemological status credited to each. Women's knowledge has been described variously as intuitive, emotional, and irrational, seeming to lack the clarity and precision of male rationality (Bordo, 1987). Paradoxically, however, subordinates, and especially perhaps female subordinates, often attain detailed knowledge of the workings of the epistemology of dominants. They learn to use this system both to function in the limited public domains they are allowed and also to predict the behavior of dominants. This feature of subordinate knowledge, sloganized in the 1970s as the epistemological advantage of the oppressed, is a sort of open secret, whose frank acknowledgment supposedly would occasion cultural revolution (French, 1985; Janeway, 1980). Hidden in this discussion, however, are questions that our discipline must now engage: What is the relation of power to knowledge? In what ways does our accumulated wisdom reproduce cultural patterns of inclusion and exclusion? How has the masculine tradition of rationality shaped our concerns, our discourse? What has it meant to have dichotomized affect and thought and to have associated affect with irrationality?

Second, questions regarding knowledge lead to new understandings, and perhaps to puzzles, regarding the knower. In the traditional construction, the unit of analysis for all categories of interest, whether thought, affect, morality, or economic behavior, is the individual. The individual is stereotypically male: autonomous, giving definition to rather than being defined by connections to other entities, and ontologically separated from the objects of his consideration (cf. Scheman, 1983). Empirical research done from the standpoint of the knower who is subordinate, however, reveals a quite different picture: Knowledge, feeling, morality, and perhaps even the self may exist not as entities but as relations. The implications here are staggering: What has been aberrant, pathological, or even impossible in most of our theories may be normative for large numbers of persons (Belenky et al., 1986; Gilligan, Ward, & Taylor, 1989). Furthermore, perhaps the masculine model of autonomy is itself a myth, depending for survival on hidden, often trivialized forms of connection (Parry, 1989). Rich (1979) compared this phenomenon to a tapestry: The clarity and distinctiveness of objects on the front depend on complicated, intricate, and hidden connections on the back. According to Scheman (1983), the objects of psychology have had a traditional construction as singular, autonomous selves. That construction now appears in need of dramatic revision.

Finally, these considerations highlight the critical role of various forms of context in the creation and maintenance of our theoretical constructions. The epistemological and ontological positions previously discussed show the effects of having been constructed in particular sociopolitical (and metaphysical) contexts and are now being challenged or changed in different contexts. This virtual truism leads, however, to a host of problems with which feminist thinkers are attempting to grapple: What constitutes relevant context? How can we both live the construction of our contexts and simultaneously examine and alter them? Perhaps most important, how does a construction rooted in a context relate to lived experience: Is constructionism, although analytically useful, yet another form of subject–object dichotomizing that limits or reduces the meaning of experience to the people living them, usually not those doing the theorizing (Allen, 1989)?

These issues, we suggest, do not yield simple solutions. They require active engagement if psychology is to evolve in ways that reflect and address the diverse experiences of persons of different cultures.

Specific Theoretical Contributions

The aforementioned considerations imply matters of more immediate concern for professional psychology. Perhaps the most basic of these is methodology. As Harding (1983, 1986) and others pointed out, traditional methods of investigation in the social sciences are reliant on subject–object dualism along with attendant assumptions about the independence of the two and on the epistemological superiority of the subject (investigator). Various methods, usually modeled on anthropological researches or adapted from phenomenological investigation, have been proposed as alternatives. They may, indeed, yield richer information but have not yet fully addressed the basic issues. Some critics, in fact, suggest that the language of investigation itself incorporates such cultural bias that knowledge across the dominant–subordinate divide may not be possible (Belenky et al., 1986). Even without such radical limitations, work such as that of Gilligan (1982), Gilligan et al. (1989), and Belenky et al. (1986) demonstrated that, given more opportunities to structure the investigation in their own terms, women tell considerably different stories about their lives than when questions are structured for (about) them. Methods, both experimental and clinical, will continue to need to be informed by greater sensitivity to the meanings of subjects who cannot be reduced to objects.

Second, from the previous discussion of ontology, psychology in general, and professional psychology in particular, is faced with the task of rethinking its definition as expressed in its choice of the individual as the basic unit of analysis. Although intriguing questions regarding individual existence are likely to persist, they must be held in potentially productive tension with pressing questions of the nature of social or collective realities that also structure psychological meaning.

Third, the very work characterized at the outset as quilt making requires a new appreciation, understanding, and incorporation of change processes into the content of psychological theory. Social constructionism and various historical researchers have contributed to our realization that our understanding of what constitutes our core has changed markedly (e.g., Peterson, chap. 3). However there is still tremendous pressure in the social sciences and in the philosophy of science on which they are based to assume a static nature for psychological entities (Harding & Hintikka, 1983; Lakoff, 1987). Feminist critiques and reformulations press the point not only that the canons of knowledge and skill should be opened but that they routinely are. The ways in which this should and does happen could be profitably considered.

The contribution of these and related points that feminist theorists have been raising seems to us to emphasize the critical need in professional training to structure a curriculum that is fitted to the worlds of those whom we serve rather than to the history of the discipline. This perspective is all the more pressing because women, who have historically been excluded from processes of both generation and consumption of psychological knowledge, are rapidly becoming the majority of trainees and practitioners of professional psychology. The discipline must understand and respond to this change.

Training and Educational Processes

In developing graduate-level training programs, the emphasis has been generally on what training to provide, how to provide it, and how to assess its effectiveness. Little attention has been given to modification of training processes in response to differences between students. This lack of attention can be seen as a function of the traditional uniformity among graduate students in terms of age, gender, race, cultural background, and sexual orientation. However, attracting and training a more diverse student body requires challenging the assumption that conventional educational processes are equally appropriate for all students. Of specific relevance is the impact of gender on training because professional psychology graduate students are increasingly female, and women now constitute the majority of students in most doctorate-level professional training programs.

Research and theory suggest that the professional development of women and men differs at both the graduate and postgraduate levels. Implications of this research for the graduate training of women are examined in the following sections.

Graduate-Level Training

Professional role models. Entry into professional roles is facilitated by the presence of role models, important figures within the field with whom one can identify. Within the field of psychology, there is a long history of gender inequality in training and career opportunities, compensation, achievement, and recognition (Over, 1983). Women who have contributed significantly to the field have been ignored in textbooks and in courses on the history of psychology (Russo & Denmark, 1987). Thus, the opportunity for female graduate students to identify with experiences of their successful predecessors is limited not only by historical realities but also by neglect of the contributions that women have made. Recent publications that bring to light the history of women in psychology are an important step in filling this gap (Russo & Denmark, 1987; Scarborough & Furumoto, 1987). Incorporation of this material into course work and into general textbooks remains a pressing need.

Mentoring relationships. Mentoring relationships are generally identified as an essential component of professional development. They can facilitate progress through training programs, help in the development of professional identities, and directly assist in entry into the profession through coauthored publications and presentations and through establishment of professional contacts. The importance of such relationships for men entering professional roles is well known (Levinson et al., 1978). Mentoring relationships may be even more important for women (Gilbert, 1985). At the same time, establishment of successful mentoring relationships is likely to be more difficult for women (Bogat & Redner, 1985).

Same-sex role models may be particularly beneficial to women (Gilbert, Gallessich, & Evans, 1983; Goldstein, 1979). Female students seek out female mentors, even when they are fewer in number, less available, and less senior than male faculty (Gilbert, 1985). Female mentors may provide modeling and support particularly appropriate to the needs of female students. For example, although both men and women place importance on the mentor's professional skills and personal characteristics, female students also look for role models who can demonstrate integration of family and work roles (Erkut & Mokros, 1984; Gilbert, 1985) because this is a crucial issue in the professional development of many women.

At the same time, availability of female faculty who can serve as mentors is limited. The majority of faculty in clinical and other professional programs continue to be male (Pion, Kohout, & Wicherski, 1989). In addition, the majority of female faculty members are in nontenured, assistant professor positions (Pion et al., 1989). Increases in numbers of female faculty members have not expanded into higher faculty or administrative ranks. Evidence that established senior faculty are more likely to serve as mentors (Bogat & Redner, 1985) suggests that the very limited numbers of women at this level seriously restricts development of successful mentoring relationships.

Mentoring relationships between male faculty members and female students may have their own inherent problems. Reluctance of male faculty to invest in the professional development of female students is long-standing (Hirschberg & Itkin, 1978; Trow, 1977). Although overt prejudices against women students may have diminished during the last decade, a new ambivalence about women entering psychology has emerged. Many in the profession have become concerned and even alarmed that the increasing presence of women will result in the decline in income and in status to those traditionally associated with female occupations. As in other traditionally male professions that are experiencing an influx of women, it can be difficult to go beyond an attitude of grudging acceptance. To the degree that these attitudes are present, they necessarily undermine faculty investment in the professional development of female students.

Sexualization of male faculty member–female student relationships also continues to be a problem. Complaints to ethics boards and surveys of female graduate students suggest that this problem persists in many graduate programs despite recognition that such relationships are detrimental to the student and constitute abuse of unequal status and power within the professor–student relationship (Keith-Speigel & Koocher, 1985).

Teaching and training processes. On the basis of their extensive interviews of young adult women, Belenky et al. (1986) argued that educational programs for women should reflect the learning styles and the academic experiences of women rather than imposing those based on men. They found that the traditional educational format in which the authoritarian expert dispenses information to be absorbed by the novice student undermines the intellectual development of women. Confirmation that their knowledge and skills provide a foundation for further learning and provision of a collaborative professor–student context for learning are prerequisites for the intellectual development of women. These findings have important implications for the ways in which graduate programs help women develop the confidence and skills required to acquire knowledge critically rather than to absorb it uncritically.

Postgraduate Career Development

Although, in general, professionally oriented men prepare for and experience a direct, linear pattern of career development, this is not the experience of most women (Havighurst, 1982). Within our culture, the responsibilities of family relationships (raising children, attending to domestic crises, caring for aging parents) continue to fall on women. As a result, preparation for and development of a career is shaped by the need to balance the demands of family and work. Women are more likely than men to struggle with psychological integration of professional and family identities, to begin preparation for and to enter careers "off time," and to structure work roles to accommodate family needs. Little is known about the impact of this process on the personal experiences of women (Baruch, Biener, & Barnett, 1987). In addition, little attention continues to be given to restructuring the profession to facilitate an integration of, rather than a choice between, family responsibilities and career advancement. For example, requirements for full-time commitment to graduate study and reluctance to commit training resources to off-time older students are likely to have a differential impact on women entering the field. Similarly, once in the field, the extent to which consistent, full-time career commitment is essential to success is likely to have a negative impact on opportunities for advancement available to women.

Conclusion

The increasing number of well-qualified women applying to professional training programs demonstrates that women are experiencing a strong interest in the career roles and opportunities available in psychology; they are an essential resource for the future of the field. The feminist critiques and reformulations of psychology intellectually support and are supported by this development. Acceptance of women into doctorate-level programs in professional psychology indicates a commitment to their training and career advancement. The challenge confronting programs is to construct a high-quality "quilt" of professional training that combines the changes in content, structure, and processes to which these women are entitled.

20

ETHNIC DIVERSITY AND THE CORE CURRICULUM

Elizabeth Davis-Russell and Wesley T. Forbes
California School of Professional Psychology
Fresno, California

Joseph Bascuas
Antioch New England Graduate School
Keene, New Hampshire

and

Eduardo Duran
Pacific Graduate School
Palo Alto, California

It is vital that the core curriculum in professional psychology contain more than current facts and psychological knowledge about ethnic minority individuals and groups. A thorough understanding of the paradigms that traditionally have guided the production of supposedly relevant psychological knowledge is essential. Indeed the adoption of a new paradigm for work in this area is a further critical step. An understanding of current paradigms and the adoption of a new one are two additions to the Davis-Russell (1990) list of knowledge, skill, and attitude competencies that must be integrated in a core curriculum that trains psychologists to participate effectively in the process of evaluating and generating new knowledge pertaining to ethnic diversity.

These epistemological competencies become particularly crucial for two reasons. First, if as is often said the life expectancy for psychological knowledge is about 10 years, the process by which old knowledge becomes obsolete and new knowledge comes to guide our scientific and clinical enterprises is central. Second, "critical contemporary scholarship maintains that the subject matter for study is no longer the external and distant content of the formal curriculum" (Hatfield & Jacobs, 1989, p. 4). The formal core curriculum necessarily must include current material from a rapidly changing knowledge base.

Traditional Paradigms and Ethnic Diversity

More than a dozen years ago, Rappaport (1977), in his attempt to define community psychology, provided an interesting and thought-provoking analysis of the role of paradigms in science and a brief examination of the traditional paradigms used by American psychology in its scientific inquiry. As we attempt to delineate the core curriculum for professional psychology, Rappaport's work suggests an outline for the type of knowledge competency we should provide.

Borrowing from Kuhn (1970), Rappaport (1977, p. 17) defined a paradigm simply as "a set of shared ways of viewing a world of concern." The paradigm or view of the world dictates all theorizing, conceptualizing, and methodology used in scientific inquiry. Thus, when scientists or a scientific discipline adopts a paradigm, that discipline has also adopted a set of rules for problem solving and a set of "permissible" problems (Rappaport, 1977, p. 17). Paradigms not only delineate which events should be attended to, but the use of different paradigms will necessarily lead scientists to see the same data in quite different ways. We can illustrate this by paraphrasing an example from Rappaport (1977): When medical scientists began to view psychopathology as an illness rather than as a result of demonic possession, they stopped seeing devils and began to see symptoms of illness. Rappaport (1977) described the paradigm that he believed professional psychology typically used to guide its inquiry. He characterized this worldview as one that "sees everything in terms of individuals and their adjustment to a single standard" (Rappaport, 1977, p. 19). Rappaport (1977) explained that this paradigm has led psychology to develop an "idealized standard" for human beings and, as a result, to rank order people as more or less meeting that standard of competence rather than to attempt to maximize each person's unique potential.

Psychology's overemphasis on the search for universals has led us to believe that "current research strategies and approaches, as well as mental health practices, are adequate and appropriate in application to various minority groups" (Sue et al., 1982, p. 46). Many scientists, several of whom are of ethnic minorities, have provided convincing documentation that refute this myth. Gordon (1985) argued that despite the social sciences' long history of searching for the relationship among human behavior, experience, and system, it has neglected to study the unique impact that culture, ethnicity, and gender have on human behavior and on social systems that are expressive of behavior. Others, such as Bryde (1971), Padilla and Ruiz (1974), Samuda (1975), Smith (1973), Sue and Sue (1972), Thomas and Sillen (1972), and Williams (1970), also lended credence to the argument that challenges that myth.

This tendency of the social sciences to exclude culture and ethnicity systematically in their theoretical conceptualizations has resulted in a narrowing of the knowledge base of the social sciences. This in turn has resulted in a failure to create a realistic understanding of ethnic minorities in America (Sue et al., 1982). Nowhere is this more evident than in the study of Black Americans. When one attempts a serious examination of the literature, it becomes unmistakably clear that the approach has been "to understand the life experiences of socially diverse groups through a narrow cultro/ethnocentric perspective and against an equally narrow cultro/ethnocentric standard. Thus, the issue of cultural and ethnic diversity has been incompletely or inadequately assessed and has insufficiently influenced knowledge production" (Gordon, 1985, p. 118).

This restriction of knowledge production has had its impact both on the curricula and practice of professional psychology. The core curriculum contains courses whose assumptions often border on White supremacy, thereby forcing non-White students to accept and to comply with theories and practices that are not only exclusive of their worldview but see them and their cultural groups as inferior.

Assessment instruments and procedures reflect these aforementioned assumptions. A case in point is intelligence tests. Although Wechsler (1974) revised his instruments with a view toward their improvement, his assumptions are reflective of a Eurocentric worldview.

In reviewing the Wechsler Intelligence Scale for Children-Revised (WISC-R), it is evident that his intentions have remained unchanged and that he has designed an instrument intended to measure general intelligence of all populations. He believed that general intelligence does exist, that it is possible to measure it objectively, and that by so doing one can obtain a meaningful and useful index of a subject's mental capacity. Wechsler (1974) also believed that the "*much challenged and berated IQ in spite of its liability to misinterpretation and misuse* [italics added] is a scientifically sound and useful measure" (p. iii). For this reason, he has "retained the IQ as an essential aspect of the revised Scale. But the new WISC, like its predecessor, has broader applications than just providing a reliable Intelligence Quotient, important as this index may be" (p. iii).

The new tests were tried out with 2,200 subjects who constituted the standardization population. Wechsler selected a stratified sample of boys and girls 6½ to 16½ years old, including Black and other minority groups in proportions equal to those reported in the 1970 U.S. Census. He felt that, different than the sample used in the standardization of the original WISC introduced in 1949, this was more representative of the country as a whole. Wechsler spoke of the revision being a cooperative enterprise of the publisher and himself and of the assistance of many persons. He failed to acknowledge and to caution the user that both the assumptions underlying his tests and their typical use are racially biased. The tests must be used contextually.

The traditional research curriculum is a worse culprit in its perpetuation of the status quo reflected in Euro-American paradigms. Methods that were and are currently being devised reflect a domineering manifest-destiny mind-set. Students are required to learn research methods that are foreign and offensive to ethnically diverse groups. The fact that many ethnic groups do not conceptualize the world in a Socratic linear fashion, if known, is completely ignored as researchers embark on their applications of Euro-American principles to populations that are often resentful of insensitive probing.

The individual differences paradigm that has guided our discipline has of necessity forced psychology to disdain differences and to identify them as deviance rather than to appreciate and to value diversity. All of the data that have been gathered from predominantly White, middle-class college sophomores at major research universities no doubt have less generalizability than was once thought. More important, these data never should have been used to develop a supposed universal standard for behavior.

It is apparent that the existing paradigm has gravely influenced the preparation and training of clinical psychologists in particular and has perpetuated poor preparation to provide services to ethnically diverse clients.

New Paradigm for the Understanding of Ethnic Diversity

Just as one paradigm can limit the range of events to which we may attend, the adoption of a new paradigm can allow us to be open to things that could not be seen before. According to Kuhn (1970), this is, in fact, how science progresses.

Tyler, Sussewell, and Williams-McCoy (1985) identified the need for a paradigmatic shift that incorporates at least three elements. First, psychological paradigms must incorporate the importance of culture, race, and ethnicity in defining their constructs, concepts, and parameters. Second, psychological paradigms must fully acknowledge their clients as "knowing individuals who shape their worlds and destinies through conceptual frameworks (which they develop about the world), and their lives" (Tyler et al., 1985, p. 311). Third, psychological paradigms must acknowledge the role of the system and of individual interactions in their formulations about how people function and organize their lives.

In addition, we could be guided by Rappaport's (1977) recommendations made with regard to community psychology. He proposed that the appropriate paradigm for community psychology should be based on the values of "respect for human diversity, the right to be different, and the belief that human problems are those of person–environment fit, rather than of incompetent (inferior) people or inferior psychological and cultural environments" (Rappaport, 1977, p. 22).

Faculty and Pedagogy

How do we provide the skills to learn about different individuals and groups using a paradigm that respects and values diversity? The great American philosopher Yogi Berra is popularly purported to have said that "you can observe a lot by watching." It is *what* and *how* we watch, however, that may determine what we will observe. We have already discussed at some length how our theory, worldview, or paradigm determines what we will watch and thus what we will observe. Therefore, we need to make students aware of the fact that each of us looks through our own individual and unique set of lenses and that this set of lenses is a product of our own personal history, including our own culture. The classroom then becomes the site for

> *citizens of a multicultural community to initiate a continuing discourse . . . no one cultural or ethnic orientation is given the power or authority to define and complete this pluralistic discourse. . . . The new curriculum becomes the multiple life history of all classroom inhabitants, with the student's cultural orientation and identity the source of the new and emerging text that will provide the source for the dialogical exchange. (Hatfield & Jacobs, 1989, p. 3)*

As we attempt to define what and how we watch, our faculty and students of color can be instructive. According to Hatfield and Jacobs (1989), students and faculty of color have "a unique narrative voice, a voice suppressed and unrepresented previously in the official materials of formal institutions of learning. Their historical odyssey not only enlightens their present condition and situation but explains the present attitudes and mentality of students (and faculty) who do not share that experience" (p. 8). Such a focus requires a shift from the Euro-American concept of faculty.

> *They are no longer the official curators of the sacred icons of the dominant Euro-American culture but mediators of the various cultural communities that merge into the single community of the classroom. Faculty have an intellectual and ethical responsibility to nurture and sponsor the knowledge and wisdom of students of color as they begin to speak from the context of their origins and world view. (Hatfield & Jacobs, 1989, p. 9)*

As the community of the classroom expands, it must include the voices of the ethnic minority communities: those nonstudents who can be instructive of their cultural values and who are the "official curators of the sacred icons" of their cultures. Through consultation, colloquia, and representation on advisory boards, they add their truths to the curriculum: truths that are replete with cultural, psychological, and other significance.

The development of a pedagogy to impart the necessary knowledge, skills, and attitudes may not be simple, yet it is a critical task. Perhaps we could borrow from cultural anthropology, which sees participant observation as the foundation of its research methodology (Bernard, 1988). Perhaps we should examine the influences of constructivist thinking within our own discipline. One possibility would be the Milan approach to family therapy (Selvini-Palazzoli, Boscolo, Cecchin, & Prata, 1978). Their perspective on therapy as a process in which the observer is included and participates in a system to construct reality may be a useful model. However, regardless of which approach we adopt, an integral part of this pedagogy must be an understanding of one's own cultural identity and sensitivity to how one's cultural heritage has helped create the set of lenses through which we perceive the world. If we are able to accomplish this, then the learning community, now expanded to include the ethnic minority communities, becomes the validator of knowledge. Such a process becomes a dynamic one. As the discourse attempts to incorporate multiple possibilities from a wide range of cultural and ethnic orientations, we will see new versions considered, modified, and reshaped. As we engage in this process, the effort is "not to collect, in the conventional institutional habit, low level data or information about another culture from one of its speakers, but to integrate ways of knowing and seeing into possibilities of understanding the world" (Hatfield & Jacobs, 1989, p. 11).

Conclusion

The success of implementing such a curriculum is contingent on the creation of a multicultural learning community and faculty who are not wedded to their role as the "official curators of the sacred icons of the dominant culture." Therefore, faculty who understand and can teach clinical and research psychology from such perspectives must be retained, encouraged, and supported in their work.

If we see the curriculum as the core of the actual propagation of knowledge and methods in our psychology training programs, it becomes imperative that such a curriculum include fundamental relevant thinking derived from non-Euro-American cosmologies. Our students must graduate with the ability to integrate an array of ways of knowing and seeing into possibilities of understanding the world, a world that is ethnically diverse.

PART IV
CONFERENCE RESOLUTIONS

21

NATIONAL COUNCIL OF SCHOOLS OF PROFESSIONAL PSYCHOLOGY CORE CURRICULUM CONFERENCE RESOLUTIONS

James D. McHolland
Illinois and Minnesota Schools of Professional Psychology
Chicago, Illinois

Introduction

The San Antonio conference on the core curriculum in professional psychology, sponsored by the National Council of Schools of Professional Psychology (NCSPP), adopted a detailed set of resolutions that appear in this chapter after some introductory comments. Four curricular values were explicitly identified: a broadened view of the educational domain of professional psychology; the existence of multiple ways of knowing; necessary mastery of professional knowledge, skills, and attitudes; and the preparation for lifelong learning. The conferees affirmed the value of "diversity and inclusiveness as fundamental elements of human experience" (p. 159, current chapter), the necessity of education of the personal and professional self of the student, the importance of preparation for multiple professional roles, a broadly defined view of curriculum, the centrality of relationships to the clinical enterprise, and the importance of the responsible use of power and authority.

The San Antonio conference is one of a series of annual conferences sponsored by NCSPP that enable the systematic and intentional explication of standards for the education and training of professional psychologists. At the pivotal Mission Bay conference in 1986–1987, NCSPP members endorsed the view that professional applications of psychology should be related to an evolving knowledge base and to the recognition that knowledge, skills, and attitudes are equally important parts of the training experience.

Six core areas were identified: relationship, assessment, intervention, research and evaluation, consultation and education, and management and supervision. Reaffirming and expanding on the Mission Bay resolutions, the San Antonio conferees developed and endorsed more specific explications of these six professional core curriculum areas.

Curricular Values and Conference Themes

The preamble to the core curriculum conference resolutions affirms general values relevant to professional psychology supported by NCSPP before moving to articulate particular curricular values. Taken together, they reflect significant conference themes. The values and themes to which the conferees committed are not readily apparent in many psychology training programs. Here are some of the most important elements of the resolutions along with selected commentary.

Broadened Educational Domain

The educational domain of professional psychology is characterized by scholarly, disciplined thought that is grounded in science, in the humanities, and in personal and professional experience and is enhanced by interdisciplinary studies. Although nearly every graduate program describes the scholarly discipline of psychology as scientific, the conferees broke new ground by asserting that the discipline also is grounded in the humanities and in personal and professional experiences.

Multiple Ways of Knowing

There are multiple ways of knowing. These include both objective and subjective methods. Few would debate that psychological knowledge derives from empirical investigation. However, to maintain that valid knowledge also derives from subjective methods, such as the client–psychologist relationship, is a departure from conventional views of how psychological knowledge is obtained.

Knowledge, Skills, and Attitudes

The demonstrated mastery of knowledge, skills, and attitudes and their integrated application to the practice of psychology is essential. Whereas, traditionally, doctoral programs have expected the mastery and demonstration of knowledge, skills, and attitudes relevant to research, the conferees asserted the importance of comparable systematic training in the knowledge, skills, and attitudes relevant to professional practice.

Lifelong Learning

Consistent with the value of lifelong learning, the core curriculum should be seen as initiating the process of lifelong professional development and not as an end in itself.

This perspective assumes that there is an ongoing growth of competence in the practice of psychology and necessitates mechanisms to monitor competence.

Valuing Human Diversity

The valuing of human diversity and inclusiveness as core and fundamental elements of human experience and thus as a part of the core curriculum of professional psychology education was reaffirmed. Before the San Antonio conference, NCSPP (i.e., the Mission Bay conference participants and the NCSPP 1988–1989 Puerto Rico conference participants) unanimously enacted resolutions that endorsed the centrality of considerations of diversity in education and training. At San Antonio, the conferees acted on the premise that "considerations of diversity should be integrated throughout the scientific–academic and professional elements of the curriculum" (p. 159, current chapter), and they intentionally integrated this concern into each of the six competency areas of the professional psychology core curriculum. Participants recognized the need for curricular innovations and reconstruction to integrate diversity truly into the education of students.

Education of the Personal Self

NCSPP members affirmed the value premise that subjective methods of knowing are important in educating psychologists. This explicit theme focused on education of the personal as well as the professional self of students. The foundation of training professional psychologists is the recognition that all professional psychology is relationship centered. Thus, the first professional competency area—relationship—was defined and the knowledge base identified. NCSPP members asserted that the core curriculum should include the intentional education and training of students in the development of interpersonal skills, empathy, and respect for others. Essential elements of curriculum design and implementation for the relationship competency were specified as experiential learning, opportunities for self-reflection and awareness, direct observation of relationship behaviors, and feedback by peers and experts. A significant feature of relationship knowledge, as endorsed by NCSPP members, was the recognition that (a) inequalities of power and authority determine the nature of relationships, and (b) power and authority can be used responsibly.

Multiple Roles

Preparation for multiple roles as a professional psychologist was a clear, well-documented theme of the conference. The array of possible roles of the practicing psychologist was identified as including assessor, intervener, educator, consultant, supervisor, administrator, program developer, researcher, and program evaluator. NCSPP members endorsed core competency areas that prepare students for these multiple roles as the organizing principle for a coherent approach to curriculum construction. The clients to be served by professional psychologists were defined broadly to include individuals, couples, families, groups, organizations, social systems, and sociopolitical structures. Both the roles of practicing psychologists and their potential clients require schools that train professional psychologists to give careful consideration to the relevance and to the verifiability of the educational objectives of their core curricula.

Some of the roles ascribed to professional psychologists are commonly accepted and are included in the core curricula of most programs. Although the emphasis on degree of mastery may vary, research, assessment, and intervention knowledge base and skills exist, to some extent, in most training programs. Almost all training programs, however, ignore or minimize training for the roles of educator, consultant, administrator, supervisor, program developer, and program evaluator. When these roles were considered at the Mission Bay conference, participants endorsed their inclusion in the list of professional core competencies. Yet few NCSPP member programs actually had or have now articulated curricular means of achieving these competencies. As member schools systematically and intentionally have considered the designated professional core competencies, recognition of their importance has increased. A random review of the program bulletins of several American Psychological Association (APA)-approved nonprofessional school doctoral programs revealed that none directly addressed teaching, consultation, program development, or management. When supervision was taught, curricular emphasis usually was on the student receiving supervision, not learning how to supervise others.

Conference Conclusions

Several conclusions can be drawn from NCSPP's core curriculum conference. The core curriculum was seen as dynamic not static. The content areas of the knowledge base that were endorsed were similar to those specified in APA's accreditation criteria, with some notable additions. NCSPP members promoted knowledge and skill bases that were broader than those designated by APA, and the members specified that they must take into consideration the self of the student, diversity in all its forms, and the actual roles psychologists are required to assume in the marketplace. In addition, issues of power, authority, and sociopolitical structures must be included in the training of professional psychologists.

Most important, NCSPP participants resolved that the core curriculum must include an integration of theory and practice such that effective use of theory can be demonstrated in solving human dilemmas. Critics have assumed that, sometimes incorrectly, research skills are devalued when doctoral education is provided by professional schools. One of the required six professional core competencies endorsed by NCSPP was research and evaluation, defined in part by the concept of local clinical scientist (see Trierweiler & Stricker, chap. 14). At the Mission Bay conference, NCSPP participants emphasized the importance of evaluation (McHolland et al., 1987).

A final conclusion to be drawn from the core curriculum conference is that NCSPP is taking seriously its stated purpose to "advance the development of the highest quality of graduate training in professional psychology" (Bent, 1987, p. vii). The conferees at the Mission Bay conference defined the parameters of NCSPP's mission. Now NCSPP systematically is defining and is committing itself and its member schools to a set of standards for the practitioner model of education and training of professional psychologists. Diversity issues and standards were made explicit at the Puerto Rico conference. Now for the first time in American psychology, the core curriculum of professional psychology has been defined to include practice competencies. In 1991 the NCSPP conference will focus on women's issues. Evaluation will be the focus of the 1992 conference.

Each of these conferences can be expected to carry forth the explication of the standards to which professional schools of psychology aspire and against which they will measure their effectiveness in the education and training of professional psychologists.

The actual NCSPP core curriculum conference resolutions are presented in the remainder of this chapter. The resolutions were developed through a complex political process that included (a) drafts composed by subgroups; (b) line-by-line scrutiny during plenary sessions; (c) particular editorial changes of words or phrases proposed by members; and (d) ultimately, a series of votes on the document, sometimes attending to sections as small as a paragraph.

NATIONAL COUNCIL OF SCHOOLS OF PROFESSIONAL PSYCHOLOGY CORE CURRICULUM CONFERENCE RESOLUTIONS

Preamble

The primary goal of education for professional psychology is preparation for the delivery of human services in a manner that is effective and responsive to individual needs, societal needs, and diversity. The learning environments, including resources and curriculum, should be designed in a manner that accomplishes this goal, and should be open to continuous development and evaluation.

The curriculum comprises a broad set of explicit learning experiences that include courses, seminars, practica, and experiential learning. There also are socialization processes that comprise an implicit curriculum in professional psychology that includes educational methods, faculty characteristics, the nature of student–faculty relationships, program culture, and the attitudes and values of the total educational community. The synergistic relationship between the explicit and implicit components of the curriculum must be considered in curriculum design and implementation.

The primary task of education in professional psychology is preparation for effective functioning in the multiple roles graduates will fill during the course of their careers. These roles might include, but are not limited to: assessor, intervener, educator, consultant, supervisor, administrator, program developer, researcher, and program evaluator.

Preparation in professional psychology involves the education of the personal and professional selves of students. Furthermore, all of professional psychology is relationship centered. A central and integrating feature is the awareness of self and self–other relatedness. Professional socialization experiences should be designed to foster student awareness of how students' personal and professional selves affect and are affected by their professional relationships, their profession, their training, the culture of their programs, and their clinical work. The knowledge of how inequalities of power and authority determine the nature of relationships and the promotion of responsible use of power and authority are critical elements of this experience.

Professional psychology values diversity and inclusiveness as fundamental elements of human experience. We understand diversity to include, but not be limited to, gender, race, ethnicity, class, sexual preference, religion, age, physical and mental challenge, culture, and worldview. Considerations of diversity should be integrated throughout the scientific–academic and professional elements of the curriculum. Curricular innovations with regard to diversity require particular attention and reinforcement.

Attitudes, Aptitudes, and Values

We reaffirm the Mission Bay resolutions with regard to attitudes, aptitudes, and values together with the following additions and clarifications:

1. In order to function most effectively in varied professional roles, a professional psychologist should demonstrate certain personal characteristics and attitudes, including but not limited to the following:
    a. Intellectual curiosity and flexibility.
    b. Scientific skepticism.
    c. Open-mindedness.
    d. Psychological health.
    e. Belief in the capacity for change in human attitudes and behavior.
    f. Appreciation of individual and cultural diversity.
    g. Interest, courage, and compassion in providing human services, especially to underserved populations.
    h. Personal integrity and honesty.
    i. Capacity for developing interpersonal skills (empathy, respect for others, personal relatedness).
    j. Self-awareness.
2. The theory and application of professional psychology are characterized by a disciplined scientific attitude.
3. Diversity in personal and academic background on the part of faculty and students enhances education and performance as professional psychologists. Student admission committees and faculty recruitment committees are encouraged to seek out and promote such diversity of personal and academic background.
4. Professional consultative relationships within and external to professional psychology are a valuable means of enhancing the quality of professional judgments in the professional applications of psychology.
5. Professional psychology programs should participate actively in the evolving health care delivery system in the best interest of society.
6. Professional psychology programs must make their values explicit as they relate to the student's education and training.
7. Professional psychology programs should provide educational and training experiences that focus on inculcating professional identification among faculty and students.
8. Professional psychology programs should devote sufficient resources to faculty development that supports professional attitudes and values.

Curricular Values

With regard to the core curriculum of professional psychology, the following curricular values are of particular importance:

1. The educational domain of professional psychology (e.g., its theories, research

methods, and applications) is characterized by scholarly, disciplined thought that is grounded in science, the humanities, and personal and professional experience and is enhanced by interdisciplinary perspectives.

2.   There are multiple ways of knowing that inform and enrich each other. These include both objective and subjective methods.

3.   The demonstrated mastery of knowledge, skills, and attitudes and their integrated application to the practice of psychology is essential.

4.   Consistent with the value of lifelong learning, the core curriculum should be seen as initiating the process of lifelong professional development and not as an end in itself. The ongoing maintenance and growth of competence in the practice of psychology should be monitored through processes that include but are not limited to continuing education, self-reflection, consultation, and peer review.

Resolutions With Regard to NCSPP in Support of Curriculum Development

1.   NCSPP shall support efforts to communicate the variety of curricular designs on learning. Approaches to curricular construction should encourage diversity, innovation, and experimentation in the service of reaching well-defined curricular goals.

2.   NCSPP shall establish a learning resource center as a repository of relevant audio-visual resources, written material, course syllabi, experiential learning formats, interactive computer technologies, administrative policies, programs, and strategies for implementing change. Resources should incorporate and support perspectives of diversity.

3.   NCSPP shall develop a resource bank of members who can act as consultants on curricular issues for member schools.

4.   NCSPP shall promote and facilitate collaborations among member schools on scholarly activities and projects such as textbooks and grants.

Resolutions With Regard to Member Institutions in Support of Curriculum Development

1.   Program descriptions should make explicit the attitudes and values that underlie the curriculum and how these attitudes and values manifest themselves in the total program.

2.   Programs should ensure that students of professional psychology are taught by faculty who model these values and attitudes and who reflect a diversity of perspectives in their teaching and in their practice of psychology (i.e., as in settings, populations, and orientations).

The Professional Psychology Core Curriculum

The competency areas of professional psychology represent key related clusters of activities that are characteristic of practicing psychologists and that are related to relevant knowledge, skills, and attitudes. The core competencies identified at Mission Bay (relationship, assessment, intervention, research and evaluation, consultation and education, management and supervision) are reaffirmed and are the organizing principles for a coherent approach to curriculum construction. Each of the competency areas has been conceptualized separately for heuristic purposes. However, it is important to remember that the competencies develop together and often remain inextricably intertwined in professional practice. Professional psychologists serve clients, conceptualized in the broadest sense to include individuals, couples, families, groups, organizations, social systems, and sociopolitical structures.

Within the broad framework of the six core competency areas, program diversity, built around the academic and professional interests of faculty, should be encouraged. It is the fundamental responsibility of each program faculty to develop and to articulate clearly the program's coherent goals and sequentially organized objectives in order to achieve those goals. The broad-based knowledge areas should be integrated carefully with these program goals and objectives. Programs should write verifiable educational objectives pertaining to the knowledge, attitudes, and skills requisite to the development of the competencies.

These professional competencies are related to an evolving and developing knowledge base that should include the following areas:

1. Biological bases of behavior.
2. Cognitive-affective bases of behavior.
3. Cultural bases of behavior.
4. Dysfunctional behavior and psychopathology.
5. The historical and philosophical context of psychology.
6. Life span development.
7. Professional ethics and standards.
8. Psychological measurement.
9. Social bases of behavior.
10. Theories of individual and systems functioning and change.

Instruction in these areas should be carefully integrated with the development of the six competency areas throughout the learning process and should be consistent with the mission and objectives of the program.

Relationship

Relationship is the capacity to develop and maintain a constructive working alliance with clients. In the development of relationship skills of professional psychologists, special attention should be given to diversity, including but not limited to gender, race, ethnicity, class, sexual preference, religion, age, physical and mental challenge, culture, and worldview.

The relationship competency is the foundation and prerequisite of the other competencies. Therefore, its articulation in the core curriculum is of primary importance.

The relationship competency area is particularly informed by, but not limited to, (a) theories of individual and systems functioning and change, cultural bases of behavior, life span development, dysfunctional behavior and psychopathology, and professional ethics and standards; (b) knowledge of the self, and (c) knowledge of others.

Curriculum design and implementation should include education and training in attitudes essential for the relationship competency, including but not limited to (a) intellectual curiosity and flexibility; (b) open-mindedness; (c) belief in the capacity to change in human attitudes and behavior; (d) appreciation of individual and cultural diversity; (e) personal integrity and honesty; and (f) a value of self-awareness.

Curriculum design and implementation should include education and training in the development of interpersonal skills, including empathy, respect for others, and personal relatedness. An essential element of training in this area is experiential learning, with self-reflection and direct observation of behavior and feedback by peers and experts. Training should embody the principles inherent in the competency (i.e., constructive working alliances among faculty and students).

Assessment

Assessment is an ongoing, interactive, and inclusive process that serves to describe, conceptualize, characterize, and predict relevant aspects of a client. The assessment process uses a multimethod and multitheory approach that takes into account the sociocultural context and that focuses not only on limitations and dysfunctions but also on competencies, strengths, and effectiveness.

Assessment is a fundamental process that is involved and interwoven with all other aspects of professional practice. In recent years the emphasis of assessment appropriately has shifted from a narrow focus on tests, individuals, and psychopathology to a more comprehensive approach addressing a broader range of clients and client functions. Although training in formal techniques of assessment may occur in particular courses, it is critical that assessment, whether formal or informal, be integrated as a critical component of all aspects of the professional curriculum.

Historically, assessment has been linked to theories of individual development, psychological measurement, dysfunctional behavior, and psychopathology. With the broadening of the process, however, assessment increasingly is addressing the relationship between the individual and his or her system context; the entire life span of the individual; the biological, social, and cultural bases of behavior; and larger systems, including families, groups, organizations, and social systems. Knowledge of ethical and legal foundations is an essential aspect of competency in assessment.

The assessment curriculum is not limited to individual content courses but embodies a sequenced pattern of experiences covering general principles as well as specific techniques. These principles include, at minimum, psychological measurement theory and the logic of clinical inference. Supervised skill training is an essential component of the assessment curriculum.

Assessment training should include awareness of ethical, sociocultural, legal, and administrative issues.

The curriculum must include issues of diversity in all stages of the assessment process. Such stages include identification of the client, formulation of questions, selection of methods, gathering of information, arriving at interpretations and conclusions, verification and cross-validation of findings, and dissemination of findings.

Intervention

The intervention competency is conceptualized as activities that promote, restore, sustain, and/or enhance positive functioning and a sense of well-being in clients through preventive, developmental, and/or remedial services.

The integrative goal of the core curriculum is to establish the capacity for effective intervention. Historically, as a profession, we have trained most effectively at the level of remediation. However, clients have needs that are remedial, developmental, and preventive, and therefore, we advocate the development of broad-based curricula addressing intervention at all of these levels. As a profession, we also typically have focused on intervention with a relatively narrow range of clients. Consequently, we also recommend development of curricula for training in intervention with a greater diversity of clients.

The intervention competency relies especially on the following knowledge base: theories of individual and systems change, including the functioning and change of sociopolitical structures; theories and strategies of intervention; methods of evaluation and quality assurance; professional ethical principles and standards of practice.

Along with the information derived from psychotherapy research, the knowledge and methods appropriate to the understanding of self and the self–other relationship, as well as to the significance of power and authority, are particularly relevant.

Education and training in intervention should reflect diversity through the use of teaching materials, types of client populations, choice of teachers and supervisors, and service systems.

Research and Evaluation

Psychological science is a systematic mode of inquiry involving problem identification and the acquisition, organization, and interpretation of information pertaining to psychological phenomena. It strives to make that information consensually verifiable, replicable, and universally communicable. Professional psychologists systematically acquire and organize information about psychological phenomena and often engage in the general practice of science. Nonetheless, it is recognized that, because of the particular conditions that frequently limit inquiry in the local contexts of professional psychological practice (e.g., nonrepeatability of phenomena in time, privacy, etc.), the scientific goals of consensual verifiability, replicability, and universal communicability are attainable more in principle than in practice. Despite these practical realities, we endorse a view of the professional psychologist as a local clinical scientist: an investigator of local psychological phenomena who engages in the rigorous, critical, and disciplined thought engendered in striving toward scientific goals. Therefore, research training in professional psychology should be viewed as an essential tool for developing and enhancing critical thinking in students, and it should be integrated throughout the curriculum. All of our graduates are expected to function as local clinical scientists; some of our graduates may engage more directly in the application of research methodology in roles such as program evaluator. The application or diffusion of research results into practice is an important process that should be enhanced and encouraged through research training.

Training for research competency consists of (a) designing and critiquing approaches to systematic inquiry using qualitative and quantitative methods; (b) analyzing data using various techniques, including descriptive, inferential, and both univariate and multivariate statistics, and methods appropriate to qualitative data; (c) conducting a scholarly project on a meaningful problem typically associated with professional practice in psychology with a strategy of disciplined inquiry appropriate to the problem.

Research is not content-free and must draw on, and is instrumental in expanding, the knowledge base of psychology. In addition, particular importance is attached to the principles of psychological measurement, application of professional ethics and standards, and the historical and philosophical context of psychology.

Research occurs in a social context and invariably carries embedded values. The methods and conclusions of research should be appropriate and sensitive to the diverse populations to which they are applied. Care must be taken that generalizations are appropriate to the sample studied.

Professional psychologists, in their roles as researchers, are self-critical with respect to the methodological, sociopolitical, and philosophical implications of inquiry. They make efforts to ensure that the conclusions are consistent with the limits of research designs and that consideration particularly is given to the likelihood of negative impact on underserved populations.

It is recognized that difficult ethical and epistemological questions regarding the applications of research methods remain to be addressed.

Consultation and Education

Consultation refers to the planned collaborative interaction between the professional psychologist and one or more clients or colleagues in relation to an identified problem area or program. Psychological consultation is an explicit intervention process that is based on principles and procedures found within psychology and related disciplines in which the professional psychologist has no direct control of the actual change process. Psychological consultation focuses on the needs of individuals, groups, programs, or organizations.

Education is the directed facilitation by the professional psychologist for the growth of knowledge, skills, and attitudes in the learner.

The practice of consultation and education competency is informed by the knowledge base of psychology, particularly theories of individual and systems functioning and change; life span development; cognitive–affective, social, and cultural bases of behavior; and professional ethics and standards.

Students should be required to complete experiential tasks in consultative and educational activities. These experiences occur in classes, in practica, and on internship.

Consultation and education require the ability to interact effectively with diverse populations. A particularly essential element of effective interaction with diverse populations is ongoing evaluation and feedback. In the practice of consultation and education, psychologists work to enhance their clients' and learners' respect for diversity.

Management and Supervision

Management consists of those activities that direct, organize, or control the services of psychologists and others offered or rendered to the public. Self-management concerns the application of similar principles to effective functioning in a professional role.

Supervision is a form of management blended with teaching in the context of relationship directed to the enhancement of competence in the supervisee.

Because the majority of graduates of professional psychology programs are employed in positions requiring management and supervisory skills, these competencies should occupy a more developed status in the core curriculum.

Issues of diversity and the development of alternative management and supervisory models should be emphasized.

The management competency is informed by the following knowledge base: professional ethics and standards, theories of individual and systems functioning and change, psychological measurement, evaluation, styles of management, service delivery and case management in a variety of settings, planning and financial management, cultural bases of behavior, and the use of technology.

The supervision competency is informed by the following knowledge base: professional ethics and standards, theories of individual and systems functioning and change, dysfunctional behavior and psychopathology, cultural bases of behavior, theoretical models of supervision, awareness of considerations of diversity.

Self-management processes and structures should be provided for students through such methods as workshops, seminars, in vivo consultation, or advisement. Demonstrated competency in supervision should include the development of receptivity to receiving supervision and the acquisition of skills in doing supervision.

Diversity shall inform all aspects of the management and supervision competency areas.

REFERENCES

Albee, G. W. (1970). The uncertain future of clinical psychology. *American Psychologist*, *11*, 1071–1080.

Albee, G. W. (1986). Toward a just society: Lessons from observations on the primary prevention of psychopathology. *American Psychologist*, *41*, 891–898.

Allen, J. (1989). Women who beget women must thwart major sophisms. In A. Gary & M. Pearsell (Eds.), *Women, knowledge and reality* (pp. 37–46). Boston: Unwin Hyman.

Altman, I. (1987). Centripetal and centrifugal trends in psychology. *American Psychologist*, *42*, 1058–1069.

American Psychiatric Association. (1980). *Diagnostic and statistical manual of mental disorders* (3rd ed.). Washington, DC: Author.

American Psychiatric Association. (1987). *Diagnostic and statistical manual of mental disorders* (3rd ed., rev.). Washington, DC: Author.

American Psychological Association. (1979). *Criteria for accreditation of doctoral training programs and internships in professional psychology*. Washington, DC: Author.

American Psychological Association. (1982). *Report of the APA task force on education, training, and service in psychology*. Washington, DC: Author.

American Psychological Association. (1988). APA-accredited doctoral programs in professional psychology: 1988. *American Psychologist*, *43*, 1065–1072.

American Psychological Association. (1989). *Task force on the scope and criteria for accreditation*. Washington, DC: Author.

American Psychological Association Committee on Training in Clinical Psychology. (1947). Recommended graduate training in clinical psychology. *American Psychologist*, *2*, 539–558.

American Psychological Association Committee on Training in Clinical Psychology. (1949). Doctoral programs in clinical psychology: 1949. *American Psychologist*, *4*, 331–341.

Anderson, H., & Goolishian, H. (1988). Human systems as linguistic systems: Preliminary and evolving ideas about the implications for clinical theory. *Family Process*, *27*, 371–394.

Arkowitz, H., & Hannah, M. T. (1989). Cognitive, behavioral, and psychodynamic therapies: Converging or diverging pathways to change? In A. Freeman, K. M. Simon, L. E. Beutler, & H. Arkowitz (Eds.), *Comprehensive handbook of cognitive therapy* (pp. 143–168). New York: Plenum Press.

Bakan, D. (1956). Clinical psychology and logic. *American Psychologist*, *11*, 655–662.

Barlow, D. H., Hayes, S. C., & Nelson, R. O. (1984). *The scientist practitioner: Research and accountability in clinical and educational settings*. New York: Pergamon Press.

Baruch, G. K., Biener, L., & Barnett, R. C. (1987). Women and gender in research on work and family stress. *American Psychologist*, *42*, 130–136.

Belar, C. D., Bieliauskas, L. A., Larsen, K. G., Mensh, I. N., Poey, K., & Roelke, H. J. (1989). The national conference on internship training in psychology. *American Psychologist, 44*, 60–65.

Belenky, M. F., Clinchy, B. M., Goldberger, N. R., & Tarule, J. M. (1986). *Women's ways of knowing: The development of self, voice, and mind.* New York: Basic Books.

Bent, R. J. (1986). Toward quality assurance in the education of practicing psychologists. In J. E. Callan, D. R. Peterson, & G. Stricker (Eds.), *Quality in professional psychology training: A national conference and self-study* (pp. 27–36). Norman, OK: Transcript Press.

Bent, R. J. (1987). Foreword. In E. F. Bourg, R. J. Bent, J. E. Callan, N. F. Jones, J. McHolland, & G. Stricker (Eds.), *Standards and evaluation in the education and training of professional psychologists: Knowledge, attitudes, and skills* (pp. vii–ix). Norman, OK: Transcript Press.

Bent, R. J., & Cannon, W. G. (1987). Key functional skills of a professional psychologist. In E. F. Bourg, R. J. Bent, J. E. Callan, N. F. Jones, J. McHolland, & G. Stricker (Eds.), *Standards and evaluation in the education and training of professional psychologists: Knowledge, attitudes, and skills* (pp. 87–97). Norman, OK: Transcript Press.

Bent, R. J., & Jones, N. F. (1987). Knowledge and skills in professional psychology programs. In E. F. Bourg, R. J. Bent, J. E. Callan, N. F. Jones, J. McHolland, & G. Stricker (Eds.), *Standards and evaluation in the education and training of professional psychologists: Knowledge, attitudes, and skills* (pp. 35–44). Norman, OK: Transcript Press.

Bernard, H. R. (1988). *Research methods in cultural anthropology.* Newbury Park, CA: Sage Publications.

Berson, R. C. (1989). The social construction of childhood sexual abuse: Towards new theory and research. (Doctoral dissertation, Antioch University New England Graduate School, 1989). *Dissertation Abstracts International, 50/04-B,* 1641.

Bickman, L. (1987). Graduate education in psychology. *American Psychologist, 42,* 1041–1047.

Black, H. (1963). *They shall not pass.* New York: Morrow.

Bogat, G. A., & Redner, R. L. (1985). How mentoring affects the professional development of women in psychology. *Professional Psychology: Research and Practice, 16,* 851–859.

Bordin, E. S. (1979). The generalizability of the psychoanalytic concept of working alliance. *Psychotherapy: Theory, Research and Practice, 16,* 252–260.

Bordo, S. (1987). The Cartesian masculinization of thought. In S. Harding & J. O'Barr (Eds.), *Sex and scientific inquiry* (pp. 247–264). Chicago: University of Chicago Press.

Boring, E. G. (1957). *A history of experimental psychology.* New York: Appleton-Century-Crofts.

Bourg, E. F., Bent, R. J., Callan, J. E., Jones, N. F., McHolland, J., & Stricker, G. (Eds.). (1987). *Standards and evaluation in the education and training of professional psychologists: Knowledge, attitudes, and skills.* Norman, OK: Transcript Press.

Bourg, E. F., Bent, R. J., McHolland, J., & Stricker, G. (1989). Standards and evaluation in the education and training of professional psychologists: The National Council of Schools of Professional Psychology Mission Bay Conference. *American Psychologist, 44,* 66–72.

Brayfield, A. H. (1965). About special privilege—and special responsibility. *American Psychologist, 20,* 857.

Breger, L. (1968). Psychological testing: Treatment and research implications. *Journal of Consulting and Clinical Psychology, 32,* 176–181.

Bryde, J. F. (1971). *Indian students and guidance.* Boston: Houghton Mifflin.

Burns, S. M., DeLeon, P. H., Chemtob, C. M., Welch, B. L., & Samuels, R. (1988). Psychotropic medication: A new technique for psychology? *Psychotherapy: Theory, Research, and Practice, 25,* 506–515.

Callan, J. E., Peterson, D. R., & Stricker, G. (Eds.). (1986). *Quality in professional psychology training: A national conference and self-study.* Norman, OK: Transcript Press.

Carlsen, M. B. (1988). *Meaning making: Therapeutic processes in adult development.* New York: Norton.

Carson, R. C. (1983). The social-interactional viewpoint. In M. Hersen, A. E. Kazdin, & A. S. Bellack (Eds.), *The clinical psychology handbook* (pp. 143–153). New York: Pergamon Press.

Clark, R. (1973). The socialization of clinical psychologists. *Professional Psychology, 4,* 329–340.

Community Mental Health Centers Act of 1963. Public Law 88–164, Title II, 77 Stat. 290 (Title 42, §§2681–2687).

Cook, T. D., & Campbell, D. T. (1979). *Quasi-experimentation: Design & analysis issues for field settings.* Boston: Houghton Mifflin.

Cronbach, L. J. (1982). *Designing evaluations of educational and social programs.* San Francisco: Jossey-Bass.

Dana, R. H. (1987). Training for professional psychology: Science, practice, and identity. *Professional Psychology, 18,* 9–16.

Dauer, F. W. (1989). *Critical thinking.* Oxford, England: Oxford University Press.

Davis-Russell, E. (1990). Incorporating ethnic minority issues into the curriculum: Myths and realities. In G. Stricker, E. Davis-Russell, E. Bourg, E. Duran, W. R. Hammond, J. McHolland, K. Polite, & B. E. Vaughn (Eds.), *Toward ethnic diversification in psychology education and training* (pp. 171–177). Washington, DC: American Psychological Association.

Derner, G. F., & Stricker, G. (1986). Quality control in professional psychology: Avoiding the decline of excellence. In J. E. Callan, D. R. Peterson, & G. Stricker (Eds.), *Quality in professional psychology training: A national conference and self-study* (pp. 37–43). Norman, OK: Transcript Press.

Ekstein, R., & Wallerstein, R. (1958). *The teaching and learning of psychotherapy.* New York: Basic Books.

Erickson, F., & Schultz, J. (1982). *The counselor as gatekeeper: Social interaction in interviews.* New York: Academic Press.

Eriksen, S. C. (1958). The core curriculum is a dependent variable. *American Psychologist, 13,* 56–58.

Erkut, S., & Mokros, J. R. (1984). Professors as models and mentors for college students. *American Educational Research Journal, 21,* 399–417.

Fleming, J., & Benedek, T. (1966). *Psychoanalytic supervision.* New York: Grune & Stratton.

Flexner, A. (1910). *Medical education in the United States and Canada.* Boston: Merrymount Press.

Flexner, A. (1925). *Medical education: A comparative study.* New York: Macmillan.

Fowler, R. D. (1990). Psychology: The core discipline. *American Psychologist, 45,* 1–6.

Fox, R. E., & Barclay, A. (1989). Let a thousand flowers bloom: Or, weed the garden? *American Psychologist, 44,* 55–59.

French, M. (1985). *Beyond power*. New York: Summit Books.

Friedson, E. (1970). *The professionalization of medicine*. New York: Dodd, Mead.

Gergen, K. J. (1982). *Toward transformation in social knowledge*. New York: Springer-Verlag.

Gergen, K. J. (1985). The social constructionist movement in modern psychology. *American Psychologist, 40*, 266–275.

Gianetti, R. A., Peterson, D. R., & Wilkins, W. (1986). From description to evaluation: Criteria for educational excellence. In J. E. Callan, D. R. Peterson, & G. Stricker (Eds.), *Quality in professional psychology training: A national conference and self-study* (pp. 163–170). Norman, OK: Transcript Press.

Gilbert, L. A. (1985). Dimensions of same-gender student-faculty role-model relationships. *Sex Roles, 12*, 111–123.

Gilbert, L. A., Gallessich, J., & Evans, S. (1983). Sex of faculty role model and students' self-perceptions of competency. *Sex Roles, 9*, 957–608.

Gilligan, C. (1982). *In a different voice*. Cambridge, MA: Harvard University Press.

Gilligan, C., Ward, J., & Taylor, J. (Eds.). (1989). *Mapping the moral domain*. Cambridge, MA: Harvard University Press.

Goldfried, M. R., & D'Zurilla, T. J. (1969). A behavioral-analytic model for assessing competence. In C. D. Spielberger (Ed.), *Current topics in clinical and community psychology* (Vol. 1, pp. 151–196). New York: Academic Press.

Goldstein, E. (1979). Effects of same-sex and cross-sex role models on the subsequent academic productivity of scholars. *American Psychologist, 34*, 407–410.

Gopelrud, E. N. (1980). Social support and stress during the first year of graduate school. *Professional Psychology, 11*, 283–290.

Gordon, E. W. (1985). Social science knowledge production and minority experiences. *The Journal of Negro Education, 54*, 117–133.

Gross, M. L. (1962). *The brain watchers*. New York: Random House.

Guggenbuhl-Craig, A. (1971). *Power in the helping professions* (M. Gubitz, Trans.). Irving, TX: Spring Publications. (Original work published 1971)

Gumprez, J. J. (1982). *Discourse strategies*. New York: Cambridge University Press.

Gustad, J. W. (1958). The core curriculum is an independent variable. *American Psychologist, 13*, 655–656.

Harding, S. (1983). Why has the sex/gender system become visible only now? In S. Harding & M. Hintikka (Eds.), *Discovering reality: Feminist perspectives on epistemology, metaphysics, methodology and philosophy of science* (pp. 311–324). Boston: D. Reidel.

Harding, S. (1986). *The science question in feminism*. Ithaca, NY: Cornell University Press.

Harding, S., & Hintikka, M. (Eds.). (1983). *Discovering reality: Feminist perspectives on epistemology, metaphysics, methodology and philosophy of science*. Boston: D. Reidel.

Harré R. (1986). *Varieties of realism: A rationale for the natural sciences*. New York: Basil Blackwell.

Hatfield, J. T., & Jacobs, R. C. (1989, October). *Students of color as subject and text in the multicultural university*. Paper presented at Multicultural University Conference, Oakland, CA.

Havighurst, R. J. (1982). The world of work. In B. Wolman & G. Stricker (Eds.), *Handbook of developmental psychology* (pp. 771–787). Englewood Cliffs, NJ: Prentice-Hall.

Hawkesworth, M. E. (1989). Knowers, knowing, known: Feminist theory and claims of truth. *Signs: Journal of Women in Culture and Society, 14,* 533–557.

Higginbotham, H. N., West, S. G., & Forsyth, D. R. (1988). *Psychotherapy and behavior change: Social, cultural and methodological perspectives.* New York: Pergamon Press.

Hirschberg, N., & Itkin, S. (1978). Graduate students' success in psychology. *American Psychologist, 33,* 1083–1093.

Hoch, E. L., Ross, A. O., & Winder, C. L. (Eds.). (1966). *Professional preparation of clinical psychologists.* Washington, DC: American Psychological Association.

Holt, R. R. (1967). Diagnostic testing: Present status and future prospects. *Journal of Nervous and Mental Diseases, 144,* 444–465.

Janeway, E. (1980). *Powers of the weak.* New York: William Morrow.

Jones, N. F. (1987). A model for defining the knowledge base in professional psychology. In E. F. Bourg, R. J. Bent, J. E. Callan, N. F. Jones, J. McHolland, & G. Stricker (Eds.), *Standards and evaluation in the education and training of professional psychologists: Knowledge, attitudes, and skills* (pp. 75–80). Norman, OK: Transcript Press.

Keith-Speigel, P., & Koocher, G. P. (1985). *Ethics in psychology: Professional standards and cases.* New York: Random House.

Kiesler, D. J. (1982). Interpersonal theory for personality and psychotherapy. In J. C. Anchin & D. J. Kiesler (Eds.), *Handbook of interpersonal psychotherapy* (pp. 3–24). New York: Pergamon Press.

Kimble, G. A. (1984). Psychology's two cultures. *American Psychologist, 39,* 833–839.

Koocher, G. P. (1979). Credentialing in psychology: Close encounters with competence. *American Psychologist, 34,* 696–702.

Kopplin, D. A. (1986). Curriculum and curricular review. In J. E. Callan, D. R. Peterson, & G. Stricker (Eds.), *Quality in professional psychology training: A national conference and self-study* (pp. 97–123). Norman, OK: Transcript Press.

Korman, M. (Ed.). (1973). *Levels and patterns of professional training in psychology.* Washington, DC: American Psychological Association.

Korman, M. (1974). National conference on levels and patterns of professional training in psychology. *American Psychologist, 29,* 441–449.

Kuhn, T. S. (1970). *The structure of scientific revolutions* (2nd ed.). Chicago: University of Chicago Press.

Kurtz, P. D., Marshall, E. K., & Banspach, S. W. (1985). Interpersonal skills-training research: A 12-year review and analysis. *Counselor Education and Supervision, 24,* 249–263.

Lakoff, G. (1987). *Women, fire and dangerous things.* Chicago: University of Chicago Press.

Lambert, M. J. (1986). Implications of psychotherapy outcome research for eclectic psychotherapy. In J. C. Norcross (Ed.), *Handbook of eclectic psychotherapy* (pp. 436–462). New York: Brunner/Mazel.

Lamiell, J. T. (1987). *The psychology of personality: An epistemological inquiry.* New York: Columbia University Press.

Lamiell, J. T., & Trierweiler, S. J. (1986). Personality measurement and intuitive personality judgments from an idiothetic point of view. *Clinical Psychology Review, 6,* 471–492.

Larson, M. S. (1977). *The rise of professionalism.* Berkeley, CA: University of California Press.

Lawrence, G. W., & Miller, E. J. (1976). Epilogue. In E. J. Miller (Ed.), *Task and organization* (pp. 361–366). London: Wiley.

Leary, M. R., & Maddux, J. E. (1987). Progress toward a viable interface between social and clinical-counseling psychology. *American Psychologist, 42*, 904–911.

Levinson, D. J. (1977). The mid-life transition: A period in adult psychosocial development. *Psychiatry, 40*, 99–112.

Levinson, D. J., Darrow, C. N., Klein, E. B., Levinson, M. E., & McKee, B. (1978). *The seasons of a man's life.* New York: Knopf.

Levinson, D. J., & Gooden, W. (1985). The life cycle. In H. Kaplan & B. Sadock (Eds.), *Comprehensive textbook of psychiatry* (4th ed., pp. 1–13). Baltimore: Williams & Wilkins.

Levy, M. R., & Hayward, M. F. (1975). Psychological testing is alive and well. *Professional Psychology, 6*, 420–424.

Lewin, K. (1951). *Field theory in social science.* New York: Harper & Row.

Lincoln, Y. S., & Guba, E. G. (1985). *Naturalistic inquiry.* Beverly Hills, CA: Sage Publications.

Lubin, B., Larsen, R. M., Matarazzo, J. D., & Seever, M. F. (1986). Selected characteristics of psychologists and psychological assessment in five settings: 1959–1982. *Professional Psychology, 17*, 155–157.

Lubin, B., & Lubin, A. W. (1972). Patterns of psychological services in the U.S.: 1959–1969. *Professional Psychology, 3*, 63–65.

Mahon, B. R., & Altmann, H. A. (1977). Skill training: Cautions and recommendations. *Counselor Education and Supervision, 17*, 42–50.

Manicas, P. T., & Secord, P. F. (1983). Implications for psychology of the new philosophy of science. *American Psychologist, 38*, 399–413.

Marden, C. F., & Meyer, G. (1978). *Minorities in American society.* New York: Van Nostrand.

Maslow, A. H. (1962). *Toward a psychology of being.* Princeton, NJ: Van Nostrand.

Matarazzo, J. D. (1987). There is only one psychology, no specialties, but many applications. *American Psychologist, 40*, 893–903.

Mayhew, L. B., & Ford, P. J. (1971). *Changing the curriculum.* San Francisco: Jossey-Bass.

McHolland, J., Peterson, D. R., & Brown, S. W. (1987). Assessing skills in professional psychology: A triadic strategy for developing methods. In E. F. Bourg, R. J. Bent, J. E. Callan, N. F. Jones, J. McHolland, & G. Stricker (Eds.), *Standards and evaluation in the education and training of professional psychologists: Knowledge, attitudes, and skills* (pp. 105–128). Norman, OK: Transcript Press.

Meehl, P. E. (1954). *Clinical versus statistical prediction.* Minneapolis: University of Minnesota Press.

Meehl, P. E., & Rosen, A. (1955). Antecedent probability and the efficiency of psychometric signs, patterns or cutting scores. *Psychological Bulletin, 52*, 194–216.

Meeks, B. N. (1987, February). The quiet revolution. *Byte*, pp. 183–190.

Meltzoff, J. (1986). Un-vailing the professional model: Implications for quality control. In J. E. Callan, D. R. Peterson, & G. Stricker (Eds.), *Quality in professional psychology training: A national conference and self-study* (pp. 23–26). Norman, OK: Transcript Press.

Menne, J. W. (1981). Competency-based assessment and the profession of psychology. *Journal of Professional Practice in Psychology, 2*, 17–28.

Messer, S. B. (1988). Psychoanalytic perspectives on the therapist-client relationship. *Journal of Integrative and Eclectic Psychotherapy, 7*, 268–277.

Messick, S. (1965). Personality measurement and the ethics of assessment. *American Psychologist*, *20*, 136–142.

Miles, M. B., & Huberman, A. M. (1984). *Qualitative data analysis: A sourcebook of new methods*. Beverly Hills, CA: Sage Publications.

Miller, J. B. (1976). *Toward a new psychology of women* (1st ed.). Boston: Beacon Press.

Miller, J. B. (1986). *Toward a new psychology of women* (2nd ed.). Boston: Beacon Press.

Mink, W. D. (1982). The challenge: Educating students to meet challenges. *Teaching of Psychology*, *9*(1), 35–38.

Mishler, E. G. (1986). *Research interviewing: Context and narrative*. Cambridge, MA: Harvard University Press.

Mission Bay conference resolutions for professional psychology programs. (1987). In E. F. Bourg, R. J. Bent, J. E. Callan, N. F. Jones, J. McHolland, & G. Stricker (Eds.), *Standards and evaluation in the education and training of professional psychologists: Knowledge, attitudes, and skills* (pp. 25–29). Norman, OK: Transcript Press.

Moghaddam, F. M. (1987). Psychology in the three worlds: As reflected by the crisis in social psychology and the move toward indigenous third-world psychology. *American Psychologist*, *42*, 912–920.

Mogul, K. M. (1979). Women in midlife: Decisions, rewards, and conflicts related to work and career. *American Journal of Psychiatry*, *136*, 1139–1143.

National Conference on Graduate Education. (1987). Resolutions approved by the national conference on graduate education in psychology. *American Psychologist*, *42*, 1070–1084.

New York Public Library. (1989). *Desk reference*. New York: Stonesong Press/Webster's New World.

Over, R. (1983). Representation, status, and contributions of women in psychology: A bibliography. *Psychological Documents*, *13*, 1–25.

Padilla, A. M., & Ruiz, R. A. (1974). *Latino mental health: A review of the literature* (HSM 73-9143). Washington, DC: U.S. Department of Health, Education and Welfare.

Parry, S. (1989, March). *Re-thinking autonomy and dependence*. Paper presented at the meeting of the Association of Women in Psychology, Newport, RI.

Pinsof, W. M. (1988). The therapist-client relationship: An integrative systems perspective. *Journal of Integrative and Eclectic Psychotherapy*, *7*, 303–313.

Pion, G. M., Kohout, J., & Wicherski, M. (1989). *Characteristics of graduate departments of psychology: 1987–1988*. Washington, DC: American Psychological Association.

Raimy, V. C. (Ed.). (1950). *Training in clinical psychology*. Engelwood Cliffs, NJ: Prentice-Hall.

Rappaport, J. (1977). *Community psychology: Values, research, and action*. New York: Holt, Rinehart & Winston.

Rich, A. (1979). *On lies, secrets and silence*. New York: W. W. Norton.

Roe, A., Gustad, J. W., Moore, B. V., Ross, S., & Skodak, M. (Eds.). (1959). *Conference on graduate education in psychology*. Washington, DC: American Psychological Association.

Rogers, C. (1957). The necessary and sufficient conditions of therapeutic personality change. *Journal of Consulting Psychology*, *21*, 95–103.

Rogers, C. (1965). *Client-centered therapy*. Boston: Houghton Mifflin.

Rorty, R. (1979). *Philosophy and the mirror of nature*. Princeton, NJ: Princeton University Press.

Russo, N. F., & Denmark, F. L. (1987). Contributions of women to psychology. *Annual Review of Psychology*, *38*, 279–298.

Sampson, E. E. (1985). The decentralization of identity: Toward a revised concept of personal and social order. *American Psychologist, 40*, 1203–1211.

Samuda, R. J. (1975). From ethnocentrism to a multicultural perspective in educational testing. *Journal of Afro-American Issues, 3*, 4–18.

Samuels, R., Hatcher, C., & Cannon, W. G. (1988, February). *Implications of pharmacological interventions by psychologists.* Paper presented at the meeting of American Psychological Association Divisions 29, 42, and 43, Scottsdale, AZ.

Sarason, S. B. (1981). An asocial psychology and a misdirected clinical psychology. *American Psychologist, 36*, 827–836.

Sarason, S. B. (1982). Individual psychology: An obstacle to understanding adulthood. In S. B. Sarason (Ed.), *Psychology and social action: Selected papers* (pp. 211–231). New York: Praeger.

Sarason, S. B. (1986). And what is the public interest? *American Psychologist, 41*, 899–905.

Scarborough, E., & Furumoto, L. (1987). *Untold lives: The first generation of American women psychologists.* New York: Columbia University Press.

Scheman, N. (1983). Individualism and the objects of psychology. In S. Harding & M. Hintikka (Eds.), *Discovering reality: Feminist perspectives on epistemology, metaphysics, methodology and philosophy of science* (pp. 225–244). Boston: D. Reidel.

Seashore, C. (1975). In grave danger of growing: Observations on the process of professional development. *Social Change: Ideas and Applications, 5*(4), 1–3, 7–8.

Selvini-Palazzoli, M., Boscolo, L., Cecchin, G., & Prata, G. (1978). *Paradox and counterparadox.* New York: Jason Aronson.

Shakow, D. (1976). What is clinical psychology? *American Psychologist, 31*, 553–560.

Shotter, J. (1985). Social accountability and self specification. In K. J. Gergen & K. E. Davis (Eds.), *The social construction of the person* (pp. 167–188). New York: Springer-Verlag.

Shotter, J. (1989). Social accountability and the social construction of "you." In J. Shotter & K. J. Gergen (Eds.), *Texts of identity* (pp. 133–152). London: Sage Publications.

Simmons, W. L. (1971). Clinical training programs, 1964–1965 and 1968–1969: A characterization and comparison. *American Psychologist, 26*, 717–721.

Singer, D. L. (1982). Professional socialization and adult development in graduate professional education. In B. Menson (Ed.), *New directions for learning: Building on experiences in adult development* (pp. 45–63). San Francisco: Jossey-Bass.

Singer, D. L., Astrachan, B. M., Klein, E. B., & Gould, L. J. (1975). Boundary management in psychological work with groups. *Journal of Applied Behavioral Science, 11*, 137–176.

Smedslund, J. (1985). Necessarily true cultural psychologies. In K. J. Gergen & K. E. Davis (Eds.), *The social construction of the person* (pp. 73–87). New York: Springer-Verlag.

Smith, D. (1987). *The everyday world as problematic: A feminist sociology.* Toronto: University of Toronto Press.

Smith, E. J. (1973). *Counseling the culturally different black youth.* Columbus, OH: Charles E. Merrill.

Starr, P. (1982). *The social transformation of American medicine.* New York: Basic Books.

Stern, S. (1984). Professional training and professional competence: A critique of current thinking. *Professional Psychology, 2*, 230–243.

Stiles, W. B., Shapiro, D. A., & Elliott, R. (1986). Are all psychotherapies equivalent? *American Psychologist, 41*, 165–180.

Stricker, G. (1986). Admission to schools of professional psychology. In J. E. Callan, D. R. Peterson, & G. Stricker (Eds.), *Quality in professional psychology training: A national conference and self-study* (pp. 77–82). Norman, OK: Transcript Press.

Stricker, G., & Callan, J. E. (1987). Attitudes and aptitudes of a professional psychologist. In E. F. Bourg, R. J. Bent, J. E. Callan, N. F. Jones, J. McHolland, & G. Stricker (Eds.), *Standards and evaluation in the education and training of professional psychologists: Knowledge, attitudes, and skills* (pp. 129–140). Norman, OK: Transcript Press.

Stricker, G., Davis-Russell, E., Bourg, E., Duran, E., Hammond, W. R., McHolland, J., Polite, K., & Vaughn, B. E. (Eds.). (1990). *Toward ethnic diversification in psychology education and training*. Washington, DC: American Psychological Association.

Stricker, G., & Keisner, R. H. (1985a). The relationship between research and practice. In G. Stricker & R. H. Keisner (Eds.), *From research to clinical practice* (pp. 3–14). New York: Plenum Press.

Stricker, G., & Keisner, R. H. (Eds.). (1985b). *From research to clinical practice*. New York: Plenum Press.

Stromberg, C. D., Haggarty, D. J., Leibenluft, R. F., McMillian, M. H., Mishkin, B., Rubin, B. L., & Trilling, H. R. (1988). *The psychologist's legal handbook*. Washington, DC: Council for the National Register of Health Service Providers in Psychology.

Strupp, H. (1972). On the technology of psychotherapy. *Archives of General Psychiatry*, *26*, 270–278.

Sue, D. W., Bernier, J. E., Durran, A., Feinberg, L., Pedersen, P., Smith, E. J., & Vasquez-Nuttall, E. (1982). Cross-cultural counseling competencies. *The Counseling Psychologist*, *10*, 45–52.

Sue, D. W., & Sue, S. (1972). Ethnic minorities: Resistance to being researched. *Professional Psychology*, *2*, 11–17.

Sugarman, A. (1978). Is psychodiagnostic assessment humanistic? *Journal of Personality Assessment*, *42*, 11–21.

Taylor, S. (1986, October). *Learning from the inside out: Approaches to pedagogy with women in transition*. Paper presented at Antioch University Convocation and Planning Conference, Yellow Springs, OH.

Taylor, S. (1987, April). *Transition: Inner work, outer work*. Paper presented at Psychology Department Colloquim, Antioch University, Seattle, WA.

Thomas, A., & Sillen, S. (1972). *Racism and psychiatry*. New York: Brunner/Mazel.

Trow, M. (1977). *Aspects of American higher education, 1969–1975*. Berkeley, CA: Carnegie Council on Policy Studies in Higher Education.

Tyler, F. B., Sussewell, D. R., & Williams-McCoy, J. (1985). Ethnic validity in psychotherapy. *Psychotherapy*, *22*, 311–320.

Ullman, L. P., & Krasner, L. (1969). *A psychosocial approach to abnormal behavior*. Englewood Cliffs, NJ: Prentice-Hall.

Urdang, L., & Flexner, S. B. (1969). *The Random House dictionary of the English language* (college ed.). New York: Random House.

Varnedoe, K. (1986). *Vienna 1900: Art, architecture & design*. New York: Museum of Modern Art.

Vickers, K. (1974). *Supervisory effects on novice therapists' therapeutic style and orientation*. Unpublished doctoral dissertation, Adelphi University, Garden City, NY.

Watson, N., Caddy, G. R., Johnson, J. H., & Rimm, D. C. (1981). Standards in the education of professional psychologists. The resolutions of the conference at Virginia Beach. *American Psychologist*, *36*, 514–519.

Wechsler, D. (1974). *Manual for the Wechsler Intelligence Scale for Children-Revised*. New York: Psychological Corp.

Wellner, A. M. (Ed.). (1978). *Proposal for a national commission on education and credentialing in psychology*. Washington, DC: American Psychological Association.

Whyte, W. H., Jr. (1956). *The organization man*. New York: Simon & Schuster.

Willensky, H. (1964). The professionalization of everyone? *American Journal of Sociology, 70*, 137–158.

Williams, R. L. (1970). Black pride, academic relevance and individual achievement. *The Counseling Psychologist, 2*, 18–22.

Winnicott, D. W. (1965). *The maturational processes and the facilitating environment*. London: Hogarth Press.

Zindell, D. (1988). *Neverness*. New York: Bantam.

NCSPP SAN ANTONIO CONFERENCE PARTICIPANTS

NCSPP MEMBER SCHOOL REPRESENTATIVES

Alan Barclay	*Wright State University*
Russell J. Bent	*Wright State University*
Kathi Borden	*Pepperdine University*
Edward Bourg	*California School of Professional Psychology: Berkeley/Alameda*
Joanne Callan	*California School of Professional Psychology: San Diego*
W. Gary Cannon	*California School of Professional Psychology: Fresno*
Peter Chang	*California School of Professional Psychology: Berkeley/Alameda*
John Court	*Fuller Theological Seminary*
Richard Cox	*Forest Institute of Professional Psychology*
Elizabeth Davis-Russell	*California School of Professional Psychology: Fresno*
Frank De Piano	*Nova University*
Evelyn Diaz	*Caribbean Center for Advanced Studies: Miami Institute of Psychology*
James Dobbins	*Wright State University*
Eduardo Duran	*Pacific Graduate School of Psychology*
Glenace E. Edwall	*Baylor University*
Keith Edwards	*Biola University*
Helen Evans	*Illinois School of Professional Psychology*
Philip Farber	*Florida Institute of Technology*
Lucy Ferguson	*California School of Professional Psychology: Berkeley/Alameda*
Martin Fisher	*Adelphi University, Derner Institute*
Wesley Forbes	*California School of Professional Psychology: Fresno*
Samuel Friedman	*Wisconsin School of Professional Psychology*
Abraham Givner	*Yeshiva University*
Steven N. Gold	*Nova University*
Beverly Goodwin	*Indiana University of Pennsylvania*

Jeffrey Grip	*Chicago School of Professional Psychology*
John Gruber	*Forest Institute of Professional Psychology*
Archibald D. Hart	*Fuller Theological Seminary*
Laura Hines	*Yeshiva University*
Jacqueline S. Jackson	*Pacific Graduate School of Psychology*
Nelson Jones	*University of Denver*
Mary Beth Kenkel	*California School of Professional Psychology: Fresno*
Dennis Klos	*California School of Professional Psychology: Los Angeles*
Thomas Lombardo	*Forest Institute of Professional Psychology*
Perry London	*Rutgers University*
Marc Lubin	*Illinois School of Professional Psychology*
Hector Machabanski	*Chicago School of Professional Psychology*
Ethel Magidson	*Massachusetts School of Professional Psychology*
James McHolland	*Illinois School of Professional Psychology*
John McNeill	*University of Denver*
Carey Mitchell	*Pepperdine University*
Robert Morgan	*Pacific Graduate School of Psychology*
Robert Moriarty	*Forest Institute of Professional Psychology*
Terri Needels	*Forest Institute of Professional Psychology*
Nancy Newton	*Chicago School of Professional Psychology*
Rodney A. Nurse	*California Graduate School of Family Psychology*
R. Paul Olson	*Minnesota School of Professional Psychology*
Ruth Ann Parvin	*Oregon Graduate School of Professional Psychology*
Roger L. Peterson	*Antioch New England Graduate School*
Kenneth Polite	*Biola University*
Lisa Porche-Burke	*California School of Professional Psychology: Los Angeles*
Salvador Santiago-Negron	*Caribbean Center for Advanced Studies*
Saul Siegel	*Wright Institute*
David L. Singer	*Antioch New England Graduate School*
Eloise Stiglitz	*Antioch New England Graduate School*
Mark Stone	*Alfred Adler Institute of Chicago*
George Stricker	*Adelphi University, Derner Institute*
Siang-Yang Tan	*Fuller Theological Seminary*
Veronique Thompson	*Wright Institute*
Thomas Titus	*Spalding University*
Jerry Treppa	*Forest Institute of Professional Psychology*
Steven J. Trierweiler	*Antioch New England Graduate School*
Raymond Trybus	*California School of Professional Psychology: San Diego*
Leon VandeCreek	*Indiana University of Pennsylvania*
Billy E. Vaughn	*California School of Professional Psychology: San Diego*
Edwin Wagner	*Forest Institute of Professional Psychology*
Frank Webbe	*Florida Institute of Technology*
Bruce J. Weiss	*Massachusetts School of Professional Psychology*
Barbara Williams	*Spalding University*

INVITED PARTICIPANTS/OBSERVERS

Cynthia Baum	*American Psychological Association*
David Downs	*American Board of Professional Psychology*
Glenn P. Fournet	*East Texas State University (CAMPP)*
Bruce Fretz	*National Register*
Jessica Kohout	*American Psychological Association*
Susan Moses	*American Psychological Association Monitor*
Robert Reynes	*United States Air Force, Wilford Hall (APIC)*
Edward Sheridan	*Northwestern University (COGDOP)*
Charles Spielberger	*University of South Florida*